DIFFERENTIATED COACHING

A Framework *for* Helping Teachers Change

Jane A. G. Kise

CORWIN PRESS
A SAGE Publications Company
Thousand Oaks, California

For information:

Corwin Press
A Sage Publications Company
2455 Teller Road
Thousand Oaks, California 91320
www.corwinpress.com

Sage Publications Ltd.
1 Oliver's Yard
55 City Road
London EC1Y 1SP
United Kingdom

Sage Publications India Pvt. Ltd.
B-42, Panchsheel Enclave
Post Box 4109
New Delhi 110 017 India

Printed in the United States of America.

Library of Congress Cataloging-in-Publication Data

Kise, Jane A. G.
Differentiated coaching : a framework for helping teachers change / Jane A.G. Kise.
    p. cm.
Includes bibliographical references and index.
ISBN 1-4129-1642-9 (cloth) — ISBN 1-4129-1643-7 (pbk.)
   1. Teachers—In-service training. 2. Teaching—Psychological aspects.
3. School personnel management. I. Title.
LB1731.K57 2006
370'.71'55—dc22   2005023005

This book is printed on acid-free paper.

06 07 08 09 10 9 8 7 6 5 4 3 2 1

Acquisitions Editor:	Rachel Livsey
Editorial Assistant:	Phyllis Cappello
Production Editor:	Jenn Reese
Copy Editor:	Barbara Ray
Typesetter:	C&M Digitals (P) Ltd.
Proofreader:	Victoria Reed-Castro
Indexer:	Nara Wood
Cover Designer:	Rose Storey

Contents

Acknowledgments

Although the need to protect the identity of the specific teachers, students, and administrators in the stories and case studies prevents me from naming individuals, I want to thank all of those I worked with for allowing me into their classrooms and sharing their experiences, beliefs, frustrations, and perspectives. I also want to acknowledge their willingness to partner with me in trying new techniques and lessons in their classrooms. The teachers, especially, devoted hours to reflection as we worked together to evaluate whether the concepts of personality type could be useful for urban teachers.

Dr. Elizabeth Murphy not only provided the research version of her type instrument for children for my work, but also shared her insights on working with teachers and children. The Center for Applications of Psychological Type provided scoring services and materials. Dr. Gordon Lawrence read early drafts of the opening chapters and provided several key insights for improvements. Thank you also to Len Tallevi, Dr. Daniel Robinson, Sandra Krebs Hirsh, and other members of the personality type community who gave suggestions and shared training ideas and methods.

The support of the Myers and Briggs Foundation was also instrumental in developing *Differentiated Coaching*, providing funding for staff development time for teachers to study how personality type related to learning styles and classroom management.

Finally, I developed much of the content of this book as I worked on my dissertation. I would like to acknowledge the significant contributions of my dissertation committee and thank Dr. Huber for her wisdom in helping me address my own biases; Dr. Payne for her insights into teacher education and other models for reform; and my chair, Dr. Kramer, for the generous amount of time, effort, and patience he devoted to helping me understand the ethics of the work I do and think beyond my own practices and beliefs.

The contributions of the following reviewers are gratefully acknowledged:

Marilee Springer
Professional Development Consultant
Peoria, IL

Lois Easton
Coach and Consultant
Former Director of Professional Development
Eagle Rock School and Professional Development Center
Estes Park, CO

Janet Crews
Instructional Mentor
Clayton School District
Clayton, MO

Steve Hutton
Adjunct Instructor
Northern Kentucky University
Villa Hills, KY

Donna Walker Tileston
Author, International Consultant
Strategic Teaching and Learning (ST&L)
Dallas, TX

Kathryn Kee
Leadership Coach & Consultant
Coaching School Results, Inc.
Shady Shores, TX 76208

Charles F. Adamchik, Jr.
Corporate Director of Curriculum
Learning Sciences International
Blairsville, PA 15717

About the Author

Jane A. G. Kise, EdD, is an educational consultant, specializing in teambuilding, coaching, and school staff development. She is also the coauthor of nearly 20 books, including *Introduction to Type and Coaching, Using the MBTI Tool in Organizations, LifeKeys,* and *Work It Out.* She holds an MBA in finance from the Carlson School of Management and a doctorate in Educational Leadership from the University of St. Thomas.

Kise has worked with diverse organizations, including Minneapolis Public Schools and various public and private schools, The Bush Foundation, and numerous other institutions. She is a frequent workshop speaker and has presented at NSDC, World Futures, and APT International conferences. She has taught writing at the university level. She is a faculty member of the Center for Applications of Psychological Type and an executive board member of the Association for Psychological Type.

For Dr. Beth Russell
In appreciation of her unwavering support, advocacy, and belief
that these strategies for coaching teachers could bring about change

Part I

Staff Development That Changes Classroom Practices

Imagine having almost 90 minutes of staff development time every week. My first experiences with school change took place at a small suburban school with just that luxury. Slowly, I introduced the 25 teachers to a learning styles model and helped them use it to plan differentiated lessons and assessments. They walked out of each session with ideas or activities to use with students right away.

To collect data on our efforts, I ran student focus groups, asked teachers to e-mail descriptions of classroom experiences, and conducted interviews to understand what teachers found helpful or useless in the materials. Each week I asked, "What did you try? What did you see?"

The "eager beaver" teachers told stories of increased class participation, fewer behavior problems, more student engagement in projects, and higher work quality. Little by little, other teachers tried the practices they heard their colleagues raving about. By the end of the year, even two of the most reluctant teachers decided to attend the extra six hours of training (on their own time) to become certified to use the differentiation model with students and adults.

Fast-forward a year. The principal moved to an urban middle school that was three times the size of her previous assignment, with 60 percent students of color, 60 percent of its students qualifying for free or reduced lunches, and almost no staff development budget. Rather than cut corners on the quality of our efforts, we decided that I would work with a volunteer pilot team. We hoped that they would eventually advocate the framework to the rest of the staff—much as the "eager beaver" teachers had done at the first school. The principal offered to provide research access to her building in exchange for my staff development work. That research became the basis for my doctoral dissertation as I collected data via interviews, classroom observations, teacher journals, student focus groups, student data such as grades and behavior referrals, and analysis of student work.

As you will see in *Differentiated Coaching*, the pilot team—who knew me, understood what they were volunteering for, and eagerly met with me week after week—didn't change. They listened. They asked questions. They planned lessons. They scheduled *extra* meetings with me. But they didn't try anything.

Have you been there? Have you

- Selected school reform strategies, curriculum, or collaboration models *and* implementation methods, using scientifically based research in your decision-making process
- Trained teachers and administrators following established standards for professional staff development, perhaps even investing in instructional coaching
- Evaluated student data to establish priorities, monitor progress, and adapt adult learning to continue moving toward implementation goals

. . . only to see no significant advances in student achievement? Or even significant changes in classroom practices? Let me suggest that the above strategies are only half of what is needed for effective school reform.

The other half is a common framework that allows you to understand *why* teachers aren't changing. As you'll see in the first part of this book, progress with the pilot team came when I grasped that I wasn't just getting them to adopt a common learning styles framework—I was asking them to change their educational beliefs. That magnitude of change is difficult even when we believe that the change will be for the better, let alone if we've seen change after change bring little improvement in student academic performance, as is the case for many teachers.

WHY READ THIS BOOK?

The first half of *Differentiated Coaching* lays out six key elements for effective staff development that allow for differentiation to meet the needs of each teacher, just as we are asking them to meet the needs of each student in their classrooms. The second half introduces a model that helps identify patterns in teacher beliefs, needs, and learning styles that, while not eliminating the difficulty of change, adds understanding and a common framework for coaching and for discussing teaching and learning.

If you are a principal or administrator, these pages will help you

- Develop a schoolwide framework for teaching and learning so that conversations can focus on which students each educational practice will reach rather than on who is "right" or "wrong"
- Understand your own strengths and beliefs and how they influence your goals and implementation strategies—and how they may bring about resistance in teachers who are least like you
- Anticipate those patterns of resistance and adjust both the *content* and *delivery* of staff development to meet the needs of the teachers for whom the changes will be hardest.

If you are a staff development provider or teacher educator, these pages will provide new tools to

- Create staff development experiences that teachers look forward to (instead of assuming, "There'll be nothing in it for me")
- Help teachers collaborate at a deep, reflective level
- Increase teachers' willingness to implement in their classrooms what they learn during classes or seminars.

If you are a teacher, the brunt of school reform initiatives falls on you and your colleagues. Sometimes the efforts make sense. At other times, the changes seem potentially harmful to some of your students. This framework will allow you to

- Stand back from your own practice and evaluate the changes through the framework to determine which children are being served, who is being left out, and where your own practices might need adjustment
- Present your analysis in a factual, logical manner when reform, analyzed in the above unbiased way, *does* seem to harm some students
- Collaborate more effectively with colleagues in ways that increase your collective wisdom
- Advocate for your own needs during the change process.

If you are a coach or mentor (and administrators, staff developers, and teachers all may serve as coaches), these pages will help you

- Tailor your coaching practices to meet the needs of each teacher
- Understand how to "translate" school or district mandates into practices or implementation methods that use a teacher's strengths, not weaknesses
- Develop a neutral methodology for evaluating *why* teachers won't change and then using their *wisdom* to improve reform goals and methods.

Does this sound like hard work? Change *is* hard work, even when we want to change and are convinced it's worth the effort. Yet all too often, teachers are expected (not even asked) to change without clear explanations or evidence of how the changes will be better than what they are doing now. If we are asking teachers to meet the needs of all students, we need to model with them how it is possible by meeting their needs as they engage in the difficult work of changing their classrooms.

1

What Do Teachers Believe?

This chapter introduces three of the six key elements of effective staff development:

- Using a common framework for unbiased reflection on education
- Understanding the teachers' strengths and beliefs about teaching and learning
- Providing information and evidence that can influence those beliefs.

Josh,[1] an experienced sixth-grade social studies teacher, wanted to change his classroom. He and the other members of his team chose to work with me on differentiation as their team staff development plan for the year. Before we started, Josh told me,

> I know my curriculum is too standard and quite boring, so all last year my kids were quite bored. Someday the kids will rebel or something . . . but I'm afraid that if I use other methods, chaos will be created and I won't be able to manage it, or I'll make mistakes and look dumb. Someone will find out that I'm not that great of a teacher or parents will get mad at me or test scores will go down or more students will fail.

Josh admitted that he never felt adequate as a teacher, at least not in the high-poverty school where he taught. Close to 20 percent of his students were English language learners, and an additional 15 percent had learning disabilities. Students of color, from diverse backgrounds, made up nearly two-thirds of the school's student body. "How do I differentiate for all *that*?" he lamented.

Despite his self-doubts, Josh articulated several key strengths that my observations of his classroom verified:

- He built relationships with his students, chatting during passing time and remembering who'd had a ball game the night before.
- He stressed organization. He helped students keep track of materials and provided detailed directions for assignments.
- His drama skills, which he used for reading aloud and classroom management, kept students focused.
- He'd developed solid methods for teaching basic skills such as outlining, note taking, text summarizing, and learning vocabulary words.

Josh put in long hours, too, organizing lessons and trying to correct papers overnight to give his students rapid feedback. Still, too many students—as many as 25 percent—failed his classes. "I want to help them be more successful," he said.

A FAILURE TO COLLABORATE

At a team meeting, Josh asked for help planning his upcoming unit on ancient civilizations. "Usually I read aloud and give an open-note quiz every few days," he told us. "But I thought I'd start by having them journal on what would be the same and different about living a couple thousand years ago."

We all commented that his journal exercise would produce some fun responses. Then I asked what he'd do with students who preferred reading on their own, as I would have. Josh answered, "They still need to participate in class discussions, so they'll have to pay attention."

"What about letting them read from different sources, then report to the class on them?" the language arts teacher suggested.

"Or give enrichment activities," the science teacher added. "I always have extensions of experiments for students who finish first."

Josh didn't reply. I sensed that he was determined to stick to reading aloud, so I said, "What about concentrating on themes that catch student interest instead of sequential notes?" I added that providing something to manipulate, like note cards, might help some students keep listening.

Josh sighed. "They all need to be doing the same thing or too many of them will get lost." We brainstormed more ideas. Josh nodded politely, noncommittally.

Josh eventually differentiated for ability by making two separate packets, a "high" and a "low" one, for students to work on as he read aloud. The worksheet activities varied: short-answer questions, puzzles, basic vocabulary and note-taking drills, and a few what-if or connections questions. The result? Focus-group students reported that they loved the information he read to them. "I could almost see the Aztecs climbing up the temple steps," one student said. Still, over 30 percent of his students received D's or F's on the unit, and 15 percent never turned in their packets. The grades were comparable to results on similar large units the other teachers on his team experienced. Josh had hoped his structure would bring better results and was disappointed when that didn't happen.

Instead of judging how Josh taught the unit, we're going to examine *why* he taught it the way he did, then look to cognitive theories to understand the implications for coaching teachers for change.

A TEACHER'S STRENGTHS AND BELIEFS

Here are several of Josh's beliefs about education, gathered through interviews and verified through classroom observation.

Josh believed that for his particular students, reading aloud was essential for basic comprehension. With so many English language learners and students with learning disabilities, he seldom had them read to themselves or aloud to each other, even in pairs. In a team meeting, someone mentioned "popcorn reading," where a student reads as much or as little as is comfortable and then calls the name of another student, who reads next.

Josh: I still don't get popcorn reading.

Team member: It's not round robin. They only have to read a sentence if they want to stop. Most of the kids love it. Even [a struggling student] read a whole page today.

Josh: Well, maybe for a novel, but they might miss something in an article if someone pronounces things wrong.

Josh dismissed *all* of the different reading techniques we discussed for mixed-ability classrooms. Remember, dramatic reading was one of Josh's core strengths. Further, the students loved it. One said, "I like when he does that 'cause it lets you get into stuff more. He changes his voice for different people." His ability to keep the students' interest while he read kept him from questioning the practice despite its obvious flaw: Students need to read materials themselves to develop decoding and comprehension skills.

Josh believed that his students learned best in a structured environment. Note that again it was one of Josh's strengths. Further, sixth grade was the first year his students had multiple teachers. Many in fact did misread directions or forget deadlines.

Josh himself recognized drawbacks in his emphasis on organization, yet he continued to teach through this strength.

> I think that I'm good at trying to make sure that everybody "gets it," that everybody understands, but again that turns into a weakness when the people who've already gotten it, they're bored. But I want to make sure that the low kids get it.

Josh believed that the path to differentiation was to provide more individual help. Despite his attempts to build relationships, he didn't think it was possible to know the needs of 110 students. Further, he fully expected class sizes to increase because of budget cuts. He admitted that he didn't know how to differentiate.

> I wish that I could just work with a group of four or five, especially the English language learners or the low-level kids who just don't have the skills. But then I don't know what to do with the kids who need challenge . . . You know what would be nice, if I could have the super high level kids go work on a project in the library, but then who's going to baby-sit them and make sure that they don't do anything wrong?

Josh believed that he needed to emphasize basic skills practice. He'd thrived as a student on such instruction and sought teacher training on content area reading and other basic skills. Again, he wasn't wrong; Bloom's taxonomy lists knowledge and comprehension, emphasized in Josh's ancient civilization packets, as the first two categories of educational objectives. Many of Josh's students needed practice in these areas.

INEFFECTIVE BELIEFS

However, Josh's emphasis failed to help the very students he was trying to reach, as evidenced by the number of students who never completed the basic skills-oriented packets. Students in focus groups complained that they received far too many similar packets in other classes as well.

Student 1:   Another project that I didn't like? In social studies we had to do a big old packet.

[Groans all around]

Jane: How many of you liked learning about the pyramids and Aztec temples, just out of curiosity?

[All hands went up]

Student 2:   The stuff was awesome.

Student 3:   He always has to do those packets, though. I hate packets.

Student 1:   Especially that pink organization packet.

Student 3:   He called my house and I had to do it, so . . . Them packets, you get them and you lose them and they take a long time to finish them and it's just like, you want to be finished with them fast.

Two of the above students failed the packet; it didn't help them learn basic skills. Further, the packet in general didn't engage students in learning. When I observed Josh's classroom as he reviewed the pages with students, barely 25 percent followed along, despite his attempts to generate discussion. Most students stared at the wrong page or at blank pages; they hadn't done the work and didn't bother to fill in answers.

Josh's practices were not simply the result of laziness or bad habits—the long hours he put in attested to his dedication. Instead, his beliefs and strengths, the core of how he saw himself as a teacher, drove his classroom practices. Later, he confessed that he should have tried something new.

My problem was I had about six different resources to teach the unit, and I had a page I liked from this one and that page from another, and so I decided to copy them all off and put them in a packet, and . . . I've done that before and that bombed and you'd think I'd learn.

That's how tightly, though, all of us hold to our habits and beliefs. That's why coaching teachers for change is so difficult. I've seen similar patterns with most of the teachers I work with, not just Josh.

WHERE THOSE INGRAINED HABITS COME FROM

Habits, beliefs, opinions . . . where do they come from? For educators, many are the result of our own school experiences, as was Josh's affinity for the structured learning activities that had helped him thrive in school.

Other beliefs come from the environment in which we teach. Josh told me that the looming high-stakes state basic skills tests lessened how creative he was willing to be.

Sometimes we can't articulate exactly how we formed such beliefs because they are simply a part of us, "The way things are."

John Dewey (1910) recognized our general habit of unconsciously forming beliefs almost a hundred years ago; he described how the ideas and images in our minds are actually invisible powers that govern us. These fixed beliefs can entrap us, keeping us from freely entertaining new beliefs. He recognized that without discipline and effort, we struggle to distinguish between good and false conclusions.

In Josh's case, his beliefs matched his strengths and were so ingrained that he overlooked contradictory information, which trapped him in his classroom style. Dewey (1932/1985) points out the problem of habit:

> Habit gives facility, and there is always a tendency to rest on our oars, to fall back on what we have already achieved. For that is the easy course; we are at home and feel comfortable in lines of action that run the tracks of habits already established and mastered. Hence, the old, the habitual self, is likely to be treated as if it were *the* self; as if new conditions and new demands were something foreign and hostile. (pp. 306–307)

Asking teachers to change their practices often means asking them to do things that sound absolutely hostile to them. Josh only showed human nature when he taught his usual way. His team's suggestions seemed threatening. It shouldn't surprise us that he stuck with what he knew, given that his classroom was under control and his results were no worse than other teachers'. The real surprise is that so many teachers, or people in any other profession, are actually willing to try innovations.

HABITS AND MENTAL MODELS

Dewey's concept of habit parallels current writings on mental models. Senge, Kleiner, Roberts, Ross, and Smith (1994) describe mental models as "the images, assumptions, and stories which we carry in our minds of ourselves, other people, institutions, and every aspect of the world. Like a pane of glass framing and subtly distorting our vision, mental models determine what we see" (p. 235). Senge, Cambron-McCabe, Lucas, Smith, Dutton, and Kleiner (2000), Duffy (2003), and others point out that because people are often unaware of how their mental models control their actions, these models can block change unless we purposely unearth, examine, and challenge them.

Similarly, Costa and Garmston (1994) point out that

> While the traditional model of clinical supervision addresses overt teaching behaviors, we believe that these overt behaviors of teaching are the products and artifacts of *inner thought processes* and intellectual functions. To change the overt behaviors of instruction requires the alteration and rearrangement of the inner and invisible cognitive behaviors of instruction. (p. 16)

However, *all* of us, not just teachers, operate from mental models. In working toward school change, we need to examine our own beliefs about why teachers aren't changing. Do our own mental models trap us? Do we really understand the magnitude of the changes we are asking teachers to make?

IDENTIFYING TEACHER BELIEFS

For teacher-centered staff development, the starting point is four essential questions:

1. *What are the teachers' beliefs about how students learn?* Watch a classroom and you can discern the beliefs of any dedicated teacher. A social studies teacher I know has artwork and objects on display from many different cultures; she believes in a culturally relevant curriculum. Another teacher starts each morning advisory period with a game; she believes school should be fun. A science teacher has students building dragsters, robots, and rockets; he believes students need hands-on activities to learn science concepts.

Before designing any staff development effort, consider these four essential questions:

1. What are the teachers' beliefs about how students learn?

2. How tightly are teachers' beliefs tied to their own strengths as educators?

3. What are the teachers' beliefs about their roles in student success?

4. What else keeps teachers from trying new practices?

These are all valid beliefs. However, unexamined beliefs can have unintended consequences. For example, if the science teacher doesn't follow the hands-on activities with other kinds of learning activities, the students may remember how to use a band saw rather than the laws of force and motion. And the energetic, game-playing morning meetings, if not run within safe boundaries, may alienate some quiet students.

More important for staff development, though, is understanding that change initiatives often require changing these ingrained, habitual beliefs, which is no easy task.

2. *How tightly are teachers' beliefs tied to their own strengths as educators?* Other factors influence teacher beliefs, such as a strong mentor with a different strength, or a deliberate effort to work on a developmental need, or observation of another teacher who effectively uses a different skill. However, for the teachers I've worked with, the relationship between strengths and beliefs is very close.

Listen to a teacher's explanation of his teaching philosophy:

I set up an experience and the students take it from there. An administrator once told me that when he observed a teacher, he wasn't looking for what the teacher was doing but for what the students were doing. And that told him how good the teacher was . . . it's really a belief of mine.

This teacher excels at designing engaging, hands-on projects. Is it any wonder that he believes it's the best way to run a classroom?

Another teacher loves creative activities and integrates drama, sewing, beadwork, sculpting, and other arts into her curriculum. She tries to leave room in her assignments for students to express themselves as individuals. Is it any wonder that she resists providing too much structure in her directions for fear that she'll stifle creativity?

Successful people in any field work out of their strengths, not their weaknesses. Michael Jordan wasn't a jockey. Cesar Chavez didn't remain behind the scenes, helping individuals in quiet ways. Further, we need to use our strengths; being forced to overuse our weaknesses often leads to fatigue, illness, and stress (Quenk, 1993). Teachers' classroom practices and educational beliefs *should* correlate with their strengths.

However, here's the problem. When I've asked teachers about the students they have the most trouble reaching or feel most helpless with, they describe students who don't share their strengths or fit the mold of their educational beliefs. Look at these comparisons:

Teacher strength or belief	Type of student they describe as most difficult for them to teach
Creating a classroom where students can express themselves as individuals. Teachers need to engage them in ways that help them grow.	"The apathetic ones. It's like, 'whatever' the whole time. They may not be saying it, but it's the way they sit, they turn away. I'm more effective with students who sometimes misbehave, even, than when they don't care."
"I'm very organized and that helps provide structure, which I think a lot of kids need."	"Extremely disorganized, like oh my Lord, especially this one. You know I made him a take-home folder and a bring-back folder . . . it didn't help."
Using hands-on projects to teach concepts, and then reinforcing them through reading and lecture. Most units are therefore several weeks long.	"Ones with short attention spans . . . When I get excited about something and they're not quite staying with me, I'm like, 'Come on, this is [laugh].'"
"I make math fun. Kids come to math scared and they've had some pretty awful math teachers. They leave here, like, 'Oh, that was really fun. This was math?'"	"The quiet, withdrawn student."

Teachers need to work out of their strengths, but understanding how those strengths drive their beliefs about what "should" happen in their classrooms is key to understanding how those beliefs might affect students who are very different from them.

3. *What are the teachers' beliefs about their roles in student success?* I've watched teachers avoid actively making students write down deadlines or use their planners for fear of making the students become dependent on the teacher rather than becoming responsible. The problem is that some of the students stop believing they need to do the work—or *can* do the work.

I've watched teachers give an assignment, yet only half the students in the room take out paper and pencil to complete it. The teachers tell me that students are making their own choices about whether or not they do their work and are choosing to fail. The problem comes when the teachers stop looking for strategies to help students make better choices.

I've heard teachers say, "Those students don't care about education; they know they'll get promoted even if they fail my class." If teachers don't believe they can find ways to motivate students because of the effects of district policies, increasing class size, budget cuts, poverty, peer pressure, or home situations, they'll stop expecting students to engage in their classrooms. Staff development efforts will flounder from the start if they aren't designed to unearth, then change, such beliefs about student success.

4. *What else keeps teachers from trying new practices?* Besides the overall difficulty of change and the grasp that habits and beliefs have on us, consider what other factors might be present. For example, if previous efforts to change brought little or no positive results, teachers may be reluctant to sign on for the next one.

In urban settings, another factor that feeds reluctance to change is that teachers who can successfully manage their classrooms are fearful about the chaos new practices could bring. One teacher told me,

> I have a lot of fear and that holds me back from taking risks and trying a lot of ideas that have been forming around in my head, which could be so cool, but I'm scared of trying them because I'm afraid they'll fail . . . maybe the ideas are ideal, but I'm not always so sure my students are the ideal ones to try them with.

Change is a lot of work. Why would you do it if your classroom is under control, the majority of your students are succeeding, you're aware of significant factors contributing to student failure that are outside your control, and the changes either don't fit with your beliefs about education or require that you operate out of weaknesses?

There's an old rule of thumb that it takes 30 days of constant, conscious effort to form a new habit. That's when someone *wants* to change—and becomes conscious of beliefs that need changing! If a habit is tightly tied to one's beliefs, then the approach to change needs to be respectful, deliberate, and gradual.

INCORPORATING KNOWLEDGE OF TEACHER STRENGTHS AND BELIEFS INTO STAFF DEVELOPMENT

To understand this strengths-based, respectful approach to change, it helps to reframe the implementation by remembering that the teachers are now the students.

Dewey (1902) pointed out that the problem with traditional education, or one might say traditional staff development, is that "the center of gravity is outside the child. It is in the teacher, the textbook, anywhere and everywhere you please except in the immediate instincts and activities of the child himself" (p. 34). That's how many staff development efforts feel to teachers. The focus is test scores, curriculum, team structures, student learning—everything, it seems, but the teachers who have to do the changing.

Dewey (1902) added that in traditional schools, getting children to do things that didn't hold their interest required the traditional tools of discipline, which is all too often identified with force or drill, "and drill is conceived after the mechanical analogy of driving, by unremitting blows, a foreign substance into a resistant material" (p. 63). That's how much of the school change literature reads—how to get resisters on board, how to enforce district policies, how to monitor or supervise teachers.

Dewey (1934) described good teaching (and we are teaching during staff development) as an art which takes place when "a human being cooperates with the product so that the outcome is an experience that is enjoyed because of its liberating and ordered properties" (p. 214). Teacher-centered staff development, then, has the goal of liberating teachers, not controlling them. Here's the big point:

> The art of staff development is helping teachers understand where their strengths and beliefs lock them into practices that limit their freedom to help students succeed. It isn't freedom for teachers to do what they please, but freedom for them to entertain possibilities and stay open to new avenues for professional growth.

With this understanding of staff development, our goal changes from implementing a mandate to helping teachers develop their own sense of discipline. We want teachers to habitually examine their beliefs and practices and then move toward affirming, modifying, or changing them as necessary to help all students learn.

For staff development to do this, two elements need to be present: (1) a common framework for discussing teaching and learning and (2) an emphasis on experiences that can alter beliefs.

A COMMON FRAMEWORK

I would not have made much progress in coaching Josh if I'd told him, "You can't read aloud. You can't be so structured." For one thing, he knew his classroom practices were effective for many students. For another, I'd be attacking his core beliefs, his identity as a teacher and as a human being.

To engage in deep conversations in which we can honor different positions and acknowledge merits of diverse opinions, participants need a common framework that can help them unearth their beliefs.

In my work, personality type, popularized through the Myers-Briggs Type Indicator tool (MBTI), serves as a common framework. As Josh's teaching team grew to understand our common framework, instead of talking about "good" and "bad" teaching practices, they discussed how different lessons or instruction helped or hindered students with different learning styles. The framework created an environment where teachers could safely examine their own beliefs and practices.

> Part 2 of this book discusses developing an effective common framework, using personality type as an illustration. It will also give examples of how personality type relates to other frameworks, such as multiple intelligences. Other school reform models may meet the criteria if they have a learning styles component and help teachers understand their beliefs.

To be useful tools for creating this kind of environment, common frameworks need to meet several criteria:

- The model describes preferences for learning in a nonjudgmental way, encompassing both adult and student learning styles.
- The mental model should be strengths-based rather than describing the deficits of different styles. Effective coaching—and teaching—involves helping people use their strengths to compensate for weaknesses, not work on weaknesses. There's a difference.
- The model also needs to work within and honor different cultures. Some models are too linear, too logical, or based too directly in one culture to apply across the diverse student populations our schools now serve.

Using such a framework opens conversations about beliefs. Further, it reminds change agents of their *own* educational biases and how much they are asking teachers to change.

Once the teachers can use a common framework to identify their tightly held beliefs and habits, the next stage of the process begins: providing evidence to help them modify or change beliefs that don't fit with the reality of their students' needs.

PROVIDING EVIDENCE THAT INFLUENCES BELIEFS

As Josh's ancient civilization unit drew to a close, he asked for coaching to plan a unit on Native Americans. When we met, he tossed a few books on the table, slumped into a chair, and said, "I brought a couple ideas, but these kids complain that everything is 'boooring.'"

From his expression, I gathered that he was quite certain that none of my ideas would help him reach his students either. This would probably be my only chance to create an experience that might help Josh rethink his beliefs about teaching.

Dewey (1916) recognized the key role that experiences have in helping us grasp theories, processes, and ideas. He said,

> An ounce of experience is better than a ton of theory simply because it is only in experience that any theory has vital and verifiable significance. An experience, a very humble experience, is capable of generating and carrying any amount of theory (or intellectual content), but a theory apart from an experience cannot be definitely grasped even as theory. (p. 144)

Because of this, creating *quality* experiences requires two emphases: making them initially engaging or instructive *and* ensuring that they positively influence beliefs.

When meeting with Josh, to create an engaging experience I had to remember that our learning styles are almost complete opposites. I used our common framework to position my reaction to the ancient civilizations unit, saying, "My learning style is so much more abstract that I *couldn't* have listened day after day."

Further, I enjoyed planning lessons, whereas Josh found it stressful. Despite his drive for organization, he complained, "I want everything to be perfect. I take it down to the last detail, but I never know about timing, so what difference does planning make?"

Josh started our meeting on the Native American unit by saying that the textbook had good information.

Josh: I looked for new ideas, but they all seem impossible. Here's one for making models of different artifacts, but what a mess.

Jane: Let's start with your normal approach. Remember you start with your own style, then adjust for your opposite.

Josh: Well, a game to introduce vocabulary words, then preview the text before I read it aloud.

Jane: What about choosing topics like legends, archaeological sites, treaty rights, important leaders? We could get other resources from the library and do a station-based unit?

Josh: I don't know . . . what about the struggling readers?

Note that my ideas—chances for choice and independent work—come from my strengths as a learner. They were also in opposition to every single one of Josh's beliefs about education.

- I was asking him to let the students read materials independently instead of reading everything aloud.
- Instead of working on basic skills, the students would be researching from original source materials.
- Instead of whole-class instruction, students would work at their own pace.
- Instead of structured activities with clear directions, students would need to read directions on their own or ask for individual help.

Talk about a formula for creating stress for Josh!

Again, as a coach I needed to provide a positive, guiding experience. After deciding on topics the unit should cover, we went to the library together to look for resources. As we pored over books and brainstormed activities, Josh commented more than once, "You mean some students would enjoy doing that?" He shook his head in disbelief at suggestions for the learning style opposite his own concrete/sequential preferences.

Before leaving, I asked, "Are you sure you want to try this?"

I could see the doubt in his eyes even as he answered, with total lack of enthusiasm, "It can't go any worse than the last packet."

EXPERIENCE INSURANCE

Two days later, Josh started the unit. When I observed his classroom, some students were working alone, some in groups of two or three, but everyone had resources open, pencils in hand—unlike my observation of the ancient civilization packets.

Josh complained, "It is so *noisy* in here. They're not getting anything done." I counted, then pointed out that 17 out of 21 students were on task. Yes, stations were noisier than whole-class instruction, but that didn't mean they weren't working. Remember that our beliefs are so powerful that we tend to note only information that reinforces them. If I didn't point out the positive, Josh would continue to concentrate on the noise and the few students who were off task.

I looked over the shoulder of two girls I knew well. They'd finished one station and were chatting. Then I heard Josh say, "Remember you should complete at least one station today." The girls were doing just that, completing only one station. Josh needed more specific coaching.

- Because Josh was used to teaching from the front of the room, he seemed unsure of his role when students worked independently. I modeled "nagging," checking whether students were on task and helping two English language learners decipher a station. Josh then commented on how stations would allow him to give more individual help.
- I suggested several organizing strategies—posting sheets for students to check off which stations they'd completed, rating the stations on how long they should take, listing how many stations students needed to complete for an A, a B, or a C. Once I provided a few ideas, Josh's natural organizing strengths helped him improve on my suggestions.
- I e-mailed comments to Josh about the positive things I saw.
- I provided immediate feedback about the stations from the student focus groups that met with me. Their comments, which surprised Josh, included,
  - o I think it's interesting, I think it's fun. We have all the different stations and it kinda makes you work faster and harder if you know that you have more stations done than somebody else. Or, if you have less than someone, you want to work more.
  - o I think it was good 'cause he let us work with partners to do it. And because it's a lot funner than having to sit down and read a book and then write and then read a book and write.
  - o What's good is you're getting an education. I'm going to do all 15 stations, get my A.

Still, Josh e-mailed me, "I just feel like I did this all wrong! We should be done with the stations by now, moving on to final projects. But the more time I give them, the longer it gets. They just keep socializing so much, or just sit there because they don't want to think and work." I e-mailed back, reminding him that urban students consider "nagging" a sign that the teacher cares about them (Wilson & Corbett, 2001), and added, "Everything they're doing is reading comprehension. The stations aren't more or less important than the final unit projects."

POINTING TO THE EVIDENCE

Josh needed constant help, like many of us would in a similar situation, to see what was going right—until he saw the grades for the unit. Here's the comparison:[2]

	Ancient civilizations packet	Native American stations
% of students who received an F	26%	8%
% of students who received >75%	58%	70%
% of students who received >85%	32%	55%
% of students who received >95%	9%	36%

Josh exclaimed, "Wow, look at all the A's." Together we looked at the data for each student subgroup. On the previous ancient civilization packets, 35 percent of the English language learner students had received F's, and only 10 percent received A's. On the Native American station work, 45 percent received A's. None of them failed. Josh reflected, "With the stations, I had more time to help them individually since so many students were capable of working independently."

Then, as students talked with him about their unit project choices, he *heard* how much knowledge they'd retained. These results helped Josh decide that there *were* alternatives to direct instruction.

Later we talked about the difficulty of change:

Josh: I'm afraid of trying something new because, you know, what if? That's why it was nice with the stations, trying it with you there. I still have ideas in my head as to how to improve that. I should have spent more time planning it.

Jane: Could you have done any better without seeing what happened?

Josh: No . . . I mean, you have to have the experience to know what needs improving.

The trick is making that first experience, with something as foreign as stations were to Josh, positive enough to motivate a teacher to try them again.

Josh needed three kinds of evidence before his beliefs changed:

- Evidence that his own beliefs had failed. The results on the ancient civilization packet gave me a window of opportunity to convince him to try something else.

- Evidence that contradicted his beliefs. The focus-group comments and grades on the stations helped him believe that his students could learn in ways other than direct instruction.
- Evidence that helps form new beliefs. The experience helped Josh believe he could provide the individual help that many students needed.

On the final project for the Native American unit, Josh came up with 38 different ways students could show what they learned, differentiated for learning styles. Going from one assignment to 38 choices showed a major shift in what Josh thought his students could accomplish. Proof positive of the change in Josh's beliefs about reading aloud was his commitment to use literature circles the next year on historical novels rather than read one aloud to the class!

THE GOAL OF EXPERIENCES

Again, the goal is to create experiences that cause teachers to question their beliefs and make them aware of avenues for further growth. In essence, with Josh I tried to design the kind of experiences that Dewey believed would move individuals toward true freedom: not the ability to do what one wants in the moment but the degree to which we understand our own possibilities for growth.

For teachers, that kind of freedom means believing that they can help more students be successful. It means being able to question their classroom practices without feeling threatened to the core of their being. It may mean that they need support in moving from habitual beliefs to the freedom to grow.

Do staff development efforts provide teachers with these kinds of experiences? Review a recent effort and ask specifically

- Did the experience provide knowledge, theoretical or practical, explicitly connected with the teachers' needs? If not, it may seem a waste of time. One teacher articulated the feelings of many others: "When you first started working with us, I thought, 'She's all excited because it's her life, but is this really going to work in a classroom?' And that's my bottom line . . . otherwise I don't want to hear about it."
- Did the teachers walk away with immediate applications for their classrooms? Often, workshops fill teachers with enthusiasm instead of ready-to-go activities to reinforce what they've learned. They place the new information aside with good intentions to use it, but weeks slip by.

- Were the teachers fully engaged during the experience? And, did it help teachers develop the attitude that staff development is worth their time or something to be avoided? As I will discuss in Chapter 2, teachers have different needs for information and learning experiences. Classroom differentiation begins with modeling the process in staff development by meeting the learning needs of each teacher, especially when we are asking for significant change.

Coaching Josh for change involved six key elements for effective staff development:

- Use a common framework for unbiased reflection on education. This provides the platform for the other key elements.
- Understand the strengths and beliefs of the teachers, instead of relying on our own ingrained beliefs of why teachers resist change.
- Provide information and evidence to influence teachers' beliefs about how students learn.
- Meet the needs of individual teachers, often through coaching. Not all teachers would want a coach in their classrooms to the extent that Josh did. Chapter 2 covers how to differentiate for teacher needs.
- Focus on the problems teachers want to solve. Chapter 3 provides a thorough discussion of defining and working through problems.
- Encourage deep, reflective collaboration. Chapter 4 covers moving toward effective collaboration.

Although literature exists on all of the above elements, it says little about the critical role of a common framework, not just common goals, that lets people examine and discuss their educational beliefs without bias.

Further, the literature brushes aside the difficulty of change in general. Monitoring school reform efforts for uniform implementation is seldom effective because the teachers themselves are different. The changes affect them differently—they'll have different struggles, different successes, and different needs. Josh responded to differentiated, not just instructional, coaching, a process described in the next chapter.

NOTES

1. Names and details have been changed. Parts of Josh's story are composites of several teachers.

2. Note that descriptions of assignments were altered to protect identities, making comparison of results difficult. However, about 25 percent of the students had been failing major projects in *every* class. The station assignment showed a significant departure from that pattern.

2 What Do Teachers Need During Change?

The fourth key element for effective staff development: Meeting the needs of each teacher.

Michael Fullan (1993) summarizes well what school reformers have learned over the past decades:

> The hardest core to crack is the learning core—changes in instructional practices and in the culture of teaching toward greater collaborative relationships among students, teachers and other potential partners. Stated differently, *to restructure is not to reculture*—a lesson increasingly echoed in other attempts at reform. Changing formal structures is not the same as changing norms, habits, skills and beliefs. (p. 49)

Fullan points out that influencing or changing teacher beliefs often involves changing the person the teacher is, which is exactly what I experienced as I worked with Josh to help him reach more students in his classroom. I had to meet his individual needs to help him make changes that were foreign to his beliefs about education. Meeting the teachers' needs is the fourth key element for effective staff development.

Although coaching is still new in the field of education, it has a long track record in the world of business—there, having a coach is a mark of your value to a corporation. Think of the root of the word *coach*. Witherspoon and White (1997) point out, "the root meaning of the verb 'to coach' is to convey a valued person from where he or she was to where he or she wants to be." Witherspoon (2000) also identifies a continuum of coaching, depending on the needs of the executive being coached. He differentiates between

- Coaching for skills: helping the coachee gain specific proficiencies for current tasks or responsibilities. Most instructional coaching, including literacy coaching, is at this level and is often conducted most effectively within collaborative groups (Annenberg Institute, 2005a).
- Coaching for performance: assessing the individual's strengths, blind spots, confidence, and motivation, then tailoring strategies to meet those needs—in short, the methods I used with Josh to build on his strengths. This requires an understanding of an individual's approach to both learning and change. A general understanding of adult learning processes isn't sufficient.

Instructional coaching often fails to reach resistant teachers (Annenberg Institute, 2005a). Literature on coaching treats resistance in teachers as if teachers are the cause of the problem, rather than considering whether the reform effort, or the coaching strategies, may be implemented in a way that does not take into account the individuals' differing needs or the huge changes they're being asked to make.

To examine more closely what teachers need to change, let's look at a team of teachers who *wanted* to change.

THE CASE OF THE PARALYZED PILOT TEAM

Meet Kay, Pete, and Sara, the rest of Josh's team of sixth-grade teachers who volunteered as a pilot team to learn about the differentiation framework I use, personality type, which I explain in Chapters 5 and 6. During September, they met with me once a week. I worked with them in their classrooms, modeling activities that helped students identify their own learning styles. By the end of the month, the teachers, not me, insisted that we jump right into lesson planning. They even scheduled two meetings in one week!

To accommodate the teachers' different learning styles, I followed the techniques I'd used successfully in other schools. I provided some reading materials, gave a few mini-lectures on the theory, encouraged debate and questions, brought examples of completed lesson plans and sample student work, and made sure we touched on applications for each of their subject areas.

- Kay, the language arts teacher, read everything I provided and came with notes.
- Pete, the science teacher, skimmed the materials in advance. He brought handouts of the learning styles model he already used.
- Josh had read the "essential pages" I'd asked them all to get through.
- Sara, the math teacher, hadn't read anything before our meetings. She interrupted my overview with so many questions that Pete finally asked her to let me finish.

Hoping to engage Sara, for the next session I asked the teachers to bring in lesson plans for upcoming units they would be teaching.

- Kay asked for suggestions on her novel unit, and Josh asked for help on archaeology, as described in Chapter 1.
- Pete, Kay, and Josh discussed several ideas.
- Sara didn't participate. She corrected papers and said she didn't need any help with her lessons, adding, "I think the math curriculum is good enough already."

Neither Kay nor Josh used the team's suggestions in their classrooms.

I thought that perhaps I'd been too open-ended. Maybe the team didn't grasp the planning process because I'd overfacilitated the brainstorming. So, I developed a planning grid that they could use to organize their ideas. I completed one for Josh's archaeology unit. Sara said, "This is all I need to do? Fill out an organizer?"

Still, no one created or even modified lesson plans.

WHY WEREN'T THEY CHANGING?

I was puzzled—and frustrated. The teachers kept setting up meetings with me. They asked me to design teamwide reflection activities for students—they specifically didn't want to call them final activities, telling me, "We're going to work with these concepts all year long, helping the students grasp how they really learn." If they were that committed to our work, why weren't they trying anything new in their classrooms?

They had the theory and the process; they'd helped with planning. Maybe I wasn't being concrete enough. For our fourth meeting on lesson planning, I brought a full-fledged lesson plan for a true sports story entitled

"Full Court Courage"—two days' worth of activities scripted out, the planning grid showing which activities fit which learning styles, graphic organizers for the students to use, and a list of differentiated final activities. Surely now they had a model for planning other lessons.

When I handed it out, Sara glanced through it and said, "This is good, this is—can I use it tomorrow? In my reading class?"

She did use it and e-mailed me to report that the students were very engaged. She asked if I would help her plan another lesson. Three months after we began meeting, someone finally tried a differentiated lesson with their students. And it was Sara, who until this point had been the most disinterested—even resistant—in planning lessons during our meetings.

Later, when Sara and I talked about what made her shift from being the most resistant to the most willing member of her team to try new lessons, she told me,

> My whole master's degree was theory. I can't stand the stupid— I took this class in ethics and couldn't stand it. You know, theories. And I'm like, "This is not going to help me tomorrow." That story— I saw how I could use it!

In short, I'd finally given Sara the information she needed to change— a lesson plan she could try, giving her concrete experience with what I was talking about.

Barger and Kirby (1995) asked over 2,000 workshop participants what they needed during times of changes. The responses (summarized on pages 133–135) showed clear differences in the kinds of information people with different personalities and learning styles need, how they process and react to that information, and what factors make change more stressful. They noted that resistance to change increases when these needs are not met and found that *leaders in general* failed to recognize and deal effectively with these needs.

INFORMATION: THE *CONTENT* OF STAFF DEVELOPMENT

It is essential, then, to provide teachers with the kinds of information they need to embrace a change effort. This does not mean providing just oral and written versions, along with time for discussion or questions. Let's look at the different informational needs of the four teachers on Sara's team.

Immediate applications. Although making staff development relevant to the classroom is recognized as a key element for success, teachers may not recognize what is relevant if, like Josh, their teaching habits come from their own strengths and they struggle to envision how things might be different.

What Information Do Teachers Want?

During staff development, the varying informational needs of different teachers may include

- Immediate applications
- The impact on individual students
- The details, not the big picture
- A deep understanding of the theories and models
- Implementation mechanics
- A say in the plan
- Substantive background materials
- Proof that the changes are better than the present.

Think back to your last staff development effort. How many of these needs did it meet? Note that some are in direct conflict with others!

Sara needed immediate applications before she was willing to invest time in understanding the differentiation framework. She flourished when I showed up with lesson ideas and choices. To her, planning lessons was the least enjoyable part of teaching; she needed to see how things worked before making the effort to plan and apply the concepts herself. She felt more competent planning math lessons than reading, so over the next weeks we concentrated on the latter. For a novel she hoped to teach, I brought ideas from different Web sites, introduced her to different read-aloud strategies, and helped her write out sample journal entries. She tried most of the ideas we came up with.

A vision of how each student will be affected. In contrast to Sara, Kay needed information about the children she taught. In team or individual meetings, whenever I suggested a new practice, Kay immediately questioned how different groups of students would be affected. What about the English language learners? The students who disliked working in groups? The students who had failed the previous quarter? The boy who rushed through his work? The twin who wasn't doing as well as her sister?

No matter how big of an improvement they might show, statistics and group studies will not convince these teachers that a new practice is worth trying. They need to consider atypical students and situations. Without a common framework for reflection on teaching and learning, it is very difficult to meet the informational needs of teachers like Kay, as they will continue to come up with students whom they don't think the proposed changes will help.

The details, not the big picture. Josh and Sara both struggled to concentrate on the big picture until we'd worked out the details of how something would actually work. For example, at one meeting the whole team decided to enforce student use of planners. Sara immediately opened up her planner and asked questions about how to adapt it for the students' block scheduling and where students would write daily agendas, homework assignments, and long-term goals. Hargreaves (1994) noted that many teachers test an idea against the reality of their particular classroom—can *they* make it work in the time they have, with the materials they have? That describes Sara.

A deep understanding of the theories and models being used. In contrast to Josh and Sara, with their focus on implementation details, Pete and Kay started with the big picture, asking questions about the research behind the suggested strategies. Pete, in particular, questioned each of my ideas and debated whether the personality type framework I used contradicted the Gregorc Mind Styles model he'd used for years (see page 81 for a comparison). Pete's questioning helped him fit my suggestions into the mental model he'd developed through extensive study and experiment. Only then could he make sense of why he needed to make changes in his classroom.

Pete told me, "I don't like just knowing or memorizing things, I like to *understand* things. It isn't enough for me to know which activities appeal to which kinds of learners. I have to know *why.*" Further, teachers like Pete may also need to see how a proposed change effort fits in with the big picture of district initiatives, past staff development efforts, or a school improvement plan. Telling them to "just do it" or answering their questions with "the decision's already made" often fuels resistance.

Implementation mechanics. Some teachers focus on timelines, deadlines, goals, and the paperwork required of them. They may also raise practical questions such as, "Where will we get the time to do this? What will be left undone? What specific steps need to be taken?" They want to see all of this at the start because they'll allocate their efforts accordingly—and they plan their own work in this style. Often, they've experienced change efforts that were big on vision and ended up being much more complicated or time-consuming than plans allowed for, so they're wary of efforts in which the up-front plan isn't established.

A say in the plan. Although top-down change initiators might view vocal teachers as resistant, in fact the teachers are often systems thinkers. They've constructed their own ideas of how things should change. Inviting them into some part of the planning phase and carefully considering their critiques is often key to gaining their buy-in and improving the change process.

Substantive background materials. Some teachers need to digest the rationale for change themselves. Even if they have no power to influence the direction of change, they may still need to review options *not* chosen as well as read for themselves the information that led to determining the change process. Kay functioned this way, reading entire books before discussing with me how to change her classroom.

Proof that the change is better than the present. Some teachers embrace new ideas and theories, whereas others require proof that the new is better than the present. Their motto isn't just "If it works, don't fix it" but "A known problem is less risky than an experiment when it comes to my classroom."
  Sparks (1997) points out that

> teachers' skepticism about the latest staff development program is a sign that they are not brain dead. It only makes sense that numerous negative experiences would condition someone to avoid the source of that discomfort. We must face the fact that most teachers and administrators have not been well served by staff development efforts that have been advanced in the name of change. (p. 1)

The proof needed to motivate teachers to change takes different forms for different people, including

- Statistical studies
- Stories and examples from peers who have used the ideas
- Expert testimony
- Books and papers that explain methods or theories
- Logical explanations of the changes
- Analysis of values underlying the changes
- Data on costs, commitment of staff development time, expectations, and responsibilities
- Specific, step-by-step instructions
- General directions with room for individual adjustments and ideas.

Schools that habitually neglect some of the above forms of information may see clear patterns of resistance from the same teachers—the teachers who need the information that's not being provided. And, like it or not, "scientifically based research" isn't sufficient for many types of learners because it encompasses neither the holistic view they have of education nor the particularities of their own classrooms.

RESISTERS? WHO?

Unfortunately, without a deep understanding of the informational and coaching needs of teachers as different as Kay, Josh, Pete, and Sara, it would be all too easy to label Kay (who delayed as she digested background information) as unmotivated, Josh (who sought my input continually) as needy, Pete (who debated my every suggestion) as cynical, and Sara (who didn't participate at first) as resistant. Those are the kinds of labels assigned to teachers when school reform efforts fail. Evans (2001) describes a continuum of competence, involvement, and growth, with "key members" as the stars of the school who are on the cutting edge of education and who bring enthusiasm to the workplace. Next are "contributors" who are competent and caring but may not seek change. Further from the top are "stable and stagnant" teachers who "are at best passable, who mostly go through the motions" (p. 107). Last on Evans's continuum are the "deadwood," whom he describes as teachers who were never particularly competent and have now retired on the job. Although he acknowledges the role of midlife issues and teachers' lack of efficacy brought about by increasing demands and decreasing resources, he still looks to the teachers as the problem in resistance.

Tye (2000) presents a similar taxonomy of how teachers react to change:

A group such as a school faculty consists of *innovators,* who are often in the forefront of any new project and who are recognized risk-takers; *early adopters,* also open to trying something new; and an *early majority,* who wait in the wings to see how their more adventurous colleagues are doing or if the change seems likely to stick. The *late majority* are resisters, and the *laggards* simply refuse to participate, and may even attempt to sabotage the program. (p. 151)

Yet, with the right information, Sara turned from a "laggard" to an early adopter. Josh actually moved to "innovator," taking huge risks if I joined him in his classroom for the first tries. All four moved toward being "key members" as they got the information they needed.

Complicating this change effort further, the four teachers differed widely on how they wanted that information delivered. Each wanted it tailored to their own needs, in the form of examples from which they could extrapolate, via debate or via collegial teaming. Because of the deep, deep changes I was asking them to make, differentiated coaching was necessary.

DELIVERY: THE *PROCESS* OF STAFF DEVELOPMENT

Coaching is at one end of a continuum of ways to package staff development. The traditional method of all-staff workshops is at the other. Before we turn to coaching, let's look at the pros and cons of some of the other methods.

Large-group staff development. All-staff meetings are best for conveying new missions or philosophies, launching the school year, or beginning new initiatives. If differentiated in design (see Chapter 6), they can be very effective. However, look back at the broad range of informational needs teachers have. Ponder how long a staff development session would have to be to meet all of them for major changes—and how teachers behave when their needs aren't being met. The "big picture" people tune out during discussion of the details, and, during the presentation of the big picture, teachers like Sara correct papers until the presentation answers, "What does this mean I'll be doing?" Providing differentiated content and delivery takes more planning and effort than staff development usually receives; hence, teachers come late, tune out, or leave early.

Professional learning communities. Having teachers gather in small groups to read and reflect works well for exploring specific topics such as brain research or peer mediation. Professional learning communities have the potential to build productive, collaborative relationships; help teachers learn to meet the needs of diverse students; improve school culture, teacher practice, and student learning; and engage educators in continuous professional development (Annenberg Institute, 2005b). Further, effective instructional coaching often takes place within these communities, providing for examination of data and student work.

However, if deep change is required, this method won't meet the needs of those who want specific examples, chances to ask questions of an expert, or help in integrating the information into their classrooms. Further, for many theoretical topics, teachers whose styles are similar to Sara's may not deem relevant the information provided in books or research summaries.

Off-site workshops. These all-day or summer opportunities allow schools to share the costs of expertise and provide intensive training on intricate areas. However, teachers often come back to the classroom full of good intentions that never come to fruition because of a lack of continuing support. Or, the workshop content doesn't connect directly with the current practices and is therefore too difficult to integrate. The training materials sit on their shelves.

Team-based initiatives. Although allowing teaching teams to identify their own staff development needs can increase motivation, they often need outside guidance to break out of current patterns. Little (1990) found that teams rarely progress to reflective discussions on the ethics and purposes of their current teaching practices. Further, this method is of minimal use when seeking schoolwide change. It often results in what Hargreaves (1994) labels "contrived" collaboration.

Differentiated coaching. What at first seems like a resource drain may actually be the most cost-effective method when seeking deep change. Given the high level of effort required for teachers to change their classrooms, and given that individuals need different information and scaffolding to succeed, coaching teachers in their own styles may be the only viable strategy in many situations.

DIFFERENTIATED COACHING: WHY MENTORING AND INSTRUCTIONAL COACHING OFTEN MISS THE MARK

Although the National Staff Development Council (NSDC) has provided guidelines for preparing coaches for working with teachers, including "considerable facility in working with adult learners" (Neufeld & Roper, 2003), the guidelines make no mention of adapting coaching techniques to meet the styles of the individuals being coached; in fact, they emphasize coaching as a tool for having teachers uniformly implement the same practices. Further, when teachers resist, they recommend that either district administrators or principals intervene to make it clear that all teachers must adopt the new instructional strategies. Once again, the blame for resistance falls on the teachers rather than on the coaching strategies or the suitability of the methods being taught.

In business settings, coaching has a very different flavor. To be singled out for coaching is often a mark of an employee's value to the organization because of the time-consuming, and therefore costly, nature of coaching. The whole idea of coaching someone involves tailoring learning to meet that person's needs, not implementing a districtwide mandate or practice. A coach asks, "What does this individual need to see the value of the mandate? How does it meet his or her needs? What will provide the right evidence?" Coaching may involve helping the person see exactly why a mandate is necessary and why he or she should embrace it. To change the beliefs, as happened with each member of the "paralyzed pilot team," makes it possible to change the classroom.

A LESSON FROM THE WORLD OF SPORTS

For a moment, let's look at a full-blown sports analogy. As I worked on my own philosophy of executive coaching, developed through consulting in the world of business, I thought back to my springboard diving days. Athletes cannot expect to become competitive divers simply from attending workshops and practicing alone day after day, without advice as to whether they are appropriately implementing what they have learned. No, athletes receive individual coaching before, during, and after each event.

Diving is an individual sport, much as teachers are solo performers in their classrooms. Yet, a diver's overall performance counts toward the swim team's ranking, just as a teacher's success with his or her classroom influences the success of a school. A coach works to help each team member reach a personal best.

Some divers are natural twisters, and others natural spinners. They all have "sweet" dives, ones they can count on to bring high scores. Teachers, too, have "sweet" teaching techniques and practices. A good coach builds on strengths while making suggestions and providing techniques and training exercises to work on problem areas.

Coaches play a far different role than that of a teacher or a facilitator. Although a whole team occasionally needs the same information or practice, more often each member works on different dives. Coaches know each team member's individual strengths and needs. They understand which changes will be hard and which will be easy. My own coach let one diver stand on the board for as long as she needed before trying a new dive; from experience, he knew that she was building a mental model of how to do it and would nail it the first time. On the other hand, he'd tell me to try it within a couple of minutes or quit the team; he knew the longer I waited, the more nervous I got. If the goal is for teachers to adapt their current classroom practices to meet the needs of more students, then they, too, need instruction tailored to their needs.

On those occasions when the whole team practices the same dives, the coach's instructions to each person are different. Teachers, too, need information and coaching in forms that meet their individual needs and learning styles, especially when major change is sought. Yet in the world of education, general workshops for teachers are the most common method for motivating them to change their classrooms. When some resist, the blame falls on the "deadwood" teachers instead of on the way the information was delivered. Further, the success some teachers have with the new information is often pointed to as proof that the entire staff had ample opportunities and resources to change.

Although current models of coaching in education may provide individual instruction to each teacher, Hargreaves (1994) noted that the process often frustrates teachers because the coaches often don't share their educational beliefs or teaching styles. The process feels contrived, not helpful. In contrast, gifted coaches, whether in the world of sports or the world of executive coaching, change their methods so they "speak the language" of the person they're coaching. In other words, successful coaches are chameleons. Either the coach needs the ability to flex or an organization needs different coaches with different styles.

CHAMELEON COACHING

Let's look again at the "paralyzed pilot team." All of them then made significant changes in their classroom practices, but the paths I guided them over were very different. Here are some of the different coaching styles I've used.

Coach as useful resource. Back when I handed the "Full Court Courage" lesson plan to Sara and she asked if she could use it the next day, I'd coached Sara in her own learning style. Hirsh and Kise (2000) say that for someone like Sara, "Use relevant subject matter that applies directly to one of their interest areas" (p. 23).

As described above, I kept providing Sara with ideas she could use immediately. Slowly, she started adapting her own lessons. For example, whereas all of the teachers taught a station-based unit, which is one style of differentiation, Sara was the first to develop her own station-based unit. She'd seen that it worked, and she was ready to use it.

Another educator, thinking of how he'd react, asked me, "Wasn't Sara insulted when you handed her a ready-made lesson plan?" I asked Sara how she'd felt at the time, and she answered, "I thought, *Cool. Wow, this is great. She really is here to help!*" Many educators *would* react negatively to the directive help I gave Sara, but it fit her particular style. Chapter 8, "Differentiated Coaching for Teachers," explains how to use personality type or another learning styles model to choose effective coaching strategies.

"Useful resource" coaching requires such things as a bag of tricks, multiple methods, and the ability to tailor them for specific subjects and situations. Teachers like Sara, especially if they teach noncore subjects, are frustrated by workshops in which the examples deal with language arts, science, or math rather than the subject they teach. They want to test something out to see if it works—they're hands-on learners. If it does work, they'll take the time to learn more.

Coach as encouraging sage. Josh wanted my help to get started. He insisted that he wasn't very creative and felt guilty about it. "As a tenured teacher, I should be able to do this on my own," he lamented. Josh told me he didn't trust his own new ideas until he'd received feedback from someone else about their merit.

Josh thrived on direct classroom help when trying a new idea. The other teachers accepted my presence, but Josh looked forward to a dialogue about his students' reactions and results as new lessons unfolded. He enjoyed receiving on-the-spot suggestions, often perfecting them overnight—and adding ideas of his own.

"Encouraging sage" coaching requires time, enthusiasm, and an ability to evaluate and give in-the-moment suggestions and encouragement. Josh took personally the day-to-day events in his classroom, assuming that deviations from perfect student behavior or performance were his fault. Often, he needed help to see what was going right and concrete suggestions to fix molehills that seemed like mountains because of his desire to help each child.

Coach as collegial mentor. Kay, the social studies teacher, cast me in an almost opposite role as coach. She was the last to schedule an individual meeting with me, which was a bit puzzling since she had pushed hard in the fall to begin working on differentiation as soon as possible.

Kay, though, had used the intervening months to absorb as much of the background material as she could. When we met, Kay had brainstormed a dozen different assessment ideas for an upcoming unit, but wanted my help in correctly matching them to learning styles. She willingly accepted my modifications to a few of her ideas. She admitted, "The hardest thing is imagining what the students whose learning style is opposite to mine would enjoy because the activities sound so awful to me!"

When we finished working on the lesson, she asked me to list specific skills that she needed to work on to be more effective. Later she told me, "I wanted to make sure I had a lot of stuff ready to show you because I needed to know how to do it on my own. There was just so much time you would be here, and I wanted feedback to see if I was getting it right."

"Collegial mentor" coaching requires patience and listening skills. Kay didn't feel comfortable sharing her ideas until she'd thought through them thoroughly. Often, she wanted to talk through several scenarios before deciding on teaching or assessment strategies.

Coach as expert. For Pete, on the other hand, I needed to be a debate sparring partner. Again, it wasn't that he doubted my expertise or strategies, but that he wanted to understand them at a deep level. Here's an excerpt from a debate we had about whether, under the principle of "Make the students do something rather than allow them to do nothing," providing an alternative test to students who didn't complete end-of-unit projects was appropriate and fair to students who finished the original assignment.

Pete: If you hadn't insisted on the fall-back assignment of taking a test at the end, there would have been a lot of students who did nothing, as usual.

Jane: But the test was one choice for the project.

Pete: Right, but that's what I'm saying. If part of your objective is to *not* give a paper and pencil test, if it's for them to create a product, are they really meeting the requirements?

Jane: There's two ways to look at this. In every class the team has had about 30% of students not completing major assignments. With the mandatory alternative of an open-book test, the failure rate dropped significantly, which means at least the kids did the work. The open-book test was about as much work as if they'd done the project. So if you look at scaffolding strategies, trying to hold kids to expectations, then that served the purpose of getting them all to do something.

Pete: Right, if the open-book test is the same amount of effort. I can see . . . if they don't turn in a portion of a science project, I could create a test that would test the same material.

Jane: And that's the expectations part. You know, maybe they can't get more than a C but at least they're forced to produce work rather than not do anything. [sigh from Pete] I'm not saying it's easy.

Pete: I'm thinking . . . for the picture portfolio where they have to find something that demonstrates or represents a concept. If they didn't complete it, I could test by presenting a whole bunch of scenarios—maybe I have a hundred pictures on the test and they have to explain what principle each one represents. But I bet that some of them, if they knew that's what the test was, wouldn't bother cutting magazine pictures because it takes longer.

Jane: Yet it was really interesting watching how hard kids fought in Josh's class not to take a test, where you might think the opposite would be true. The number that spent lunch hours catching up?

Pete: Yeah, yeah right.

Pete didn't argue that what the other teachers had done to help more students succeed was illegitimate. Instead, he debated when, how, and where it was appropriate. Had we really met our goal of making all students do the work? He wasn't resisting implementing the ideas in his classroom; he was trying to understand at a deep level whether we had truly accomplished our own goals.

"Expert" coaching requires depth of knowledge and objectivity. Pete expected me to have the expertise to answer his questions. Often, teachers with Pete's learning style are viewed as contrary, resistant, or abrasive rather than the deep thinkers they are. If their needs are met and they embrace the changes as valid and important, they often become enthusiastic supporters of a change effort.

MOVING TOWARD DIFFERENTIATED COACHING

The complexity of knowing how to coach each teacher is overwhelming, unless you have a common framework—a common mental model or neutral language—of teaching and learning that provides a general idea of what each person needs.

Adequate frameworks provide focus for understanding which teachers might find change most difficult, what they need to change, and how to tailor both information and processes to accommodate those needs. The model needs to focus on each teacher's strengths because, as we've seen, those strengths are tightly tied to beliefs about education. Coaching brings together several of the key elements for effective staff development and is in fact the fourth key element. To reiterate, successful staff development

- Utilizes a common framework for unbiased reflection on education. This forms the platform for the other key elements.
- Begins with understanding the strengths and beliefs of the teachers.
- Provides information and evidence that can influence those beliefs.
- Meets the needs of each teacher in a change process, which may involve individual, differentiated coaching.

Changing beliefs touches on the very essence of how teachers see themselves. The information teachers receive must help them reevaluate their core beliefs while validating who they are. Only then can deep change take place.

In my years of working with teachers, both as a parent and as a consultant, I've met only a few teachers who earned the labels of deadwood or laggard—certainly not enough to account for the high, high percentage of school reform efforts that fall far short of their goals. Instead, I've seen a clear majority of teachers who would gladly implement any reform that would clearly improve the learning of all children.

Yes, it may seem cumbersome and costly to deliver staff development in ways that meet the content and contextual needs of each teacher, but let's face it: Our current methods have resulted in millions of dollars of staff development efforts with little or no impact on student learning. *If we want to change how teachers teach, we need to model what we are asking them to do. If we want them to meet the needs of all students, we need to model with them how that is possible, by meeting the needs of all teachers.*

3 What Problems Do Teachers Want to Solve?

The fifth key element for effective staff development: Relating or applying what is being learned to the problems teachers want to solve in their classrooms.

Amy was part of a team of teachers who called me on the fifth day of school. They'd heard from Josh's team about the successes they'd had with new classroom management and differentiation strategies. "We need help," they pleaded. "We've *never* seen students with these kinds of behavior problems."

I met with them a few days later and outlined the steps Josh's team had taken. The teachers chose to wait until after midquarter, hoping that the students would get more used to their routines. Then conferences swallowed every spare minute. Not until November, as second quarter was underway, did they find time to meet with me.

These teachers were overwhelmed. Around half of their students were failing one or more core classes. They asked for a list of strategies that they could implement teamwide to create an atmosphere of achievement, but another six weeks passed before they found time to discuss them. Now it was January, and we'd done nothing. The fact that they kept asking to meet with me made me believe that they thought I had something to offer. Or rather, they *hoped* I did. They were out of ideas on their own.

AMY'S PROBLEM

Finally the language arts teacher, Amy, agreed to go with me to meet with a teacher at another school whose team had implemented a uniform structure, much like I'd suggested, with a similar group of students. Amy listened intently, asked questions, made copies of handouts, and wrote down references to articles and books. Afterward she sighed and said, "I've *always* been able to manage my classes by building relationships with the students. Most classes are better than before, but my fifth hour? They don't trust anyone, not us and not each other."

I'd been in Amy's classroom several times in past years. She was right; before, she'd been able to silence reluctant learners with a smile. She continued, "I can't even get my fifth-hour class to be civil, and I've tried everything."

Her fifth-hour class had in fact become a bit legendary. At one team meeting I attended, she agreed to transfer in more problem students. "That way," her team agreed, "we can get on with teaching in the other classes." They told me that Amy's fifth-hour kids didn't care about school or were "too low" for regular classrooms.

Amy asked me to observe that class. Students would be preparing for a debate on a topic that had grabbed the attention of her other classes. She asked me to watch for

- Off-task behavior. What triggered students' disengaging from their work?
- Put-downs. Were there any patterns to when these erupted? During transitions? During seatwork? While she gave directions?
- The strategies she used to get students on task. How did she react? What worked? What didn't?
- Scaffolding needs. What further instruction or learning tools might she provide to help all students handle the content of the lesson?

The cognitive coaching framework (Costa & Garmston, 1994) is helpful for focusing on the problems teachers want to solve. The preobservation conference with Amy served to

- Build trust
- Clarify the lesson goals and objectives
- Seek Amy's input on what I should observe
- Help Amy clarify how she thought the lesson would work.

I took a seat at the back of the room. Twenty minutes lapsed as she struggled to form groups to argue for and against the issue. I counted over three dozen interruptions—phone calls, knocks on the door, student misbehavior. Then, not one group stayed on task. Once the students were in groups, they talked about anything and everything except the subject assigned to them.

In frustration, Amy canceled the debate, skipping ahead to worksheets for essays on the subject. When she asked the students to begin writing, they started talking. She sent two boys out into the hall for being disrespectful. Amy looked at me as if to say, "See what I mean?"

I asked if she wanted me to work with the two boys. In less than five minutes, they had the first two sections of the worksheet completed. They clearly had the skills to do the work. As I roamed the class, I discovered that so did 90 percent of the others.

Afterward, I expressed my admiration for Amy's calm in dealing with an overcrowded classroom filled with challenging students, citing two specific examples where her strategies had worked well. I showed her the data I'd collected and asked for her interpretations. She shook her head in defeat. "They just insult each other unless I give a concrete task like copying notes off an overhead—as if they really learn from that. Yet all of these put-downs ruin any chance for learning, too."

I probed a few more times to nudge Amy toward more reflection, but her only answer was to use direct instruction with the class. From past conversations, I knew this went against Amy's core beliefs about how students learn. She wanted students to actively process ideas through discussions and projects that required creativity and thought. Her teaching bag of tricks, though, was empty; she had no other solutions.

Carefully, I suggested a few basic strategies for adding more structure to the environment rather than just to her instruction methods. Amy nodded at my suggestions until I mentioned starting the class with a calming activity: reading from a novel that connected with the topic of the ill-fated debate. The students would complete a picture-with-caption journal entry while she read.

She laughed at me. "They won't listen. It'll be chaos."

I pointed out how the strategy fit into the learning styles framework we used, but I was honest about not being sure what would happen with her fifth-hour class. She shook her head. Then I asked, "Will you try it if I'm there?"

The first day, it took 20 minutes for us to get the students seated, with pencils and journals, ready to listen. But they did listen. They finished the journals and most of the regular class assignment. The second day, all of the students had their journals open in less than four minutes. Again, they stayed on task for the class work. Amy gave me two thumbs up and said, "Okay, let's plan my next unit together."

DEFINING THE PROBLEM THROUGH THE EYES OF A TEACHER

Although I fully agree that it is important to use student data to determine adult learning priorities within schools, which is one of the NSDC (2001) standards for staff development, it may not be the right starting place for many efforts. In fact, teachers who, like Amy's team, feel as if they're drowning might perceive data-driven staff development as offering techniques on treading water when what the teachers want—and need—is a life ring.

The trouble with starting with data about students is that it may not correctly define the root source of the problem. Perhaps basic math computation scores are low and teachers need training on how to help students master multiplication facts, but that training won't help if the teachers believe that students need to practice those facts at home—and don't have adults present to help them. If the teachers see no immediate results in their classrooms, they may say, "See? Nothing helps."

Is it any surprise that teachers don't implement new things in their classrooms if staff development focuses on reading skills but teachers think, "What I really need is help getting students to turn in homework." Or, "Teach me how to handle frustrated parents first." Or, "The kids who really need this hate to read. What am I supposed to do about that?"

Without thorough analysis of our beliefs, not just data, we may not even bring many real presenting problems to the surface. Viadero (2005) points out that quantitative results don't always unearth complete answers about why an intervention does or doesn't work; whether it was well implemented; and often, whether it produced side effects. Note that Amy and I looked at observation data in the postconference for evidence of what was and wasn't working. The data backed my hypotheses that structure could reduce the countless interruptions in that class.

Although Amy fervently wanted her students to learn, the presenting problem, in her opinion, was the students' lack of trust, resulting in lack of respect for each other and for her. Lack of trust isn't found through the examination of data on test scores and basic skills—nor would most of the students likely have expressed their feelings that way on surveys. To gain buy-in from Amy, I focused my analysis on ways to create a safer, more stable environment for the students. At first, Amy's belief that the students were "safe" only during direct instruction caused her to reject my proposed solution—and if I hadn't offered to be present, chances are she would have given up on the read-aloud, as she had on the debate, before that first 20 minutes of struggle was over.

Amy hadn't sensed any value in learning about differentiation from me because she thought that her students' behavior would prevent it from doing any good. Once the behavior problem was under control, she was eager to move on to trying to meet the needs of the varied learners in her room.

PROBLEMS: A KEY TO TEACHER BUY-IN

Let's change the definition of relevant learning from relevant to things we *should* care about to relevant to things we *do* care about. Finding out what teachers care about requires listening. And often, as in Amy's case, if we can solve their biggest concern, they're more open to working on agendas tied directly to student data. Further, we may be able to solve those problems as we wait for longer-term efforts to show fruit. In Amy's case, for example, the first step in improving student achievement was getting them engaged in the work. She *was* using several research-based strategies for improving cognitive efforts, but since the fifth-hour students weren't doing the work, how long would it take for those strategies to bear fruit in test scores?

> This doesn't mean that we focus on whatever the teachers feel like focusing on, but that we find ways to use their immediate concerns to build buy-in for the changes we hope to see. We use their concerns as a golden opportunity to show them how the proposed changes are relevant to their needs.

Here's a list of the problems teams at a K–8 school identified as things they most wanted help to fix or solve. At this school, basically all students passed the basic skills tests; the emphasis was on preparing them for high school and college.

- Kindergarten: How to redesign their report card
- First grade: Ways to work with difficult, challenging children
- Second grade: Better ways to provide enrichment activities
- Third grade: Ways to raise student confidence and overcome sloppy work by providing better motivation
- Fourth grade: Better collaboration and appreciation of each other's strengths

- Fifth grade: How to plan curriculum for a specific novel
- Middle school: How to manage their own levels of stress, work better as a team, and work with "behavior problem" students.

Although coordinating so many efforts may seem like a nightmare, when all of the teams use a common framework for teaching and learning, the efforts can be cohesive.

A second step, though, is properly defining the problem. A comparison of Amy's and my thinking processes shows the impact that changing the definition can have:

	Amy	Jane
Problem	The students are out of control and don't trust me.	Students aren't engaged; their off-task behavior fosters lack of trust in the classroom.
Solution	• Direct instruction that focuses their attention so they don't insult each other. • Individual, structured seatwork that can be easily monitored for on-task behavior. • They may not learn much, but it will be a less damaging environment.	• Exciting, engaging content so they'd learn to settle down quickly. • A structured, consistent task that engages many kinds of intelligences: kinesthetic (by being allowed to draw), interpersonal (by stepping into the shoes of the characters), and linguistic (writing). Later journal entries included logical intelligence as we asked the students to think of alternative solutions to the main character's problems. • Removal of excuses for not learning, such as lack of supplies. • High expectations: expecting and ensuring that each student would complete the journal work.

All of those factors—engagement, structure without repetitiveness, expectations—had to be in place before Amy could use the picture-journal exercise to increase students' comprehension of what they were hearing. Within two weeks of beginning each class this way, students listened to each other respectfully as they shared what they'd journaled about. Amy was able to hold productive class discussions. Now we could look at student data to set instructional goals.

GENERATING ALTERNATIVES

Once we define a problem, the next step is to generate plausible alternatives that will address it. Remember, though, that the alternatives we generate will come from our own worldview, and that view may have considerable holes in it. If teachers don't understand their own biases or assumptions, the process of generating alternatives will be stifled. Amy, for example, didn't think my ideas had a ghost of a chance of succeeding. She'd never seen the students sit still and listen, so why would they listen to a story?

Amy wasn't stubborn; she was simply operating out of her own strengths, experiences, and beliefs, just like Josh with his learning packets. When teachers say, "I've tried everything," they usually have genuinely tried everything they can think of.

Proper definition of a problem is often a key turning point in the learning experiences of both the teachers *and* the coach. Back to Josh's team: recall that, after several months of work, they still weren't differentiating, which was what I'd been asked to get them to do. For me, the turning point came when I redefined the problem I faced: I wasn't just introducing differentiation, but supporting teachers in a change process. When the problem changed, so did my basis for reflection and the possible solutions I could generate. Similarly, when Amy reconsidered whether lack of trust or lack of structure was the presenting problem, she opened up to new solutions.

Reflective thought asks us to stop to consider what other factors, besides the ones we habitually notice, might be at work. At this stage, coaches can often help teachers unearth new perspectives.

With the pilot team of Kay, Josh, Sara, and Pete, new perspectives on a problem played a vital role in generating alternative practices. Once each had tried teaching differentiated lessons, we decided to focus on the concrete problem of reducing the number of F's students received. The coaching process began with the key element of understanding their beliefs, in this case about why students fail. Through interviews, they articulated three common beliefs:

- The factors that caused students to fail were outside their control, such as unsupportive home environments and district policies.
- They had tried all available strategies. (They had tried all the strategies they were aware of. They needed a different common framework to uncover new ones.)

- Although students needed to learn to be responsible, one can't teach specific skills to get them to complete projects and homework. (The strategies the teachers had tried fit their own learning styles, but not those of students very different from them.)

Note that these beliefs put the causes of student failure outside of their control, supporting a belief that "We've tried everything."

LEARNED HELPLESSNESS

All four teachers said outright that although they were willing to try new ideas, they did not believe that they would work. Their attitude could be described in terms of learned helplessness, defined by Seligman (1998) as "the giving-up reaction, the quitting response that follows from the belief that whatever you do doesn't matter" (p. 15). His research with laboratory dogs showed that when the subjects had no control over shocks they received, they soon stopped trying and simply lay down once they realized their actions, such as jumping to get away, were futile. When he studied helplessness in people, the biggest contributing factor was a lack of hope:

> Whether or not we have hope depends on two dimensions of our explanatory style: pervasiveness and permanence. Finding temporary and specific causes for misfortune is the art of hope: Temporary causes limit helplessness in time, and specific causes limit helplessness to the original situation. On the other hand, permanent causes produce helplessness far into the future, and universal causes spread helplessness through all your endeavors. Finding permanent and universal causes for misfortune is the practice of despair. (p. 48)

Three conditions are generally considered necessary for problems to qualify as learned helplessness (Jensen, 1998). Although learned helplessness is frequently overdiagnosed, consider its root causes as they apply to the daily lives of many urban teachers.

- Trauma in uncontrollable conditions, which could include being present while bullying goes on, insensitive behaviors in classrooms, or major fights or other violent occurrences in the building, even if the person isn't present.
- Lack of control. If teachers put in long hours and extra effort to reach academic goals with students but don't have the strategies or resources to succeed, they begin to feel helpless.

- Decision. The person has to decide that they are to blame for the problems *or* that there is nothing they can do to change things, as had the teachers on my pilot team. They'd externalized all causes of student failure, which had stymied their ability to generate new possibilities.

In one study, in which dogs had given up escaping the electric shocks, researchers dragged them to safety 30–50 times before the animals began to respond on their own (Peterson, Maier, & Seligman, 1993). Peterson cited research by Villanova and C. Peterson that demonstrated that learned helplessness is even harder to overcome in humans than in animals.

The teachers felt helpless to keep students from failing—and told me so. In such cases, coaches need to become directly involved to help teachers overcome the mental model that blocks them from change. The teachers' own resources aren't enough. Reflective practice may only reinforce those mental models unless teachers receive outside perspectives and information.

DIFFERENT BELIEFS, DIFFERENT SOLUTION SETS

My reasons for why students were failing were different from those the teachers listed—I had identified a curriculum that didn't meet the needs of different learning styles, boredom, lack of skills for work completion, and frequency of passive worksheets that taught skills separate from context— so the solution set I developed included ideas the teachers had not tried before. Although normally I would have brainstormed possibilities with the teachers, they didn't think *any* possible solutions existed. So, I initially researched and evaluated strategies on my own, synthesizing my knowledge of differentiation, information on working with students of poverty, and feedback from student focus groups at the school.

I carefully considered the implications of each proposed solution and came up with the following plan, fully intending to allow the teachers to critique my ideas as well as add to the list:

- Specific class time agendas for students to copy and check off items as they complete work
- Teamwide insistence that students record homework assignments in their planners
- Use of specific techniques to teach students to break big projects into steps and consider the time needed for each one
- Backward planning from due dates, including mini-deadlines

- Insistence that all work be at C level or be redone
- Variety and choice in assignments.

To convince the teachers that students might respond to these measures, we looked at research on what urban kids say they want from teachers (Wilson & Corbett, 2001), including

- Stay on them to complete assignments.
- Provide a variety of activities for learning and homework. Give choices wherever possible to give them some control and ownership in the work.

Note that the teachers thought they had high expectations, but what they really had was high standards. High expectations mean *expecting* that all students will succeed. Although the teachers agreed to try the strategies, all in one way or another said, "They won't work." "We've tried this before." "When we try, the same number of students fail, just different students." Further, my research into learned helplessness indicates that many of the failing students were victims as well—and as Jensen (1998) reported, it can take *fifty interventions* from a teacher before the student believes he or she can learn. The teachers needed to keep trying until they saw results.

Here, a coach's role shifts from instruction to strategic intervention to produce belief-changing evidence. The pilot team needed to discuss the number of failing grades as a problem to be solved rather than as an inevitability they couldn't change. They needed evidence that supported the strategies *before* we discussed them as a team—evidence showing that their efforts could make a difference and would be well worth the difficult changes in habit and belief the new tools would require.

EVIDENCE: DID WE
SOLVE THE PROBLEM WE DEFINED?

For three reasons I decided that working with Josh would be the best way to create evidence. First, he'd told me right before spring break that he was going to try giving 38 choices for the unit projects on Native Americans, and I knew he was worried about how his students would handle the assignment. My strategies would thus fit an immediate interest of his. Second, Josh enjoyed hands-on developmental activities, as implementing these strategies would be, and he liked having me in his classroom. Third, I felt that if our first few days using the strategies produced any results, Josh would be naturally enthusiastic in sharing them at the team meeting.

I actually met Josh outside the door of his classroom early in the morning as he returned from spring break—we had no chance to communicate in advance. He agreed without hesitation after a glance at the "No More F's" strategies, and we began using them with his first-hour class. We worked together during the next week to clarify explanations, engage students in reflection, and identify what skills students did and did not have. When the team met to discuss the strategies three days after Josh and I started using them, he shared his experiences, ideas, reactions, and suggestions, as I had hoped. I gained credibility with the rest of the team because Josh was already working with the strategies. I had evidence, the start of experiences that might influence the teachers to develop new habits. Perhaps one of the other teachers might have partnered with me that Monday on the spur of the moment, but my coaching framework, as well as my knowledge of the teachers' immediate needs and interests, suggested that Josh was my best option.

Again, my goal was to create experiences that would cause the teachers to question their habitual beliefs and make them aware of avenues for further growth. They all desperately wanted to help more students succeed, but they thought students would fail no matter what the teachers did. Coaching Josh first provided evidence that moved the team toward the freedom of considering different planning strategies that would help more students succeed.

Over the next few weeks, the other three teachers joined in the "No More F's" effort in significant ways. Sara developed a detailed system for students to track daily work. Pete consistently put agendas on the board and had students write down schedules. Kay followed Josh's lead in having students plan projects. All four teachers saw reductions in the number of F's. Further, they decided to teach the strategies as a team the next fall, using the first quarter's elective period to concentrate on organizational skills and study techniques. Instead of feeling trapped in a system where their students failed no matter what they did, the teachers were free to again consider actions that might make a difference in their students' lives. The teachers had hope.

PROBLEM SOLVING AND ACTION RESEARCH

When coaches help teachers gather evidence, they're helping them engage in action research. Coaching Amy, as well as Josh's team, turned into guiding them through action research that (a) focused on *their* problems and (b) provided evidence that influenced their educational beliefs. Coaches often help teachers understand the benefits of practitioner research. Many of the teachers I work with seem to suffer from "research anxiety" stemming from several causes, such as

- "It'll be too time-consuming." A coach can help reframe action research as a normal part of looking at student work—and can design easy-to-implement methods for the teacher to use.
- "I won't discover anything significant." A coach can help a teacher identify the questions he or she wants answered and why other teachers might be interested as well.
- "I'm not a researcher." A coach can help tailor a research effort to match a teacher's strengths.
- "I don't know what to measure, or how to measure." A coach can point out useful data besides standardized tests and other assessments.

One of the most significant roles a coach can play in action research is pointing out, or helping to record or gather, data sources other than tests that might show the effectiveness of practices. All of the emphasis on scientifically based research can keep teachers from trying simple action research projects, such as, "Do students write better journal entries if I provide samples?" Coaches take on several other roles, including

- Helping teachers select and define a problem that (a) interests them, (b) is within their realm of influence, and (c) involves measurable outcomes. For Amy, the research question was, "Can structuring an engaging opening activity improve classroom atmosphere?" We measured the impact of the read-aloud activity by counting the number of interruptions and behavior problems and comparing them with previous data on the class. For Josh's team, the research question was, "Can teaching specific strategies, based on Ruby Payne's work (1996) and personality type, help more students pass our classes?" Student grades provided the results. Although these kinds of research questions aren't designed to quickly show higher test scores, success with these short-term efforts increased teacher motivation to overcome their learned helplessness.
- Brainstorming solution sets. Although ideally teachers would brainstorm their own, the level of learned helplessness the teachers experience may determine the involvement of a coach. If the teachers are overwhelmed, it may be up to the coach to find new ideas.
- Providing guidance in selecting options. Chapter 9 provides a coaching and problem-solving methodology for choosing the option best suited for a situation.
- Working with teachers, observing classrooms, and offering suggestions that might help teachers get beyond their habitual beliefs.

Teachers, chronically short on prep time, may not be motivated to count grades, disaggregate data, or contrast student work until they've completed one action research project that influenced their classroom practices.

The action research process focused on their concerns and, supported with coaching, brought real, identifiable changes in Kay's, Josh's, Pete's, and Sara's teaching practices and beliefs.

For Amy, not only did she see improved behavior, but two weeks after beginning the read-aloud effort, that fifth-hour class also reached her goal of open, worthwhile classroom discussions. Further, the work completion rate went from approximately 75 percent to approximately 95 percent. These measures weren't in the original research design because Amy thought they were impossible.

During the "No More F's" effort, we tested several such hypotheses. Are students more motivated when given choices? (Yes. Some of Josh's students even asked if they could complete two of the 38 projects!) Will more students complete big projects if they receive specific training in planning those projects? (Yes.) Can students benefit from learning specific skills that will help them be more responsible? (Yes.) In each case, the teachers gathered evidence based on experiences in their own classrooms. The evidence convinced them to change some of their educational practices as well as certain beliefs about why students fail.

However, the evidence and experiences that provoked the changes were different for each of the teachers. I used our common framework to choose which experiences to offer and to decide how to approach the teachers.

Changing habitual beliefs requires defining a problem correctly, considering alternatives, collecting evidence, and reflecting on the results. Even when our beliefs aren't working, we won't change without evidence that brings hope. It's a sequential process:

- Find out what the teachers believe (Chapter 1).
- Develop a change process that takes into account the informational needs and learning needs of each teacher (Chapter 2).
- Talk with the teachers about the biggest problems they face in their classrooms.
- Reframe those problems when necessary.
- Develop alternatives, evaluate them, and choose the one with the best chance of success.
- Carefully monitor the implementation of the solution, collecting data as evidence. If the process goes against the teachers' natural strengths, it will be very difficult to implement correctly to produce the kind of evidence needed to change beliefs.

The reason I spent so much time in Amy's fifth-hour classroom, and in Josh's as he worked to reduce student failure rates, is that I needed to ensure that the efforts produced evidence that would overcome their beliefs. As Guskey (2002) puts it,

> The crucial point is that it is not the professional development *per se,* but the experience of successful implementation that changes teachers' attitudes and beliefs. They believe it works because they have seen it work, and that experience shapes their attitudes and beliefs . . . the key element in significant change in teachers' attitudes and beliefs is clear evidence of improvement in the learning outcomes of their students. (p. 384)

He points out that evidence from other sources, even the most careful research, may not convince teachers to change because change also brings with it the possibility that their students will do worse. They've seen it before—which was true for Amy and for Josh's team. Even though the suggestions I made were tightly tied to studies on learning styles (Lawrence, 1993; Murphy, 1992) and on students of poverty (Payne, 1996), strategies these teachers had been exposed to and knew had worked elsewhere, they hesitated. I evaluated when and where to start on the basis of the problems they *wanted* to solve and the evidence needed to change their beliefs.

Note that although I focused on individual efforts, those tied back to the *team's* goal of getting more students to succeed academically. Effective collaboration multiplies the knowledge and experience teachers have, but collaboration takes time, training, and, as we'll see, a common framework before it can have an impact on student performance.

4 How Can Teachers Collaborate?

The sixth key element of staff development: Deep, reflective collaboration.

Collaboration: to work jointly with others in an intellectual endeavor. That's the dictionary definition.

In my first career as a financial controller, collaboration was the norm. At each new job, colleagues shared computer programs, spreadsheet templates, and every trick of the trade they knew to get me up to speed as soon as possible. The faster I could carry my own weight, the better for all. However, collaboration continued even after I was competent. We had no choice but to collaborate, for many reasons:

- We often faced unworkable deadlines.
- Many tasks were too big for one person to handle.
- Coordination among departments was key to success.
- We needed to share resources.
- Often, tasks required skills I didn't have; I partnered with others who had the skills I needed and who needed my skills.

Look back through the list. Those same reasons apply to educators as well, yet few teachers collaborate.

When I first began working in schools, the lack of teaming astounded me. I asked Lisa Hartman, a friend who headed the world language department at a large high school, why teachers didn't work together more. She said,

> Deep down, many view it as stealing. It took me *years* to get the other teachers to share lesson plans. "Competent teachers do it themselves," was their message back to me. And finally, when they used something I'd created, students said, "Ms. Hartman, did you know someone stole your idea?" I made sure my name didn't appear on anything after that!

LEVELS OF COLLABORATION

In a sense, teachers seem to use a second dictionary definition of collaboration: cooperating with the enemy. They avoid it. Collaboration also runs counter to the competitive, individualistic culture of schools. Yes, there is a push for teaming, professional learning communities, small schools-within-a-school, and other possibilities for deeper teamwork, but most teaching teams fall into one of three different levels of collaboration:

Level I: Superficial collaboration. This includes teaming for administrative tasks such as fundraising, field trips, procuring resources, or discussing interventions for specific students. Ensuring that staff members build relationships with all students, although important, still falls within this level of teaming.

Level II: Segmented collaboration. Teaching teams might engage in cross-disciplinary efforts such as conducting an experiment in science and composing a related essay in language arts. Or, elementary teachers might divide up subjects, one teaching math in both rooms while the other teaches social studies. Team expectations for behavior or uniform rules and consequences might also fall here.

Note that both Levels I and II add efficiencies and allow for a fuller picture of both the learning profile and the special needs of certain students. However, they seldom result in significant changes in classroom practices or increases in student achievement. As we saw in Chapter 1, teachers derive their practices from their own strengths and beliefs. Without input from colleagues, they may be unaware of their own blind spots. This in turn can leave behind students with very different learning styles (remember the chart on page 13; teachers cited students with learning styles opposite theirs as their biggest problems). For teachers to understand where, how, and why to change their classroom practices, they need

> Level III: Instructional collaboration. Teaching teams engage in deep discussions about teaching and learning, serving as resources for each other in developing curriculum and lessons that meet the needs of all learners. Together, they unearth assumptions about teaching and learning, gain from each other's natural strengths, share strategies and ideas, and learn more about what is possible in the classroom. Other literature identifies this as reflective practice or critical reflection.

Research shows that few schools share this attitude toward teamwork (Fullan & Hargreaves, 1992; Rosenholtz, 1989). Fullan (2001) advocated what I describe as Level III collaboration through professional learning communities. Emphasizing how essential they are to reculturing, not just restructuring, a school, he wrote,

> Two ships have been passing in the night, stopping occasionally to do battle, in the dark. One is named Accountability, the other Professional Learning Community. Both have evil twins. One is Name and Shame and the other Navel Gazing. The future of educational change is very much a matter of whether these ships will learn to work together through the discomfort of each other's presence until they come to respect and draw on each other's essential resources. (p. 267)

Study after study shows that collaboration is essential to improving academic achievement.

- Rosenholtz (1989), in a study of 78 schools, found that when teachers developed shared meaning around goals and the organization of their work, they were more likely to try new ideas designed to improve student learning.
- Little (1981) found that school improvement resulted when teachers engaged in deep conversation about how they teach, observed each other, and collaborated on materials and lesson plans.
- McLaughlin and Talbert (1993) reported that professional learning communities produced substantial learning about teaching strategies and content.
- Several studies of collaboration show decreases in achievement gaps as well as academic gains for students (Lee, Smith, & Croninger, 1995; Newmann & Associates, 1996; Smith, Lee, & Newmann, 2001).

- Hord, in a synthesis of research on collaboration summarized by Hall and Hord (2001), found that teachers change practices more quickly and are more likely to make fundamental, systemic change when they work collaboratively.

Schools have moved toward teaming, learning circles, and other vehicles for collaboration because of this research, but the resulting impact on student achievement has been spotty. Part of the problem is in creating a shared vision of the goals and processes necessary for true collaboration.

PINPOINTING DEEP COLLABORATION

Let's be clear on what collaboration is and isn't. It is *not*

- Gathering for emotional support for the tough demands of teaching, although such support may result from Level III collaboration.
- A tool for implementing uniform teaching practices, although teachers involved in Level III collaboration may discover some practices they wish to use in all classrooms.
- Collective permission for continuing culture. In true Level III collaboration, instead of reinforcing each other's beliefs about why students aren't learning or why behavior is unacceptable, teachers work to increase each other's expectations for student achievement.

One way to highlight the essence of Level III collaboration is this: It emphasizes the importance of *professional autonomy* for teachers in meeting school goals, distinguishing that attitude from one of *personal freedom* to run one's classroom as desired, without regard to input from others or to school goals. Level III collaboration is

- Based on robust knowledge about teaching and learning. Otherwise, teachers may simply reinforce each other's incorrect assumptions or bad habits. Much of what teachers "know" comes from their own isolated experiences, which they rely on to defend what they do (Feiman-Nemser & Floden, 1986).
- Nitty-gritty deliberation about present practice and future direction. Teachers feel free to question each other about why a practice works, what kinds of students it reaches, who might be left out, and changes that might improve it or adapt it.
- An interdependency that reduces planning time, spreads effective teaching practices, develops a culture of shared meaning, concentrates resources where they are most needed, and makes the best use

of the strengths of each member of the team. The results are synergy, synthesis, reinforcement, and sharing.

Without this kind of collaboration, teachers (or people in any profession) seldom know exactly what they know, why they know it, or the true and false assumptions under which they are operating.

BENEFITS FROM COLLABORATION

Because of the way their classrooms isolate them, teachers may be unaware of alternatives to their current teaching methods. Further, collaboration provides concrete benefits and results. Collaboration

- Provides both the necessary pressure and incentives to change and the support needed to do the hard, hard work of changing (Fullan, 2001).
- Allows the coordination of efforts to improve student achievement. For example, Josh's team adopted a new policy of lunch-hour make-ups and alternative assignments so that all students did all the work. Josh introduced the policy first to improve results on a unit project. Students unused to being required to work protested loudly, "That's bogus." "No way." He said calmly, "I have high expectations for you, and you should have the same for yourself." Two weeks later, when Kay introduced the same policy, students shrugged and complied, seemingly saying, "That's the way it is around here now."
- Helps teams unearth patterns. Using too many worksheets and ignoring the needs of quiet students are two patterns that teams I've worked with have recognized through collaboration.
- Improves student achievement.

Yet teachers resist collaboration. Comments I've heard include the following: "I'm a tenured teacher and I should certainly be capable of developing my own lessons." "I worked hard on that lesson. Why would I just give it away?" "With all we have to do, taking time to talk about each other's work would be a luxury. We need to concentrate on our own curriculum." "What other teachers share with me isn't as good as what I give to them."

Most people possess few natural skills for collaboration. In business settings, team-building sessions are usually at least two days long. If team issues exist, more time is needed.

If schools are to move toward Level III collaboration, we need a clear understanding of why moving in that direction has been so difficult despite the call for professional learning communities. And, we need to understand the conditions required for deep collaboration to take place.

WHAT GETS IN THE WAY OF LEVEL III TEACHER COLLABORATION?

The traditional public school honors independence, not teaming. At least eight natural barriers keep teachers from engaging in reflective conversations at the deep level required for Level III collaboration:

- A culture of silence (Brookfield, 1995) that discourages teachers from talking about their classrooms or teaching in sustained, meaningful ways. Teachers are afraid of being viewed as incompetent, or of being censured for questioning conventional wisdom, especially given the criteria and procedures for gaining tenure.
- Teachers as individual entrepreneurs or executives. Executives do not take kindly to others' critique of their methods, decisions, or demeanor (Kaplan, Drath, & Kofodimos, 1985). Because teachers reign in their individual classrooms, they often take on executive characteristics, including positive ones such as taking responsibility for their actions. However, it is difficult for executives—and many teachers—to accept criticism without feeling that their competency is being questioned. As with executives, the fast pace of teachers' work often means that action without reflection is the norm. And, if they're successful, or at least as successful as their peers, the "you can't argue with my success" syndrome creeps in. If teachers have their classrooms under control and a majority of their students are learning, they may not be open to change, given the difficulties it presents.
- Teaching as creative expression. A common theme is that teaching can't be taught; from experience, each teacher discovers his or her own norm of practice. Teachers accept as a cultural norm tolerance of individual styles and preferences that are personally generated through learning and classroom experiences (Little, 1990).
- The culture of secrecy, in which self-disclosure leads to censure and trust is absent (Brookfield, 1995). Many teachers doubt their own effectiveness and are therefore unwilling to disclose the struggles they face in their classrooms. The perceived social or psychological costs of asking for help are simply too high. Lortie (1975) states that although sharing practices and lessons with other teachers increases the promise of praise and recognition, it also allows for more criticism and conflict. Stein, Smith, Henningsen, and Silver (2000) cite examples

of teachers' unwillingness to discuss uncertainties or provide critique of each other's lessons even during meetings held for that purpose.

- A bias toward noninterference, which doubles the impact of the culture of secrecy. In many schools, the attitude toward new teachers or staff members is that they will ask if they need help (Little, 1990). Since new teachers feel compelled to secrecy about their struggles, and veterans wait for them to ask for help, the avenues for passing on knowledge are blocked.

- Lack of common goals and meaning, which causes teachers to assign a high cost to collaboration in terms of sense of competency, status, and obligations incurred. Little (1990) writes:

  > Resource-impoverished and isolating environments may prompt teachers to hoard "a few good ideas"; resource-enriched environments in which teachers value mutual support may demonstrate a solid "return on investment" in sharing. In principle, sharing expands the collective pool of resources; in practice teachers describe the painstaking accumulation of an individual store of resources that may be diminished, depleted or compromised when revealed to others. Among the hidden costs of sharing expertise are the risk of an added planning and preparation burden (as teachers replace the ideas that have been "given away") and an erosion of the corpus of ideas, methods and materials that serve as the basis of individual reputation, giving teachers distinctive identity and status. (p. 6)

- Intensifying work. Globally, schools are viewed more as cost centers than as investments in future citizens (Smyth, Dow, Hattam, Reid, & Shacklock, 2000). As a result, schools constantly ask teachers to do more with less. With current trends in school funding cuts, accountability, and reporting requirements, little time is left for teaming, planning, or considering whether classroom practices fit with what we know about how students learn. Team meetings devoted to anything other than fulfilling mandates or taking care of administrative details are viewed as wasted time.

- The tendency of teachers to choose the profession because they would rather work with children than with adults (Lortie, 1975).

REQUIREMENTS FOR LEVEL III COLLABORATION

Obviously, care, sustained effort, and resources are necessary to overcome these kinds of barriers. Evans (2001) points out that simply telling teachers to collaborate—or setting up schedules for them to do so—doesn't deal with the fact that teachers prefer to cling to the personal freedom the status quo allows them in their classrooms:

> A truly collaborative culture cannot be implemented simply by structuring interactive opportunities and work arrangements. These may help such a culture ultimately develop, though often they lead to contrived collegiality in which teachers are put through collaborative paces that have little impact and wither away. But they work, at best, very slowly, and only as part of a larger sustained context that nurtures higher levels of mutual support and permits people to develop truly meaningful relationships rather than artificial connections— and only under a strong leader. (p. 240)

Criteria for Level III Collaboration

- Time for reflective discussion
- A common framework for discussing teaching and learning
- Trust, respect, and honesty
- A willingness to probe one's own beliefs and acknowledge boundaries of one's experience
- Articulated goals to measure effectiveness
- Rewards for teaming
- If these are not present, a coach's role is to help a team develop them.

Before beginning, everyone involved must acknowledge that collaborative skills take time to learn. Deep collaboration comes only with practice. Further, the first experiences should include coaching so that the collaboration produces evidence that convinces teachers that the hard work of self-disclosure, positive critique, and change is worthwhile. At least six criteria must be met for teams to move toward Level III collaboration.

Time for reflective discussion. Yes, time may seem impossible to find, but the alternative is to continue to be locked into habitual beliefs, using classroom practices that don't provide solutions.

For teachers to understand the value of deep collaboration, they need to experience it. Although coaches may have little control over school schedules, they can suggest initial options such as the following:

- Have teachers actively plan lessons together during a three-hour block of staff development time. This works well when a school is actively working to adopt a common framework for discussing teaching and learning. The coach begins the session with a review of the framework. The teachers can group by grade-level or content-area teams. The coach should have them come with projects to work on. At the end, he or she should ask each group to report on what they learned from each other. Usually, teachers appreciate the "gift" of so much planning time; their reports to the group include more plans to run ideas by colleagues or specific lessons they plan to work on together in the future.

- For a shorter staff meeting, one teacher can volunteer to allow his or her colleagues to critique a lesson using the common framework. Because so many teachers prefer that such exercises be applicable to what they teach, the coach should consider having separate lessons for each subject area or, for elementary schools, each grade level. This works best if the volunteers select lessons that they've used but were unsatisfied with instead of something they've worked to perfect. Often, in the midst of critiquing with colleagues, teachers see their own blind spots. Coaches who have established good rapport with the teachers can listen in on conversations, adding observations if the teachers are hesitant to critique.

- Another method is to provide a lesson that all teachers use at the same time. This gives them a common experience for reflection. The coach would then facilitate the resulting discussion, pointing out patterns in teacher reactions and methodology (an example of this type of collaboration starts on page 66).

- A coach might schedule at least one meeting with each team to demonstrate collaboration. At one such meeting, a team agreed to collaborate on helping their students write research reports. We reviewed an organizational strategy in which students place cards in envelopes labeled with different topic headings and check-off boxes. Students check off how many cards they've completed, indicating how much information they've found. Students staple the envelopes inside a folder, decreasing chances that they will lose the cards. The social studies teacher said, "It's too structured. I'll put together some kind of folder, but no kid would want to do all that." However, a teammate whose learning style was opposite to his stood up and said while motioning, "I'd want to check those off. See the progress. I'd love it!" The social studies teacher thought she was kidding at first, the idea was so foreign to him. When he realized she was serious, he said, "I haven't been helping the students like you at all, have I?"

That team already had a neutral learning styles language that enabled them to critique ideas in terms of which students they would help or hinder, without criticizing each other. Again, merely scheduling time for collaboration doesn't mean teachers will use it for anything but Level I and Level II collaboration activities. The other factors have to be in place.

A common framework for discussing teaching and learning. Without a common framework, it is difficult for teachers to put aside their own perspectives of right and wrong when listening to a colleague's ideas. Although many learning styles frameworks exist, their content is very similar (see the chart on page 81). Felder (1996) reviewed four different models: the MBTI, the Kolb Learning Style model, the Herrmann Brain Dominance model, and the Felder-Silverman Learning Style model. He stated that all four allowed him to balance instruction and meet the needs of all students in his engineering classes and added, "Which models educators choose is almost immaterial, since the instructional approaches that teach around the cycle [i.e. alternately meeting the needs of each style] for each of the models are essentially identical" (p. 8). Further, any model worth using takes time to learn.

As I discussed in Chapter 1, the framework needs to describe each learning style positively, emphasizing that all types can teach and learn. A close reading of Gardner (1999), for example, reveals his hesitations about using the language of multiple intelligences with children. Although he advocated the creation of environments rich with experiences for each of the intelligences, he saw the danger in labeling a student "spatial but not linguistic."

Thus the common framework used for learning styles should discuss how each style learns mathematical procedures or how to read rather than emphasizing which style does it best. This could be described as being "prescriptive," describing which students a given practice will reach so they can master material, rather than "diagnostic" of the material they will or won't have an affinity for.

The model is also more workable if it applies to both adults and students, as well as across cultures. Teachers can then acknowledge to each other their own needs as they work to change their classrooms. A highly competent math teacher looked at a chart of the ways students with different learning styles might practice basic multiplication tables and said, "I like some in every group—some I like even more than the ones this shows for my own style." She questioned the validity of the whole model. However, because the whole grade-level team was meeting, she also had a similar chart for basic reading skills. When she studied it, she said. "Oh. OH. I'd retreat into my own corner in reading. My competency in math makes exploration of new ways and ideas more comfortable for me. But I'd need my own style more in reading."

Another math teacher commented, "So . . . we aren't as confident out-side our subject areas . . . Hey, that's how many of our students feel about math!" The framework and the chance to collaborate gave them an incentive to add to their tried-and-true ideas of what works in their classrooms.

In the early stages of using a framework, a coach's role might include

- Assisting in keeping discussions focused on student learning rather than on "correct" and "incorrect" teaching methods.
- Facilitating discussions of student work. Before beginning, the coach might guide teachers in predicting patterns they can expect to see, based on how students with different learning styles might have approached the work. During the discussion, the coach might help the teachers probe for deeper understanding or alternate explanations. And at the end, the coach might help teachers summarize the implications of their analysis for future assignments.
- Being the "expert." Again, a coach helps teachers look past their habitual beliefs. Unlearning those beliefs takes time and considerable practice with the common framework.

Trust, respect, and honesty. Sometimes, the hard work of building relationships has to take place before teams can collaborate. Because teachers can operate autonomously and hide in their rooms, not even coming out for lunch, many teachers haven't developed skills in dealing with conflict, nor had any incentive to do so. Further, they usually have little firsthand knowledge of their colleagues' classrooms, so why would they take advice?

One teacher remarked, "If I learn that someone else is holding back, not sharing with me at the level I'm sharing with her, I feel like keeping all my ideas to myself."

Again, trust is best built through a common framework and agreed-upon goals. Administrators can help build trust and respect by making sure that teachers know that the problems in their own classrooms are similar to the problems others experience. They may need to play an active role in breaking the culture of silence.

Coaches can help teachers move from "contrived" to Level III collaboration. In fact, trust *may never* appear unless someone guides a team in developing it. The Annenberg Institute (2005b) listed outside technical assistance as essential to the establishment of effective professional learning communities. Techniques for building trust include

- *Setting group norms.* A coach might help a team establish norms for brainstorming, participation levels, and other processes. For example, I ask teachers to reflect on the personality-type information in Appendix A. They tell their team about their own strengths as teachers and what the others need to know to be most effective in working with them.

- *Evaluating sources of conflict.* In many cases, teachers (and team members in every profession) interpret basic personality differences as purposefully annoying behavior. A coach might act as a "translator," helping them see each other's points of view.
- *Guided problem solving.* Chapter 9 outlines a process for working through problems. Help the team select a real problem that isn't very controversial. The coach's role is to help teachers see how they benefit from each other's natural strengths through the process. This may sound simple, but at one school it took a team that had given up on teaming *four hours* to devise a common policy for snacks. At the end, they actually understood the very different ways each of them had approached the task and felt ready to collaborate on more meaningful tasks.
- *Case studies.* To make sure that teachers don't have to risk their colleagues' criticism, bring in student work or a lesson plan from either your own practice or a teacher at a different school. Again, use the common framework to guide the discussion so that the team members begin to understand each other's strengths.
- *Book studies.* A coach can help teachers articulate a goal for their first try at collaboration (understanding brain research, differentiating, working with difficult students, student-led conferences, home-school connections, etc.) and then find a book to study on that subject. The coach might then develop study questions to connect the book study back to school reform goals and the common framework.

A willingness to probe one's own beliefs and acknowledge boundaries of experience. I often joke with teachers that there's no need to examine their own practices if all of their students are doing A-quality work, are engaged to the extent that they often go beyond assignment requirements, are meeting rigorous standards, don't misbehave, and know how to work both cooperatively and independently. Many teachers are this successful. If so, I ask them whether they can articulate to their colleagues how they pull it off. Most can't. Most are unaware of how they know what they know or how it might work for a teacher with a very different style.

For example, I asked an urban teacher how she kept students on task so successfully. She said, "I'm consistent, but I can't really describe any specific techniques." She had no idea how different her style was from other teachers in the building. This goes back to "teaching as an art," a belief that skills are individual and can't be passed on. They can.

Or, teachers might not realize that their picture of a good classroom leaves out some crucial elements for student achievement. For example, Pete, the teacher who emphasized activities that got students excited about science, believed that if he could engage the students in learning experiences, they'd be more likely to finish their work. However, even though students were engaged, the same students who didn't complete social studies reports or math homework failed to complete his best assignments. Because not even his best lessons, as defined by his beliefs, increased student achievement, he'd accepted the failure rate as inevitable. Through collaborative teaming, he discovered that the projects were too *big* for many of his students. They couldn't see the end from the beginning and got lost along the way. He broke his units into smaller parts, collecting work along the way, and had more students finish.

To help teachers understand their beliefs and the boundaries of their experiences, coaches might

- *Help teachers experience the learning styles.* Many teachers take a "Let's not and say we did" attitude toward extended experiential learning in the different styles. Quick experiences, though, seem to work quite well. One example is to have teachers read silently "My Ideal Staff Development Day," page 115, and choose the description they prefer. Then discuss their probable reaction to a day that met the criteria of the description kitty-corner to their chosen one—the opposite learning style. Most teachers have a fairly strong reaction. You can accomplish the same effect by showing teachers four separate lesson plans for the same unit, one in each style. This works best if the lesson is *out* of their favored content area and therefore quite separate from their strengths and skills. For example, providing teachers with a math and a literacy example to review usually helps them reflect more deeply on their own reactions.

- Through these experiences, most teachers realize that they *do not* meet the needs of all learning styles in their classrooms. In fact, the suggestions for the style opposite to their own seem so foreign that the common reaction is bafflement: "You mean someone would want to do that?" "But could they actually learn anything that way?" That recognition opens the pathway for seeking input from colleagues with that learning style—for deep collaboration.

- *Video or script of collaboration.* Several case-study books and videos exist that allow teachers to work through a problem alone and then watch how others approached the task. A coach might then facilitate a discussion to connect different approaches with different learning styles.

Articulated goals to measure effectiveness. Just like for individuals, team engagement increases when teams choose goals for collaboration such as "Can we increase student engagement by giving more choices?" "Can we improve work completion?" At one school, a team started with improving student success with History Day projects. Another concentrated on differentiation through literature circles. The action research suggestions in Chapter 3 provide coaching ideas for setting goals.

Rewards for teaming. There's a threefold path to rewarding teaming. First is to see that nothing in your incentive system works against it. Second is to overcome the costs teachers perceive. For example, collaboration should be defined *as* prep time rather than taking away from teacher prep time. Third is to use whatever you have to reward deep collaboration until the practice takes hold. Examples include hiring substitutes to allow for collaboration or providing meals, money set aside for materials for units produced through collaboration, a day off bus duty for teams that collaborate, or coaching time for helping teams collaborate.

A coach's biggest role in rewarding teams is to make their collaboration efforts as effective and productive as possible—setting up intrinsic rewards that will encourage future collaboration.

AN EXAMPLE OF LEVEL III COLLABORATION

One teaching team asked me to design a lesson to help students experience and reflect on the learning styles framework we'd been using together. They agreed to a station-based poetry unit, spread out over three class periods. I would also teach one group of students, so I was both coach and team member for the project. Collaboration took place before, during, and after the unit.

Before, they asked me to draft initial plans for the four stations. Note that this allowed them to critique the coach's work, not each other's, in this first experience. At a team meeting, the four teachers tried the station activities for the learning style none of them had. Two said they enjoyed it, and the other two said they could pinpoint why it was out of their comfort zone. We talked about ways to help students feel comfortable at all four stations.

Then we talked about each station. Per the advice of the language arts teacher, we decided that students would write haiku instead of longer tanka poems. One teacher worried about the mess paints might produce as students illustrated their haiku, so we brainstormed ways to minimize spillage. The science teacher pointed out a term that students had given a different meaning in their slang vocabulary—an innuendo that would send sixth graders totally off task—and we dropped that poem!

During the unit, we continued conversations. All of our classrooms engaged in the lesson during a class period divided in half by student lunch. As the teachers and I ate together, they discussed the different ways we'd introduced the stations. Only one teacher had done it as stated in my lesson plan, giving a brief overview of each station before starting—but the focus wasn't on who had done it "right," but rather on how each teacher's technique had worked. One teacher had explained the stations as she set them up. Another, whose class had a high percentage of strong readers, had instructed the groups to read the written directions before they began each station. The teacher whose class had a high percentage of English language learners had explained the stations orally.

Our discussion then turned to our uncertainties. How loud could the overall noise level be? How much help should we give? What about students who didn't like group work or oral presentations (some stations had individual and written work)?

Afterward, we worked together to improve the lesson. No one was certain that their way was the best. We modified and then reclassified one station to a different learning style, trying to make all the stations more equally engaging. We explored having one station in each room and rotating the students so that groups practicing their rap poems wouldn't disturb the students at quiet stations (this turned out to be highly effective). We shared examples and anecdotes of some of the struggling learners' positive behaviors and experiences. The unit provided a snapshot of how several students engaged in learning when conditions met their learning styles—examples the teachers shared and could discuss.

In summary, the teachers were willing to reveal what had gone on in their classrooms, both the positive and negative, rather than keep it secret. They also offered ideas and suggestions to each other—and used the suggestions they received. Further, none of them seemed to censure their teammates. We were able to engage in collaborative reflection. This atmosphere allowed us to improve the unit before we taught it again in the fall. As we discussed changes, we had shared goals of making each station equally engaging as well as a clear experience for students who shared the learning style it represented. Our common learning styles framework facilitated open discussion about how we could best teach the unit, and in general created an environment in which the teachers could collaborate effectively.

Part II

Developing a Language for Change

W hen I pondered my experiences with Josh's team—teachers who *wanted* to change—an image came to mind that helped me understand why change was so difficult for them: the long underwear that hangs in the Mission House Museum in Lahaina, Hawaii.

With Lahaina's year-round average temperature of 85 degrees, one would think that the New England missionaries who settled there in the early 1800s might have thought they'd found paradise. But no. Just as they had in Boston, they donned their woolen long underwear on the first of October in Hawaii and wore it through the first of April. Their beliefs about proper dress during the winter months overwhelmed the evidence that the climate was different.

The missionaries also held to their belief that the Hawaiians' innate laziness and inferiority caused them to refuse to adopt the agricultural and construction techniques, developed for New England's climate, that the missionaries offered. They kept themselves and their children separate from the Hawaiians for living, playing, and burial. Yet they fervently believed that their motives, actions, and policies were in the best interest of the Hawaiians. They worked out of what they knew: church laws and policies, and New England climate and practices. They stuck to their training, and they stayed in their long underwear.

It's hard to view those long johns in the museum without thinking, "How could those missionaries have been so stupid? Who would wear long underwear in Hawaii?" Yet if one thinks of all the turmoil in the lives of the missionaries—their methods weren't working, their churches were destroyed by storms, they were thousands of miles away from the people they loved—doesn't clinging to their long underwear seem a bit more understandable? After all, their practices and beliefs were perfectly fine in New England, just unsuitable for Hawaii.

The lives of our teachers are in turmoil as well, with constant budget cuts, new standards for certification, high-stakes testing, more English language learners, and more students arriving at school unprepared to learn. As we've seen, the teachers' long underwear of what works best in the classroom may come from beliefs they formed unconsciously, just as the missionaries didn't connect long underwear with the climate where they used to live. Long underwear beliefs come from sources or influences you aren't aware of or erroneous assumptions that what worked for you, or what worked in another place, will work for others or in a new situation.

It is difficult to discover the nature of our long underwear and why we're clinging to it—especially if we're worried that without those long johns, students will suffer. Beliefs about education function like long underwear because they fit like your own skin. Shedding them leaves you vulnerable to changes you aren't sure you can weather. It isn't enough to have someone else point out that it's at least 80 degrees outside and you'll be fine without it. Somehow, with the underwear still on, you have to learn it for yourself. That makes change a very, very difficult process.

EMBRACING THE MISSION OF REACHING EVERY STUDENT

I haven't found a way to help teachers gladly give up their long underwear without a common framework for discussing teaching and learning. It can't be an "I'm right, you're wrong" debate, for two reasons. First, as mentioned before, attacking a belief is like attacking a teacher's personal identity. Instead of focusing on the belief, we need to use a neutral language that keeps the discussion focused on how related practices affect different students. Which students feel included? Who will benefit most? Who might become bored? Who might be left behind?

Second, because so many teachers feel called to their profession, asking for change is like asking them to change religions. Further, administrators, educational consultants, and parents hold equally fervent beliefs about education. Ponder for a moment the fierce debates over

- Whole-class instruction versus differentiated instruction
- Standardized curriculum versus culturally relevant curriculum

- Basic skills versus constructivist learning
- Direct instruction versus cooperative learning
- Mastery of content standards versus mastery of processes.

The debates often rage as if no middle ground exists between the polarized extremes. Although educators talk of research-based evidence, both sides of each debate manage to find studies that prove their points. And, each side remains entrenched with an almost religious fervor because of the magnitude of their mission: making a difference in the lives of the students in their charge. Again, we need a common framework so we can focus on what happens to students and not on who is right. The language I use exposes how the opposite positions of these debates actually match the learning styles of those on each side!

We know how dangerous debates over religious beliefs can be; we speak of being tolerant of other beliefs or of leaving room to disagree. We choose our words carefully. We know that past battles over religion have literally led to war. Yet, we haven't made the connection between the fervor of our educational beliefs and how debates rage over education without fundamentally changing schools. Sometimes we get so lost in battles over the particulars of the issues that we forget we're all on the same side, we're all on the same mission: improving the learning of all students.

So how do we get teachers to change? Think of treading as lightly as wise missionaries, aware that we are touching the core being of the teachers we work with. If we really want to meet the needs of all learners, reform efforts must model that goal by meeting the needs of all teachers. It may mean shedding some of our own beliefs, but like long underwear in Hawaii, shedding them might just free us up to fresh ideas about classroom realities and the difficulty of change.

A FRAMEWORK FOR AUTHENTIC SCHOOL CHANGE

But . . . few of us change beliefs just because we're told that they are wrong—not even under coercion. Again, six key elements contribute to effective staff development that helps teachers change their classroom practices:

1. **A deep understanding of teachers' strengths and beliefs.** Without understanding why we're holding tightly to the ways we teach, we won't know *how* we need to change.

2. **Concrete evidence that influences beliefs and shows that change will be worth the effort.** To be committed, teachers have to see that change will result in improved student achievement.

3. **Communication and assistance (coaching) in ways that meet each teacher's learning style and needs.** When teachers need to change core practices, they need support—and different kinds of support work for different learners.

4. **A focus on problems that concern the teachers.** Helping teachers solve their most pressing problems shows that staff development efforts are worthwhile rather than an added burden. Usually these problems relate somehow to the school's agenda. Seeing results will help motivate teachers to buy into the administration's agenda.

5. **Deep, Level III collaboration.** School schedules, teaching norms, and fears of incompetence are natural barriers to this kind of collaboration, yet it is essential for substantive school reculturing efforts.

Yet, none of these are possible without

6. **A common framework for unbiased discussion of education.** Without this, we tend to fall into traps of discussing who is right or wrong rather than understanding which students different practices and policies will reach.

    Without this, proposed changes threaten the teachers for whom the changes are least natural—most likely the changes go against their core beliefs about teaching and learning, which, as we saw in Josh's story, are a part of who they are, their core personality.

Again, an effective common framework needs to

- Describe teaching and learning in nonjudgmental ways. No one should feel labeled.
- Be strengths-based, emphasizing how each person teaches and learns rather than placing limits on what they can do.
- Describe which learning style a practice will reach.
- Apply across cultures and to both adults and students.
- Provide bridges among varying staff development efforts.

Shared goals and objectives are *not* a common framework for change. Although they describe where a school wants to go, they don't detail the ways in which different teachers and learners can get there.

Standards-based instruction and data-driven instruction are *not* common frameworks for the same reason. Further, they sometimes hide the needs of individual learners, focusing on *what* they need to learn, rather than how they might learn it—and how teachers with different styles might effectively teach the content.

A multicultural approach to learning is *not* a common framework for change, although being culturally aware is essential to meet the needs of all students. Because each culture is different, schools actually need a common framework for discussing multiculturalism.

Being a learning community is *not* a common framework, especially if all teachers are being asked to learn in the same ways.

Many of the frameworks used for learning styles are *not* common, neutral languages, for they lay out who learns and who doesn't, rather than providing pathways for each child to master material. To be effective, they need to help teachers and children know what to do when their styles *can't* be met, rather than just how to reach their style.

> "If you want to teach people a new way of thinking, don't bother trying to teach them. Instead, give them a tool, the use of which will lead to new ways of thinking."
>
> —Buckminster Fuller

In other words, the framework needs to be a useful *tool*, not just a language. Senge (1994) quotes Buckminster Fuller as saying, "if you want to teach people a new way of thinking, don't bother trying to teach them. Instead, give them a tool, the use of which will lead to new ways of thinking" (p. 28). The more ways a given tool can be used, the more useful it will be for staff development.

The best common frameworks are tools that actually connect staff development efforts regarding teaching and learning, classroom management, teaming, multiculturalism, students with some disabilities, student work completion, building relationships with students, and differentiation.

The framework through which I have successfully helped teachers change in ways that result in higher academic achievement for students is the language of personality type, the subject of the second half of this book. Throughout the next chapters, I will relate the research on type to other common frameworks to (a) draw connections between personality type and models that you are already using and (b) provide ideas for new ways to use other models as common frameworks for the hard work of change.

5 A Common Framework

Creating a Climate Where
Change Is Possible

Benchmarks for a School's Common Framework

To effectively allow for unbiased reflection on education, a common
framework needs to

- Describe teaching and learning in nonjudgmental ways. No one
  should feel labeled.
- Be strengths-based, emphasizing how each person teaches and
  learns rather than suggesting limits on what they can do.
- Describe which learning styles a practice will reach.
- Apply across cultures and to both adults and students.
- Provide bridges among varying staff development efforts.

So how do you find/develop/adopt a common framework that meets
all of the requirements? Let's step away from the world of education
for a moment to see what it might look like.

A CAMPING FRAMEWORK

Think about taking groups of teenagers out on wilderness treks, canoeing
or backpacking. Wouldn't you want them speaking your language? At

YMCA Camp Widjiwagan,[1] experienced counselors instruct all campers in "The Widji Way," a philosophy of respect for yourself, others, and the wilderness. "There may be many ways to pitch a tent, flip a canoe, paddle, pack a pack, or light a fire, but we will use the Widji Way." Why? Because teamwork and safety come from common understanding.

Campers quickly buy into "The Widji Way" because it makes so much sense. Further, it

- Describes camping in nonjudgmental ways. "The Boy Scout way isn't wrong; we just need to use the Widji Way."
- Is strengths-based instead of limit-setting, focusing on how every camper, from the 90-pound seventh graders to the high school seniors, can flip a canoe or paddle for miles.
- Describes which campers a practice will reach. For example, one-, two-, and three-person canoe-flip techniques mean that anyone can get a canoe on his or her shoulders by using different skills.
- Applies across cultures and to both adults and students. Widji campers of all ages from around the world use the same techniques. They make sense because respect makes sense.
- Provides bridges among varying efforts. The *reasons* behind various "Widji ways" are the same.

Still, campers can be individuals. The common framework creates room for individual freedom to choose different pathways for growth and skill development. Campers find their own niches in the group. Best stern paddler? Longest portager? Best pancake flipper? The ways are endless, as long as they fit into the overall philosophy of respect.

The philosophy fulfills two purposes:

- It facilitates open conversations about camping, the environment, and leadership. The actual methods change when staff members discover better ones. Biases aren't against practices per se, but against any that fall short of the philosophy of respect.
- It organizes counselor and camper skills, actions, and interactions. Methods interrelate; groups can intermix. What you learn on the lakes transfers to rivers, mountains, and tundra.

BACK TO SCHOOL

A common framework for school reform also needs to fulfill two purposes:

- It should provide a language or philosophy that allows open conversations about teaching and learning. In schools, the litmus test is,

"Will this framework allow for conversations about teaching and learning that are unbiased by individuals' own strengths, beliefs, and learning styles?"

- It should organize staff development and school reform efforts, providing synergy.

Current staff development and school reform efforts are often all too similar to a *disorganized* camping trip. If you think of each topic as a tool a teacher has to carry, a few years' worth of workshops on classroom management, diversity, behavior issues, and so on is similar to a sleeping bag, lantern, cook kit, tent, compass, camp saw, cook stove—all loose gear that is easy to drop or misplace.

Ideally, all that gear is organized in a backpack. Widji campers, because of "The Widji Way" to pack, know where to find the first aid kit, the shovel, and the matches—they can retrieve things when they need them. That's what a common framework can do for staff development: organize diverse topics around core principles or a mental model. Does this mean that schools need to dictate "Our Way" to teachers? No. Teachers would still have latitude to use their strengths as long as they've examined their beliefs and practices against the common framework and can demonstrate how they fit—how students will learn.

> A common framework helps teachers form information into meaningful patterns, fitting it in to what they already know.

A common framework *organizes* all of the diverse efforts that go into the hard work of school reform. Brain research (Coward, 1990) demonstrates that the brain naturally tries to form information into patterns; a robust common framework allows teachers to analyze new ideas, create meaningful patterns, and fit them into what they already know.

Such a framework won't be simple. Education isn't simple; any framework that truly has the potential to unify both staff development and teacher commitment to common goals will take time to learn and use well.

Your school may already use a common framework. The next pages discuss personality type, how and why it is important to education, and its implications for coaching. You've probably learned something about this theory through its most popular application, the Myers-Briggs Type Indicator tool (MBTI).

Intertwined, and in the next chapter, are notes on how this theory relates to multiple intelligences, other learning styles models, and cognitive coaching. As you read, consider

- Whether the framework of type might work in your environment.
- Whether your current models fit the criteria for an effective common framework.
- How the concept of type might enhance your coaching practice.
- The biases in our educational system that type theory highlights.

A FRAMEWORK THAT WORKS

Although many frameworks offer insights into differences among people, one of the best-researched is personality type.

This theory holds that people display normal differences in how they take in information and make decisions, two key processes in education. Further, the variations in behavior that type describes are quite orderly and consistent. Students—and teachers—need to receive information in ways that make sense to them and then make decisions about its meaning, applications, and usefulness. These normal differences are natural preferences. We didn't choose them; they are part of who we are.

Personality Type

People display normal differences in how they

- Take in information
- Make decisions.

These are two key processes in education.

What does "natural preferences" mean? Think for a moment about handedness. In the space below, sign your name with your nonpreferred hand and think of adjectives that describe the process.

_____

Most people describe writing with their nonpreferred hand as awkward, slow, unnatural, messy, or difficult. They have to think about the process.

Now, sign your name with your preferred hand.

_____

Most people describe writing with their preferred hand as natural, easy, flowing. They don't have to think about how to form the letters. It's a part of who they are.

We have a *physical* preference for which hand we write with. Although years ago, some left-handed people were forced to use their right hands, nowadays children are allowed to develop that preference naturally. Neither hand is right or wrong. They didn't choose it; it happens naturally. Further, if for some reason a person decides to become ambidextrous, with practice he or she can develop skills with the other hand.

> Other learning style theories often use continuums to show our agility with different learning modes. Type does *not* measure how much of a preference we have, just which mode we *prefer.*

Type theory holds that, similar to these physical preferences, we have four *mental* preferences. We didn't choose them. None are right or wrong. And further, if we wish to develop ones that don't come naturally, we can practice and learn skills that allow us to use them. Type doesn't box people in then, but rather provides a framework for understanding natural differences among people and pursuing personal development. We have different psychological preferences for how we

- Gain energy
- Take in information
- Make decisions
- Approach life.

These are natural, observable differences among people that influence *how* we coach and how we *want to be* coached.

Type gives us a language for discussing different work styles, communication styles, and learning styles, or even whether we prefer examining disaggregated data or individual student work. As with type preferences, data versus student work isn't an either/or or right/wrong. Both are necessary, but most of us prefer reviewing one or the other.

Because personality type deals with such fundamental information about who we are, its applications are widespread. As a "backpack" for staff development, type organizes

- Coaching needs. The coaching styles given in Chapter 3 fit definite patterns in people's personality preferences. Chapter 8 discusses the use of type as a framework for coaching.
- Leadership development, helping educators discover their best leadership style. This is the subject of the third book in this series.

- Teambuilding and collaboration, establishing effective professional learning communities. The third book also covers this topic.
- Teacher and student learning styles, allowing us to design staff development to meet their varying needs (the subject of Chapter 6) using the same model that teachers can use to design differentiated lessons for students. The second book in this series discusses the use of type in the classroom.
- Reflective practice. As we'll see, teacher beliefs and practices are tightly tied to personality type. The framework helps them objectively examine their beliefs in light of which students they are serving rather than who is right or wrong.
- Classroom management and student interactions. Chapter 10 covers this topic briefly, and the second book in this series does so in depth.

The list is almost endless—type is also widely used for career counseling, stress management, spiritual direction, parenting, and marriage counseling. Knowing your personality type allows you to access resources that will help you in all of these areas.

Often, educators say that they have "done" the MBTI tool before, but there is a difference between "doing" type and actually "experiencing" how people with different preferences view classroom dynamics, assignments, relationships, and other areas that are as vital to education as what is actually taught.

A Note on Using Type Inventories

The MBTI tool is a well-researched instrument, but it is a *self-reporting,* not a *diagnostic,* tool. It helps people sort their preferences; interpretation is needed to help people determine their own "best-fit" type. Ethically, interpretation includes

- Explanation of the theory by a qualified practitioner (the MBTI tool is a class B psychological instrument)
- Self-selection of the preferences, based on the explanation, written type descriptions, and, if possible, experiential exercises
- Explanation of MBTI tool results
- Selection of best-fit type

Anyone can become qualified to administer the MBTI tool by taking a college course in tests and measurements or an MBTI tool qualifying program.

> However, the instrument is not necessary to teach type preferences—remember, even when using the instrument, participants need to self-select and then validate their preferences. People can grasp the concepts, identify their preferences, and apply the theories independent of "taking the test," although using the MBTI tool generally speeds up the process.
>
> Although the MBTI tool is quite inexpensive, some schools may still hesitate to use it. Instead of substituting one of the many nonvalidated "type quizzes" that exist on the Internet, people are better served by experiencing the preferences in a workshop setting, "seeing" them in action, as in the term paper exercise described on pages 82–85, and deciding for themselves which preferences describe them best.

The chart on page 81 relates type to other learning styles models. Note how many of them use Carl Jung's theories—the basis of personality type as well—to develop their modalities. Not surprisingly then, the personality preferences show statistically significant correlations with the learning styles.

For coaching, type is useful because we can

- Honor each teacher's uniqueness so that they view coaching as an investment, not remediation.
- Add efficiency. Type helps us identify which coaching techniques will work best with individual teachers.
- Neutralize areas for development (see Appendix A). There is a huge difference between "I'm wrong" and "I naturally struggle in that area, and there are strategies available that have worked before for people like me!"

You may already use another learning style model or common framework. In the next pages, as I explain the theory of type, I will give links to other theories such as multiple intelligences. The examples should help you link your current practices to type and help you decide how you might adapt your coaching style.

JUDGING AND PERCEIVING: TWO GREAT APPROACHES TO LIFE

Because educators are often concerned about any framework that might label people, I start type workshops with a group exercise that is a concrete

A Comparison of Learning Styles Models

	Personality Type	Multiple Intelligences (Gardner, 1999)	Experiential Learning Model (Kolb, Experience-Based Learning Systems, 2000–2005)	Mind Styles Model (Gregorc, 1999–2005)
Basic premise	People display normal differences in how they take in information (Perception) and make decisions (Judgment)	Each of us has at least eight different kinds of intelligence available to us to improve, to gain new insights and abilities. These are not learning styles, but faculty with the content of what is being learned.	People develop preferences for different learning styles, just like they develop styles for motivation, leading, etc.	Human beings are endowed with a uniquely proportioned set of mental qualities for interacting with the world that result in specific behaviors, characteristics, mannerisms, and products known collectively as style.
Learning style/ Intelligence vocabulary	Extraversion or Introversion (energy source) Sensing or Intuition (information) Thinking or Feeling (decision style) Judging or Perceiving (approach to life)	Verbal-linguistic Musical-rhythmic Visual-spatial Logical-mathematical Bodily-kinesthetic Naturalist Interpersonal Intrapersonal	Active experimentation (**E**)[1] Reflective observation (**I**) Abstract conceptualization (**NTJ**) Concrete experience (**E**)	Concrete Sequential (**SJ**) Abstract Random (**FP**) Concrete Random (**NP**) Abstract Sequential (**IST**)
Based on	Psychological type theory of Carl Jung, research base of Isabel Briggs Myers and Katherine Briggs	Howard Gardner's theory of multiple intelligences	Synthesis by David Kolb (1984) of the work of Piaget, Dewey, Lewin, and Jung	Brain hemisphere research, Jung
Source of styles	Preferences are innate, but we can access through skills the preferences that are less natural for us.	All learners have access to each intelligence, but are stronger in some. We can use our strengths to do better with others.	All learners have access to all four styles, but use some more easily than others. Your learning style will shift if you have more learning experiences in other styles.	Each mind has a different fixed balance of the four styles, but can "overachieve" in any area to meet outside demands and expectations.

1. Bold letters represent correlations with personality type preferences, based on studies reported in Hammer (1996).

demonstration of four ideas: (1) that the preferences are normal, observable differences among people; (2) that each preference is equally desirable; (3) that each person decides for himself or herself which preferences describe him or her best; and (4) that as we mature, we develop skills that let us use the less preferred sides of ourselves. In other words, we aren't labeling people, but providing a framework to discuss differences in positive ways.

Here's the exercise:

> Imagine for a moment that you're back in school and you've just been given a major assignment—a term paper, a science project, or a report that's due at the end of the semester. When would you normally finish such a project?

I explain that I was a "Get it done before midterm break" student; I hated the feeling of work hanging over my head. Then I ask who approached schoolwork in a similar way and hand one of them a sign to hold, labeled "Done before midterm break."

Inevitably a few people groan at the very thought of finishing so soon, and I ask if they might describe their style as "Late to class, just printed it off." In every case, someone willingly takes a sign with those words. Those two signs are the endpoints of a continuum I then ask the group to form. Everyone stands and finds their spots, with the midpoint labeled "Topic chosen before midterm break."

Then I ask a few questions of the people standing at each of the far ends of the continuum. I start with the last-minute end. Here's a typical conversation:

Jane:	Did you ever try starting a project early? Perhaps a parent said, "This time you aren't staying up all night!" and tried setting a schedule for you? [Heads nod.] How did it work to start early?
Late-starters:	"It's like staring at a blank wall." "I couldn't find any energy to get going." "I didn't have any ideas." "I stared at my computer . . . and ended up doing it at the last minute, anyway."
Jane:	How was the quality of your work?
Late-starters:	"Flat." "I just couldn't do it."
Jane:	And how does it feel at the last minute?
Late-starters:	"The ideas just flow." "I'm so alive when the pressure's on." "My head is clear. I can work at top speed."

Jane:	And the quality?
Late-starters:	"Superb." "Those are my best ideas." "My work is truly top quality."
Jane [to the people at the other end]:	So the quality of their work is actually higher when the pressure is on. Now, those of you who like to start early . . . did you ever have to do a project at the last minute? Perhaps you were ill, or missed the directions, or had to wait for someone else to finish *their* part? [Heads nod.] How does it feel when you're working at the last minute?
Early-starters:	"Awful." "I'm so anxious about finishing that I can't concentrate." "I keep thinking I'll forget something."
Jane:	How's the quality of your work at the last minute?
Early-starters:	"It's harder to find mistakes." "Flat—I'm not as creative." "Not as good."
Jane [to the whole group]:	Do you see that these are two totally different approaches to life? And that we do our best work when we use our *preferred* approach? Yet our society honors one way more, doesn't it? Which end?
Group:	The early starters.
Jane:	That's right—in the United States, we expect people to be on time, to follow schedules, to meet deadlines. But . . . what if I went down to South America? Or India? [Participants point to the last-minute end.] That's right. A friend of mine on a trip to one of those countries was told, "We print the flight schedules for you Americans. Our planes leave when they're ready." And that's a rather good idea when you think about it, isn't it?

Before people sit down, I make two more points. First, neither end of the continuum is a better or worse way to be. In fact, each side has strengths and, in its extreme, a weakness. For the late starters, the extreme is when they miss so many deadlines that people stop counting on them. For the early starters, it's when deadlines become more important than the needs of the people involved.

A Note on Multicultural Uses of Personality Type

The Association for Psychological Type is an international organization. At the 2004 international conference in Toronto, representatives from 24 nations were present, including Kuwait, Egypt, Chile, India, Brazil, Sweden, Indonesia, Korea, and New Zealand—type literally goes around the world. However, even though the theory itself is universal, instruments like the MBTI tool don't cross cultures. People within those cultures develop their own culturally relevant sorting tools to help people determine their preferences—the United States version doesn't even work well in England.

Further, different cultures honor different preferences, and that influences how people behave. For example, the United States honors Judging over Perceiving—one might say that our *archetypal* preference is for Judging.

The *stereotype* of the United States is also Judging; people in other countries tend to view us as Type A, driven by the clock. One person from Africa remarked, "Ah, you Americans. You have all the watches, but we have all the time." Further, the *modal* type in the United States is Judging; about 60–65 percent of the general population reports a Judging preference.

That isn't true in all cultures. Marcela Bitran (2004), an assistant professor of medicine in Chile who has studied her culture's type preferences extensively, describes it as Perceiving, whereas her own preference is for Judging:

> From my J point of view it is easier for a Perceiving person to enjoy life in Chile . . . 9 AM is usually understood as 9:15 or 9:20, or even 10 according to the circumstances (traffic jams, last minute calls, earthquakes, "Now that I am here, why don't I buy this stuff I have been looking for" . . . and so on). Since there are no apparent consequences to being late, punctuality is not reinforced. Being on time is just not a good business. For one thing, the meeting does not get rolling until the rest show up, and—even worse—nobody notices your punctuality because usually nobody is there to witness it!! Time management is a big issue in my country. If you do not confirm one day in advance a date made the week before, your friend may not show up (RSVP requests are of no help!). It is not uncommon to have deadlines postponed, exams deferred and promises thought over. Perceiving people don't seem to be in a hurry. (p. 3)

The cultural archetype of Perceiving matches the stereotype Americans hold of many Latin American countries—Bitran also mentions how as she pursued her doctoral work in Canada, people kidded her that all they knew about Chile was "mañana" and "siesta."

In the type community, this style of analysis goes on within the culture, not from without. (See pages 171–174 for more information.)

Finally, I emphasize that no one is glued to one spot on the continuum. I give a few examples and ask people to move up or down the line for different situations. For example, what if they're on vacation at the beach? At a ski resort? An amusement park? How soon will they get going in the morning? What if they're working on a project with their boss? Will they honor their supervisor's preference? I conclude, "At times, all of us are called on to be early starters or late starters. Maturity is about developing skills to use the right preference for the moment even if it isn't our natural style."

This exercise introduces the preference pair for how we approach life, through

Judging (designated by the letter J): A preference for planning their work and working their plan. They are *not* more judgmental, but rather prefer to come to judgment (closure) on things.

Perceiving (P): A preference for staying open to the moment. They are *not* more perceptive, but rather prefer to continue to perceive (gather) more information.

In general, people with a preference for Judging like to plan ahead, set schedules, work at a steady pace, finish work before they play, and make decisions rather than leaving issues open. They're the "early starters" of the world.

> What might happen when someone with a preference for Judging coaches someone with a preference for Perceiving? (See page 145 for suggestions.)

In general, people with a preference for Perceiving like to leave schedules open, work in bursts of energy, find ways for work and play to coexist, and delay decisions while they gather new information. They are the "last-minute" people of the world.

These are psychological opposites. Both are normal. Neither one is better than the other; as we saw in the exercise, when people operate in their own preference, they actually do better work.

The following continuums are to help you sort your own preference for Judging or Perceiving. Mark the spot on the continuum that you feel best describes you. And, note that some people have worked hard at developing skills that allow them to use the other preference. They sometimes find it easier to identify their *natural* preference if they think about themselves at age 18 or 25. And remember, both preferences are great ways to approach life, so be honest with yourself.

J |_____|_____|_____|_____|_____|_____ P

I like to work on
big projects at a
steady pace

I like to do more
of the work close
to the deadline

J |_____|_____|_____|_____|_____|_____ P

I do my best work
when I'm not
under pressure

I do my best work
when an upcoming
deadline adds pressure

J |_____|_____|_____|_____|_____|_____ P

I have a built-in clock;
I *know* how long
something will take

It's hard for me to
estimate how long
something will take

J |_____|_____|_____|_____|_____|_____ P

I feel better if my work
is done before I play

I might work first,
play first, or combine
work and play

J |_____|_____|_____|_____|_____|_____ P

I know when I have too
many things to do; then
I can say no to new
commitments

I say yes to new commitments,
then struggle to keep things
under control

J |_____|_____|_____|_____|_____|_____ P

I like to scope out the
magnitude of a project,
then plan it

I like to see how a
project unfolds, work
on it as inspired

J |_____|_____|_____|_____|_____|_____ P

I naturally narrow
down my options

I naturally look for
more options

J |_____|_____|_____|_____|_____|_____ P

If plans change
without warning
I feel stressed

If plans change without
warning I'm not bothered
much

As you look at the overall patterns of how you placed yourself on the continuums, which describes you best? Circle one:

J   P
Judging   Perceiving

Remember, there is no right or wrong. However, 80–85 percent of K–12 principals prefer Judging (compared with 60–65 percent of the general population in the United States).[2] Teachers and administrators with a preference for Perceiving may sometimes feel as if they're out of the mainstream. Think of the impact of these two different preferences in terms of educators' views on

- Planning and curriculum mapping
- Homework policies
- Class time structure
- Staff meeting schedules and agendas.

> Although the Gregorc, Kolb, and Multiple Intelligences models show little correlation with the Judging-Perceiving preference pair, several Dunn and Dunn Learning Style "elements" touch on the same concepts, including Emotional Stimulus (Motivation, Persistence) and Psychological Stimulus (Impulsive-Reflective). See their Web site for more information: http://www.learningstyles.net.

You've seen the two preferences in action, haven't you? One Perceiving teacher said of curriculum mapping (which, by the way, she had completed on time), "It's like a straitjacket. I mean, I want to pick the novels we'll read based on the interests and needs of the students I have. And, each year those needs are different. If a theme doesn't work, the map seems evil." In contrast, many Judging teachers view curriculum mapping as providing a secure sense of where they're going.

Coaching Implications of Judging and Perceiving.

Perceiving types *may*

- Avoid planning very far ahead—things could change! A coach needs flexibility regarding the whens and whats of interactions.
- Resist deciding quickly about lessons or practices—or may easily change their minds with new information.

- Be more likely to over- or underestimate how long activities will take.
- Be stressed by closure: something better or more appropriate may be revealed through waiting.

Judging types *may*

- Find good practices and stick with them.
- Have things planned out and resist coaching interventions that interfere.
- Seem rigid without sufficient attention to their informational and timing needs.
- Be stressed by changes—they had it all planned!

Judging and Perceiving are the first of four preference pairs. We'll review the other three in this chapter. Then, in Chapter 6, we'll look at the impact our preferences have on how we learn.

EXTRAVERSION AND INTROVERSION: FINDING THE *ENERGY* TO TEACH AND LEARN

The next preference pair concerns how we are energized, through

Extraversion (E): Gaining energy through action and interaction, the outside world.

Introversion (I): Gaining energy through reflection and solitude, the inner world.

This preference pair is *not* about sociability. Note that in type language, Extra*v*ersion is even spelled differently than extro*v*ert. Introverts can be very social, but group gatherings can be draining even if they enjoy them.

It's not about shyness. Extraverts can be very shy around strangers, yet need contact with friends and the outside world to be energized.

It's not about being the life of the party. Introverts can be very entertaining (many actors, musicians, and sports figures are Introverts).

It's not about depth of thought. Extraverts aren't shallow, but instead increase their understanding through discussion rather than through solitary thinking. Further, they often have a wider breadth of interests, preferring to know something about a lot of things rather than a lot about a few things.

Extraverts are communal creatures, finding their comfort zone in a crowd, a busy street, a full room, a group of acquaintances, or even a group of strangers if they can talk to them. Even shy Extraverts find it a relief to be able to talk to at least one other person at frequent, regular intervals.

Introverts are independent creatures who find that their heads start to buzz in the midst of too much noise or too many people for too long. They may have lots of friends, but need less time with them—and in fewer numbers at a time. In a crowd, they may naturally drift off into daydreaming to gain back some energy, or limit the crowd by narrowing their interactions to one or two people.

In *general,* people with a preference for Extraversion focus on their environment, talk things out and say what they're thinking, enjoy interruptions as they work, and express themselves more naturally through spoken words than written forms of communication.

In *general,* people with a preference for Introversion focus on their own inner world of ideas, think things through before speaking, find interruptions distracting, and prefer written forms of communication.

Extraversion correlates with the kinesthetic mode of learning. Introversion correlates with both auditory and visual modes of learning (Hammer, 1996).

In the United States, we honor Extraversion more than Introversion. In meetings, people are rewarded for brainstorming quickly. We grade students on class participation. We worry about our own children if they are too quiet, and we often judge Introverts as being slow or shy.

Within education, think of the implications of this preference for

- Team meetings
- Classroom expectations
- Staff development workshops
- Reading and writing.

Kolb's Experiential Learning model shows the following correlations (Hammer, 1996):

- Active Experimentation: Extraversion
- Concrete Experimentation: Introversion
- Reflective Observation: Introversion.

Again, use the following continuums to help you sort your own preference. Note that as Extraverts age, they find that to regain *physical* energy, they need more downtime and may seek more time alone. However, they still need more social contact than people with a preference for Introversion.

Again, both preferences are excellent ways of being, so be honest about your own preference.

E | | | | | | I

I get my best ideas
when talking with
others

To come up with
good ideas, I need
time for reflection

E | | | | | | I

After a few hours, a
silent retreat would
get frustrating

I could take frequent,
long silent retreats

E | | | | | | I

I find it easy to share
my thoughts in
meetings

It is easier for me to share
thoughts if I have an agenda
in advance to think through

E | | | | | | I

When I have free time,
I look for people to do
things with

When I have free time,
I'm content to be alone
for long periods

E | | | | | | I

I enjoy group
projects

I enjoy working
by myself

E | | | | | | I

I need to talk about
problems to work
through them

I try to work through
problems on my own

E | | | | | | I

It's hard to
concentrate if it's
too quiet

It's hard to
concentrate if it's
too noisy

E | | | | | | I

People view me as
quick on my feet

I often feel that I'm
slow to answer

As you look at the overall patterns of how you placed yourself on the continuums, which describes you best? Circle one:

E   I
Extraversion   Introversion

Remember, there is no right or wrong.

Coaching Implications of Extraversion and Introversion

Extraverted types *may*

- Need to talk, not listen, to understand.
- Change their minds as they talk.
- Prefer act-reflect-act patterns of learning; for Extraverts, the doing gives them something to think about.
- Be stressed by too much lecture/inaction/quiet.

Introverted types *may*

- Prefer to reflect on materials or experiences in advance.
- Take on a "deer in the headlights" feeling if the meeting focus changes from what they expect.
- Prefer a reflect-act-reflect pattern of learning, anticipating, or reading about what might happen in advance of trying it.
- Be stressed by noise, changes without reflective time, or being asked to self-disclose too much information.

SENSING AND INTUITION: YOUR PREFERENCE FOR GATHERING INFORMATION

If you received the following sixth-grade mathematics assignment, what would be your reaction? What if you had to give the assignment to students?

In any form of your own choosing, prepare a final project that demonstrates what you have learned about the characteristics of, relationships among, and real-life appearances of triangles, squares, rectangles, parallelograms, quadrilaterals, pentagons, hexagons, and octagons. You may decide to present your information as a book, a poster or set of posters, a story, a report, a mobile, a movie, a slide show, or any other design of your choosing. Be certain your project shows all the facts you know about the relationships among the different shapes' edges and angles.[3]

Some teachers tell me they don't use the assignment, saying it's too ambiguous. Others have added more structure, allowing students to choose among just three or four options for presenting their information. Still others give the assignment as is. Your reaction might hint at your preference for

Sensing (S): *First* paying attention to *what is,* to information you can gather through your five senses—the facts.

INtuition (N)*: *First* paying attention to what *could be,* to hunches, connections, or imagination—a sixth sense.

* Note that the **I** was used for Introversion, so the **N** stands for **IN**tuition.

Sensing teachers and students generally think that assignment directions should let you know what to do. Intuitive teachers and students feel that structured assignments prevent students from excelling from their strengths bases. Thus, Intuitive teachers tend to think more highly of the above math assignment.

- Sensing and Judging correlate with the Gregorc category of Concrete Sequential.
- Introversion/Sensing/Thinking correlate with Abstract Sequential.
- Intuitive and Perceiving correlate with Concrete Random.
- With the Kolb model, Intuition correlates with Abstract Conceptualization; none of the styles correlate with Sensing (Hammer, 1996).

In *general,* people with a preference for Sensing like to work from experience, understand expectations, deal with current reality, and be known as practical rather than as imaginative.

In *general,* people with a preference for Intuition like to be innovative, have room for creativity, deal with future possibilities, and be known as imaginative rather than as practical.

In the United States, we honor Sensing more than Intuition; 70–75 percent of the population prefers Sensing. We value accuracy, common sense, and real-world application. Results are to be measurable—think about the importance of test scores or grade point averages in education.

However, within education itself, Sensing is more valued in the early grades (accurate arithmetic, spelling, learning to follow directions, etc.), whereas Intuition becomes more valued the higher the educational level (and is often touted as "higher level thinking"). At the elementary school level, approximately 62 percent of the teachers show a preference for Sensing. At the university level, 66 percent of professors show a preference for Intuition.

In addition, there are startling differences in the preferences of teachers among the different subject areas. For example, 64 percent of English teachers show a preference for Intuition; 62 percent of math teachers show a preference for Sensing; 65 percent of trade, industrial, and technical teachers have a preference for Sensing; and 71 percent of art, drama, and music teachers have a preference for Intuition. Remember, 70–75 percent of the population has a preference for Sensing—what does this say about the people who select lifelong interests such as English or art or music as a profession?

Within secondary schools, the fact that different disciplines attract teachers with different personalities often leads to a diverse teaching staff. However, within departments, things can be very unbalanced. A school I worked with was typical: five of seven math teachers preferred Sensing, and all but one language arts teacher preferred Intuition.

Although people who prefer Sensing have their own vibrant styles of creativity and people who prefer Intuition can be fully competent with details when they need to be, we still have a natural preference. Both are equally valuable ways of perceiving the world. I often contrast the valuable emphasis of scientists such as Thomas Edison, who work on practical applications of their knowledge to show the contribution of Sensing, and the work of scientists like Albert Einstein, emphasizing theoretical knowledge to show the contribution of Intuition. Use the following continuums to sort your own natural preference.

As you look at the overall patterns of how you placed yourself on the continuums, which describes you best? Circle one:

S   N
Sensing   INtuition

Because this preference pair deals with taking in information, it has enormous ramifications for education. We know, for example, that 82 percent of National Merit Scholarships (which are based on PSAT scores) go to students with a preference for Intuition, even though only 25–30 percent of the population has a preference for Intuition (Myers & Myers, 1993).

In Chapter 6, I will further discuss the impact of teacher and student preferences for Sensing and Intuition.

S | | | | | | N

I like clear
expectations for
responsibilities and
assignments

I like open-ended
responsibilities and
assignments

S | | | | | | N

I tend to look at *what
is real*—actual past
experiences and
verifiable information

What is real triggers my
perceptions of what
could be or reminds me
of other things

S | | | | | | N

I like to gather facts
and then decide what
they all mean

I often "know," then
look for facts to back
up my hunch

S | | | | | | N

Past experience and
reflection on what
did/didn't work are
my best guides

Inspiration and
imagination are my
best guides

S | | | | | | N

Repetition leads to
mastery when I want
to learn something

Repetition leads to
boredom, more
mistakes

S | | | | | | N

I like tasks where you
keep using proven
methods

I like work that
allows for novel
approaches

S | | | | | | N

I prefer learning
practical knowledge

I prefer learning
interesting things, even
if I won't use them

S | | | | | | N

Open-ended
assignments and test
items are frustrating
to complete and hard
to grade

Open-ended
assignments and test
items bring out my
best thinking

Coaching Implications of Sensing and Intuition

Sensing types *may*

- Want immediate applications and relevant examples.
- Prefer step-by-step implementation strategies and details to take them from what they know to what you want them to do.
- View theory as beside the point; they want to know what will work in *their* classroom.
- Be stressed by removal of what is working with no proof that the change will be better.

Intuitive types *may*

- Be less interested in isolated skills than in how they fit into overall goals and strategies.
- View curriculum or instructional practices as a starting place for innovation *unless* given clear reasons not to deviate from them.
- Respond more to metaphors or theories than to facts.
- Be stressed by details, structure, and lack of room for creativity.

THINKING AND FEELING: HOW WE MAKE DECISIONS

Not all rational decisions are logical, although people raised on the scientific method may find this hard to fathom. This preference pair describes two rational processes for making decisions:

Thinking (T): Making decisions through objective, logical principles.

Feeling (F): Making decisions by considering the impact of each alternative on the people involved.

Feelers can think; Thinkers have feelings. However, their ideal worlds are different. In an ideal world for Thinkers, rules would be universally applied. There'd be no need for exceptions. An ideal world for Feelers would have a different set of rules for each person, based on their needs. *None* of us live in an ideal world, do we? Neither the Thinking nor the Feeling way can work all the time.

During one staff development workshop at a brand-new school, after learning about the preferences, teachers met in grade-level teams to look at their type preferences and think about the impact their personalities might have on students. The seventh-grade teachers all had a preference for Thinking. After the breakout session, here's what they reported:

As a team, we'd already decided to enforce a strict homework policy: If it's late, they fail. However, now we know that as Thinkers our preference is for universal rules like that. We need to have some mechanisms that allow students an occasional second chance—perhaps because of a family commitment or sports event. So, they'll get two homework passes per quarter in each class. They don't have to explain why they're using them. But, when the passes are gone, they're gone.

These teachers came up with a *balanced* approach: a universal rule that allows for exceptions. Although we each have a preference for Thinking or Feeling, the best decisions use the strengths of both.

In general, people with a preference for Thinking might describe themselves as analytical, objective, impartial, fair but firm, and logical. "Good decisions are made with the head," they might say.

In general, people with a preference for Feeling might describe themselves as empathetic, subjective, harmonious, and accepting. "Good decisions are made with the heart," they might say.

In the United States, we honor Thinking over Feeling. Think about pay structures for jobs that require Thinking skills (law, accounting, engineering) versus those that require Feeling skills (early childhood education, nursing, social work). Further, consider the emphasis on logic and the scientific method, even in requirements for how to write papers in the humanities subject areas.

Thinkers and Feelers each account for about 50 percent of the population. However, this is the only preference pair for which there is a gender difference. More men have a preference for Thinking. Further, male culture emphasizes Thinking skills over Feeling skills. The reverse is true for women. A pop saying would be more accurate as, "Thinkers are from Mars, Feelers are from Venus." Indeed, Thinkers and Feelers almost seem to speak different languages at times.

- In the Gregorc Learning Styles model, Thinking correlates with Abstract Sequential and Feeling with Abstract Random.
- In Kolb's model, Thinking correlates with Abstract Conceptualization; Feeling shows no statistical correlation with any of the styles.
- Studies also show that Feeling correlates with field-dependent learners and Intuition/Thinking with field-independent learners (Hammer, 1996).

In education, about 75–80 percent of K–12 principals have a preference for Thinking. This is similar to trends in businesses, where a preponderance of managers are Thinkers. If they underestimate the importance of "soft" people factors when making decisions, they often find that reality varies widely from their plans. Feeling administrators, on the other hand, often struggle to make tough decisions, as they worry about the impact on people. The Thinking and Feeling preferences need each other to understand and deal with complex problems and situations.

Again, sort through your own preferences, remembering that both Thinking and Feeling are integral to good decisions, yet all of us tend toward one or the other. Ask yourself, too, whether it's a skill you've developed or something that comes naturally for you.

Without grasping these basic differences between the preferences, Thinkers might look on Feelers as wishy-washy and Feelers on Thinkers as cold or lacking compassion. Especially in education, where we are dealing with the future possibilities and present self-esteem of our students, both Thinking and Feeling processes need to be taken into account in setting standards, practices, and classroom environments. On the basis of your placement on the continuums, choose whether Thinking or Feeling describes you best and circle one below:

T   F
Thinking   Feeling

Coaching Implications of Thinking and Feeling

Thinking types *may*

- Want to know a coach is competent. Tout your credentials and experience.
- Need logic and the rationale for changes.
- Distrust nonspecific praise.
- Be stressed by displays of emotion, assumption of a personal relationship, or lack of fairness or equity.

Feeling types *may*

- Take problems or critiques personally. Start with concrete positive reinforcement.
- Be concerned about the impact of practices on the *whole* person—both teachers and students—not just academic achievement.
- Want students (and coaches) to like them.
- Be stressed by disharmony, not being listened to, or awareness that some teachers' or students' needs are unmet.

T | | | | | F
I tend to use logic (cause-
effect, if-then reasoning)
in decisions

I tend to step into the
shoes of people
involved in decisions

T | | | | | F
I think through
precedents before
considering making
an exception

The needs of an
individual outweigh
the dangers of setting
a precedent

T | | | | | F
I usually first see
what's wrong with an
idea or event

I usually first
see the positive in
an idea or event

T | | | | | F
I tend to be
objective, separating
feelings from
decision making

I tend to be subjective,
considering feelings as
important data

T | | | | | F
I invite criticism in
order to improve

I need praise first before I
can handle criticism

T | | | | | F
I put work first—I seek
competency before
camaraderie in coworkers
to be productive

I put relationships
first—I need to get
along with coworkers
to be productive

T | | | | | F
I'm good at seeing
external factors when
something goes
wrong

I'm good at seeing
the role I played
when something
goes wrong

T | | | | | F
I can easily detach
myself when
delivering tough
messages

I struggle to deliver
tough messages

EIGHT PREFERENCES, SIXTEEN TYPES

Again, personality type helps us look at normal differences among normal people. An ethical interpretation of robust instruments such as the MBTI tool (as opposed to quizzes found on the Internet) includes a thorough explanation of the preferences, the results of the instrument, and written type descriptions. These three pieces are then used to help a person find his or her best-fit type.

Some people find it easier to find their best-fit types than others do. Several factors influence this, including

Nature vs. nurture. CAT scans and other evidence reveal that a person's preferences are inborn. However, the environment does influence them. For example, my Extraverted friends from London tell me that they aren't nearly as Extraverted as their American friends with the same type preferences. Britain's more Introverted culture has influenced them. Family systems and work environments may also influence how we view our natural preferences.

Further, o*ur preferences are innate, but behavior is dynamic.* In other words, although we have preferences, we adjust our behavior to meet situations; our preferences don't box us in.

Youth vs. maturity. Although we are born with certain preferences, maturity is about knowing when we can use our natural preferences and when we need to step out of our preferences. For example, Introverted teachers need to tolerate a certain amount of noise in their classrooms to accommodate Extraverted students. Parents with a preference for Judging need to set aside their schedules and meet their children's needs in the moment. Our preferences don't change, but we learn skills to access the competencies of the other side.

Individuality vs. stereotyping. Some people view any framework that categorizes people as an attack on their individuality. Worse, they may learn about type in an atmosphere in which it is used to label rather than to understand people. We emphasize that although type explains certain basic differences among people, each person still has individual experiences, education, values, and circumstances that make them unique. Knowing a person's type might help you better communicate with them and give you some broad principles about how they approach life, but that person is *unlike* other people of his or her type in an infinite number of ways. Further, people are to choose their own preferences, not be told what they are. This is another factor that keeps it from being a labeling system.

Take a moment to capture your four preferences below. My own preferences are for INFJ. Write yours in the blanks below:

_____	_____	_____	_____
E or I	S or N	T or F	J or P

In the next chapter, we'll look at the research base and practical implications of the impact of the preferences for coaching, teaching, and learning. Chapter 7 explains how our preferences influence our needs during change.

NOTES

1. "Traveling companion for life" in the Ojibwe language.
2. All type distribution information is from the database of the Center for Applications of Psychological Type, Gainesville, Florida.
3. Adapted from Michigan State University. (1996). *Shapes and designs: Two-dimensional geometry, student edition.* Palo Alto, CA: Dale Seymour Publications, p. 76.

6 Learning Styles and Coaching

An Effective Alliance

> For educators, a robust common framework becomes a tool for letting us
>
> - Focus on which students a practice reaches rather than on who is right or wrong
> - Uncover biases and assumptions that come from our own learning style
> - Understand our reactions, both favorable and unfavorable, to suggested changes
> - Clarify, from a strengths-based model, which new practices might be easy or difficult for us, and provide strategies for adopting them.

Why do teachers teach the way they do? As we saw in Chapter 3, teachers' beliefs about education and what works in the classroom are often tightly tied to their strengths as teachers. When we ask them to change, we are often asking them to teach out of their weaknesses.

Coaching involves educating teachers through processes that lead to self-reflection. Eventually, we want teachers to coach themselves by evaluating the effectiveness of their ideas in terms of student achievement. For educators, a robust common framework becomes a tool for letting us

- Focus on which students a practice reaches rather than on who is right or wrong
- Uncover biases and assumptions that come from our own learning style
- Understand our reactions, both favorable and unfavorable, to suggested changes
- Clarify, from a strengths-based model, which new practices might be easy or difficult for us, and provide strategies for adopting them.

Personality type in particular helps teachers—and coaches—understand that *their educational beliefs are to a large extent tightly bound to their personalities*. At its heart, recall that type is about the different processes we use to take in information and make decisions. These are key processes in education. Our beliefs come from how *we* learn. When teachers look at descriptions of how students with type preferences opposite to their own learn, they react by saying either, "They can really learn that way?" or "But I'm not comfortable teaching that way."

Let's look at four teachers you've already met to see how their beliefs and personality types go hand in hand. Then we'll look at some research that correlates trends in education and type biases, then at the model itself as used for learning styles.

DIFFERENT PERSONALITIES, STRENGTHS, AND BELIEFS

In the following chart, the "General strengths for each type" come from general descriptions of the types in my other writing. The second and third columns are from interviews with the four teachers, confirmed through classroom observations. How closely the general information and individual comments relate varies somewhat from teacher to teacher, but overall, each teacher's strengths and beliefs are related. Further, note how *different* the self-reported strengths are for the teachers whose personality preferences are least similar, i.e., Kay compared to Sara or Josh. Kay emphasizes creativity, whereas Sara and Josh emphasize basic skills.

Studies of learning styles and personality type in education show evidence of the ties between teachers' personalities and their educational beliefs. Gregorc (1999–2005) puts it this way:

	General strengths for each type[1]	*Self-reported teaching strengths[2]*	*Educational beliefs*
Sara (ESTP) Extraversion Sensing Thinking Perceiving *Prefers coach as useful resource*	Paying attention to what needs doing/fixing right now Meeting practical needs in the most efficient way Reminding others of the joys of this life, this *present* time Solving problems in a straightforward, logical manner	Patience so students can discover concepts Classroom management, organization Making math fun Breaking tasks into steps	Children need multiple explanations to learn Good curriculum is key Students need to enjoy school Basic skills are key to success
Josh (ESFP) Extraversion Sensing Feeling Perceiving *Prefers coach as encouraging sage*	Adding enthusiasm, energy to workplace Communicating warmth, excitement, and acceptance Keeping track of many things at once Linking people and practical information to task at hand	Theatrical background, reading aloud Building relationships Being organized Basic skills	Reading aloud is necessary with mixed-ability classes Students who struggle need individual help Structure and organization foster school success Students need basic skills practice
Kay (INFP) Introversion Intuition Feeling Perceiving	Bringing a compassionate, caring, and personal focus	Loving children Student reflection exercises,	Teachers need to treat students as individuals

(Continued)

(Continued)

	General strengths for each type[1]	Self-reported teaching strengths[2]	Educational beliefs
Prefers coach as collegial mentor	Reminding others of their values and the worthiness of striving to meet them Providing a positive vision for the future Enriching others with creative ideas	classroom discussions Focusing team on big picture Creativity	Students need to hope, to believe in themselves before they can learn Specific big-picture focuses including writing across curriculum, heterogeneous groupings Teachers need to make learning attractive to students
Pete (ENTP) **E**xtraversion **In**tuition **T**hinking **P**erceiving *Prefers coach as expert*	Initiating new projects, direction, etc., with enthusiasm and energy Meeting challenges proactively Using synthesis as a strategy to solve problems Challenging and encouraging personal and/or organizational growth	Active teaching style Curriculum balanced between engagement and challenge Using learning styles framework Building relationships	Students need to actively participate to learn Student engagement will lead to success Students have different learning styles Learning starts with respect, knowing each student

1. From Hirsh & Kise (2000) and Kise, Stark, & Hirsh (2005).

2. Self-reported teacher strengths and beliefs are from interviews.

Teaching is a form of thought transmission and thought control. Therefore, teachers must recognize how they use their personal Mind Styles to transmit specific ideas and how they place special mediation ability demands on the student. They must understand that their mindsets create, reinforce, support and reward certain mental qualities and how their natural biases affect their approaches to classes, choices of methods, media and tests, and arrangements in the environment. Such knowledge is absolutely necessary for responsive and responsible professional behavior.

Research on personality type reveals several important areas in which our own preferences and learning styles affect teaching methodologies, subject matter, and assessment, including

- Reading and writing
- Mathematics and science
- Classroom practices
- Student behavior
- Gifted education.

> Remember, type is essentially about taking in information and making decisions. Consider where the research discussed below indicates biases in our educational system for either adult or student learners.

This means that as coaches, type can help us reframe resistance to new ideas in terms of personality strengths and biases rather than rights and wrongs. Let's look at what we know about each one of the above topics.

READING AND WRITING

> *Sensing* correlates with left-brain dominance and concrete learning processes, as well as kinesthetic modes of learning.
> *Intuition* correlates with right-brain dominance, abstract learning processes, and auditory and visual modes of learning (Hammer, 1996).

Isabel Briggs Myers, the creator of the MBTI tool, noted that because reading and writing are in symbolic languages, the natural realm of the Intuitive preference, people with a preference for Intuition have a natural affinity for reading (Myers & Myers, 1993). For Sensing types, she pointed out, "Whatever comes directly from the senses is part of the sensing types' own experience and is therefore trustworthy. What comes from other people indirectly *through the spoken* or *written word* is less trustworthy. Words are merely symbols that have to be translated into reality before they mean anything" (p. 57). Her theory holds true in a compilation of studies that compare reading scores of Sensing and Intuitive students; in every study, Intuitive students significantly outscore Sensing students (Hammer, 1996).

> How might one's preference for Sensing and Intuition influence one's adeptness with verbal-linguistic intelligence?

This in no way means that people with a preference for Sensing are less intelligent. Instead, consider that the tests are in the "native language" of Intuitives; the tests do not take into account the equally legitimate intelligence of Sensing. Myers and Myers (1993) pointed out,

> The sensing child's native language is the reality spoken by the senses. The intuitive's native language is the word, the metaphor, the symbol, spoken by the unconscious. Most mental tests are of necessity couched in the intuitive's language. The sensing child has more translating to do, and translating takes time. (p. 59)

> Note how reading aloud adds a second sense—hearing the words. The Montessori method of tracing sandpaper letters adds *touch* to the process of decoding.

Sensing students tend to reread test questions to deepen their understanding. Intuitives tend to skim for important facts and the right answer, meaning that they can cover more problems in the same amount of time. Sensing types value soundness of thought over quickness and don't trust their hunches. Sensing students usually learn to read easily when reading instruction makes clear the connections between sounds and word symbols (i.e., phonics). The bridge between the senses and the symbols has been made for them.

The following passage from *Dicey's Song* illustrates the struggles of a Sensing child, Maybeth, who wasn't taught to read through phonics, as seen through the eyes of her older sister who is tutoring her:

> You mean, what Maybeth does is sees—like the beginning of the word and then she guesses . . . And she's not a guesser by nature . . . It would make her nervous, and she'd always be waiting to be caught in a mistake, and she wouldn't hear what she was reading, so it would be hard for her to understand what she was reading. Maybeth likes—knowing how to do what she's doing. When she gets nervous, and scared—she can't think about things. (Voight, 1982, p. 143)

Our preferences influence how we teach. Josh and Sara, the two Sensing teachers, emphasized basic skills, whereas Pete and Kay, the Intuitives, emphasized creativity. Pete and Kay admitted how much they struggled to break projects down into small steps and give sufficiently detailed directions; Sara and Josh excelled in those areas.

> Josh and Sara could also be described as Concrete Sequential and Pete and Kay as Abstract Random.

Our personality preferences also have a bearing on *what* we like to read and write. For example, teachers with preferences for Introversion and Sensing are more likely to use a basal reader approach to reading instruction, whereas those with preferences for Extraversion and Intuition are more likely to use a whole-language approach (Lehto, 1990). Intuitives receive higher grades on reflective papers, and lower grades on papers that require the reporting of factual information, than do Sensing types (Fisher, 1994). In summarizing lab work, Sensing students tend to present itemized lists without an overview, whereas Intuitive students tend to write overviews that lack focus (Held & Yokomoto, 1983).

> How might literacy coaches use this information with teachers who are reluctant to introduce specific graphic organizers or other methods to help students with writing?

MATHEMATICS AND SCIENCE

Studies show that mathematics teachers tend to have preferences for Sensing and Thinking (Hammer, 1996). Traditionally, mathematics teachers use logic, and the logical scientific method is the hallmark of research methodology as well as a natural process for people with a preference for Thinking. Huelsman (2002) demonstrated how this emphasis puts Feeling students at a disadvantage; he improved results by changing his developmental mathematics classes to directly address mathematics anxiety in Feeling students.

> Consider the connections with Logical-Mathematical intelligence. Also, consider gender differences in performance in mathematical and scientific tasks and the fact that our culture's archetypes are Thinking for men and Feeling for women.

Crumpton (2000) documented the effectiveness of using hands-on manipulatives to help students understand abstract mathematical concepts. In contrast, the response of Intuitive students, especially those with a preference for Introversion, is often "Why do I have to move around slices of pizza when I can see it in my head?" In my own work with mathematics teachers, several Intuitive teachers confirmed that they try to "wean" students off of manipulatives, a reflection of their own style.

> Using hands-on manipulatives taps into kinesthetic intelligence and the Sensing preference to learn mathematical skills.

Nygren and Nygren (2000) describe how a Sensing teacher provided Intuitive-style alternatives to his usual step-by-step teaching methods and improved the grades of students who were underperforming in his precalculus class. As his teaching methods became known, Intuitive students chose his classroom. No Sensing students took the class; it appealed more to Intuitives than the traditional classes.

> One can compare the changes in teaching methods in these studies to adding more kinesthetic, Concrete Sequential techniques to coursework that had traditionally honored Logical-Mathematical intelligence and Abstract styles.

In mathematics, Intuitive students fare better on standardized testing (Hammer, 1996), just as they do in reading. They also tend to outperform Sensing students in theoretical science classes. *However,* research shows that this performance gap is more a matter of how the classes are taught than whether Sensing students can master the material. Wilkes (2005) studied first-year engineering students and found that their MBTI personality types accounted for 67 percent of the variance in grades. Over 77 percent of the Intuitive students received A's, compared with 52 percent of the Sensing students. However, in another study, when engineering classes added active, cooperative, and inductive teaching methods, Sensing students performed as well as Intuitive students, who had held the advantage when the same subject matter was covered through high quantities of abstract content (Felder, 2002).

To summarize, the most common approaches to mathematics and science instruction can put people with certain personality preferences at a disadvantage. When the approaches are changed to honor the other preferences, those students perform better.

> Coaches can use this information to help elementary teachers rethink mathematics instruction in terms of what students need.

Ponder this: more than two-thirds of elementary teachers show a preference for Feeling; for almost half of those, Feeling is their dominant function, the function that Huelsman (2002) identified with mathematics anxiety. For these students, "Rote memory and fact regurgitation have become part of a mathematics-course-passing-game that only appears to yield temporary abilities to solve standardized problems. The desire to develop critical thinking skills in a mathematics class appears to have died in these students" (p. 31). Many elementary teachers resort to fact and procedures methodology rather than the exploratory methods recommended by the National Council of Teachers of Mathematics (NCTM). Perhaps their own strengths and type preferences—and struggles with math—influence their beliefs of how children learn.

CLASSROOM PRACTICES

As noted in Chapter 1, teachers' own strengths and beliefs color their perceptions of their students. It shouldn't surprise us that Pete, who enjoyed global concepts (Intuition and Thinking; Abstract Random), struggled with students who had short attention spans for such things. Or that Kay, who tried to reach each student through creativity (Intuition, Abstract style), was frustrated with students who didn't get excited about anything not grounded in the here and now (Sensing, Concrete style). Or that Sara, full of fun and energy (Extraversion), struggled to reach quiet students (Introversion).

Study after study shows that these natural biases affect how we run our classrooms, putting students with preferences very different from our own at a disadvantage. Studies that monitor brain electrical activity establish a physiological base for the Introvert's need for quiet for concentration and the Extravert's need for more external stimulation (Wilson & Languis, 1989). Yet Introverted teachers tend to have quiet, orderly classrooms, and Extraverted teachers have classrooms with movement and noise, placing students with opposite preferences at a disadvantage. Coaches need to understand the deep source of these biases and then use the common framework to provide solid reasons for change.

STUDENT BEHAVIOR

At one school I worked with, the teachers and administrators asked me to work with students they identified as "at risk" either academically or because of behavior problems. Over 80 percent of those students self-identified as having a preference for Perceiving, twice as many as one would expect in a normal distribution. Other studies show that teachers are more likely to view normal Perceiving behaviors as problematic, which can become a self-fulfilling prophecy.

Several different studies have shown that Sensing and Perceiving students can be most frustrated in traditional classrooms. At one alternative high school, 90 percent of the students, "dropouts" from the traditional programs, were Sensing-Perceiving (Giger, 1996). The researcher characterized the students this way:

> While working with SP [Sensing-Perceiving] students in both school and treatment settings, they shared some fascinating and "true to type" information about "teacher testing." SP students enjoy the thrill of the reaction from SJ [Sensing-Judging] teachers (*My job is to teach, your job is to learn*) and find it much less exciting to test NF [Intuition-Feeling] (*Let me know what I can do to help you*) and NT [Intuition-Thinking] (*I'm here when you're ready to learn*) limits. They report that SP's (*I expect you to participate and be a team player . . .*), when they can find them, can be the most fun to engage in conflict. Many SP students, particularly Extraverted, report enjoying the adrenaline rush of confrontation and may create a situation, if necessary, to experience this feeling. (p. 388)

Note that 70 percent of all elementary teachers have a preference for Judging; perhaps this starts many Sensing-Perceiving students off on the wrong foot?

O'Neill (1986) noted that students referred for discipline purposes differed significantly from their teachers on the Sensing-Intuition scale. Given that Sensing teachers tend to emphasize order, quiet, sequential learning, and structure, and Intuitive teachers tend to emphasize choice, movement, and student voice in decisions (Lawrence, 1993), it is easy to see how clashes between the two styles could result in disciplinary referrals. This is a key concept for classroom management coaching.

GIFTED EDUCATION

Several studies of gifted high school students show disproportionate levels of Intuitive students. However, when measures of giftedness include hands-on tasks and not just tests, Sensing students are selected more frequently (Robinson, 1994). In other words, many standard methods of identifying gifted students are biased toward those with a preference for Intuition. They do not acknowledge the Sensing creative ability to improve existing ideas, processes, or products in evolutionary ways, instead recognizing only Intuitive innovation as creative (Segal, 2000).

A SIGNIFICANT FACTOR IN EDUCATION

These are just a few of the very real, very significant ways in which personality preferences influence the experiences of both teachers and students in the classroom. They color our beliefs, our biases, our practices. The studies cited above get at the underlying factors of why some students have actually become high-, middle-, and low-performing students. Personality type details *how,* not whether, each style can learn various subject content. It is a strengths-based model, emphasizing what teachers and students of each type do best.

Consider another possible source of bias in our educational system: Personality type even affects who goes into teaching. Look at the following table of elementary teachers. The selection ratio (*I*) calculates the expected number of teachers, based on their frequency in a standard population sample, versus the actual number.[1] If *I* is less than 1, people with those type preferences are underrepresented. The bold *I* values are significantly over or under 1.00.

Teachers: Elementary School
$N = 804$

ISTJ	ISFJ	INFJ	INTJ
$N = 86$	$N = 144$	$N = 41$	$N = 17$
$\% = 10.70$	$\% = 17.91$	$\% = 5.10$	$\% = 2.11$
$I = 0.92$	$I = 1.30$	$I = 3.40$	$I = 1.00$
ISTP	**ISFP**	**INFP**	**INTP**
$N = 14$	$N = 38$	$N = 37$	$N = 12$
$\% = 1.74$	$\% = 4.73$	$\% = 4.60$	$\% = 1.49$
$I = 0.32$	**$I = 0.20$**	$I = 1.05$	**$I = 0.45$**
ESTP	**ESFP**	**ENFP**	**ENTP**
$N = 7$	$N = 46$	$N = 82$	$N = 12$
$\% = 0.87$	$\% = 5.72$	$\% = 10.20$	$\% = 1.49$
$I = 0.20$	**$I = 0.67$**	$I = 1.25$	**$I = 0.47$**
ESTJ	**ESFJ**	**ENFJ**	**ENTJ**
$N = 68$	$N = 100$	$N = 58$	$N = 42$
$\% = 8.46$	$\% = 12.44$	$\% = 7.21$	$\% = 5.22$
$I = 0.97$	$I = 1.01$	$I = 2.88$	$I = 2.90$

Note that the four Sensing/Perceiving types are underrepresented (ISTP, ISFP, ESTP, ESFP), and remember that these same types made up 90 percent of the students at an alternative high school (p. 110). Why are these types so underrepresented in teaching? Were their own school experiences so miserable that they chose not to go into teaching? Or, are the selection processes we use to allow students into teacher education programs biased against these types? Or, do the students drop out because of the slant of teacher preservice education? Remember, Sensing types tend to dislike theory without immediate practical application—and do better in classes that present application and theory together. They value experience over the written word; are preservice programs of interest to them in general? Considering that they are so underrepresented in education, do our reform efforts take into account the needs of these learners? These are areas of ongoing research among type practitioners.

Again, the impact of our type preferences on how we teach and learn is very real. Although much is written on the needs of adult learners, little attention is given to the fact that they, like children, have different learning styles. As we ask teachers to change their classrooms, we need to help them change by providing them with the information that will convince them of the need to do so. That information varies, depending on their personality type preferences—their learning style.

WHY USE TYPE IN COACHING?

In a sense, using a learning styles framework for coaching is a shortcut for overcoming teacher resistance. One can use the neutral framework to uncover biases, choose activities, and build on teacher strengths.

One of the clearest incentives to consider type biases in education is the significantly higher scores on the PSAT for Intuitives than for Sensing types. Myers and Myers (1993) identified that although 70–75 percent of students are Sensing types, 82 percent of the National Merit Scholarships go to Intuitive students. Wilkes (2004), in an item-by-item analysis of student responses, found that the gap was due to the Intuitive style of guessing. The PSAT contains "detractor" items; Sensing students chose these consistently on the more advanced content questions, and the test penalizes for wrong answers. Intuitive types, who tend to remember the big picture of a concept, chose the detractor items far less often. He concluded that the test is clearly biased.

Teachers need this information to understand the source of their beliefs and why their beliefs may not be sufficient to help all students succeed academically. Teachers do not need to teach to all styles at every moment, although they should honor all styles in their classrooms some of the time. Although some argue that students need to adjust to the teachers' styles, similar to the "real world" of adapting to different managers, the research cited above clearly shows that not teaching to different styles in fact has created biases concerning who does and doesn't succeed in schools!

Coaches need this information to help teachers understand which children a given practice will reach. They can then use the learning styles model to provide the right strategies to help teachers change, on the basis of the teacher's learning style.

This doesn't mean that every coaching strategy needs to target a teacher's style, especially for instructional coaching in small groups. Sometimes we learn the most when we're slightly out of our comfort zone— being "stretched." Sometimes an activity that favors another learning style brings a freshness that makes it more appealing than our normal ways. Sometimes to go deeper in our favorite subjects and disciplines, we need to leave our preferred processes behind and learn new techniques. And, sometimes we need to observe the results and methods of people whose styles are very different from our own so that we can grasp the richness of what they have to offer.

But, understanding that an activity will be outside your learning or teaching style, your comfort zone, is very different from engaging in it without that knowledge. The latter is the path to feeling inadequate or unintelligent or even feeling like a failure as a teacher or student.

DIFFERENTIATED STAFF DEVELOPMENT: THE FIRST STEP IN COACHING

Whether for group staff development events, instructional coaching in professional learning communities, or individual coaching, differentiation addresses two issues:

- Differentiation allows teachers to receive the information they need. The forms of information listed on page 27 correlate with different learning styles.
- By differentiating, we model for teachers what they are expected to do for students: meet their learning needs. Teachers "see" what it means to meet the needs of different students, bringing their understanding to a deeper level.

Ideally, each teacher would know his or her four personality preferences. However, it is too overwhelming to expect coaches and teachers to learn and then differentiate using a 16-type model. Introducing type in phases provides immediate applications that motivate educators to learn more. Phase I is introducing the learning styles model, essential to staff development. Phase II uses Judging and Perceiving as a framework for working through planning, goal-setting, and work completion. Phase III adds more richness to the learning styles model by adding information on Thinking and Feeling—and is necessary for coaching. I describe these phases below.

PHASE I: THE LEARNING STYLES MODEL

Read through the following descriptions of an ideal staff development day, based on the four learning styles we'll work with in this chapter. Which one appeals most to you? Which one describes the majority of experiences you've had?

My Ideal Staff Development Day

__ My ideal staff development day has clear, practical goals. We know why the agenda was chosen and have an outline of the important learnings of the day. The content relates to frameworks or subjects we've learned about in the past and is relevant to my needs in the classroom. We have chances throughout the day to reflect on what we're learning, especially how we will use it, either quietly or in very small groups.	__ My ideal staff development day would consist of about six hours of independent study and an hour (maybe) with the big group. Give me the background materials to read in advance and a scenario to try them out with or exercises for thinking through the implications of what we're learning. That day, I may wish to review other related resources of my choosing and then, at the end, share my insights with colleagues and learn from them. Even better, give me choices in what I pursue—or let me be involved in selecting the choices.
__ During my ideal staff development day, I'd receive ideas and tools I could use right away in my classroom. Hopefully it builds on skills I've learned in the past. Give me a brief overview of what we're learning and why it works—go light on theory. Answer all my questions about it. Then let me discuss how it might affect my students and ways to perfect it with my colleagues. I'd prefer to try it in my classroom immediately; it'd be great if you could join me, either to co-teach or to give feedback on what I did effectively as well as where I need improvement.	__ For an ideal staff development day, I'd have a role in the planning, making sure the content and activities are novel enough to keep everyone's attention. Any new focus could be interesting—brand-new areas for exploration are best in my book. Give us plenty of time for group activities and discussion. Changing agendas in the midst of the day is fine, too, if our discussions take us in a new direction. And, forget the details. I can read those later when necessary.

IS Introversion Sensing	**IN** Introversion Intuition
ES Extraversion Sensing	**EN** Extraversion Intuition

Which description best matches your learning style? Clockwise from the top left, these describe the *quadrants* of the type table: IS, IN, EN, and ES.

Can you think of different learning experiences you've participated in that match each description?

In your experience, does staff development consistently slight or leave out one or more of the learning styles described?

Although all eight of the preferences are important in designing lessons, atmospheres, and assessments for adult and student learning, Phase I provides a starting place because it uses the quadrants of the type table. The quadrants cover

- Extraversion and Introversion—do adults (or students) have enough energy for learning? The key concept here is that without action and interaction, Extraverts use their energy to try to remain still. They have little left for learning tasks. In contrast, Introverts lose energy for learning in atmospheres that are either too noisy or too fast-paced, because neither allows for reflection.
- Sensing and Intuition—are adults (or students) receiving the kind of information they need to master the concepts being presented? Remember, Sensing types begin with the details or step-by-step processes, then work toward the big picture. Intuitives prefer to begin with the big picture, then gather details to support their insights.

The following chart describes the four learning styles. As you read, consider how different coaching techniques (modeling, observation, cognitive coaching, team teaching, etc.) fit into each style:

The Four Learning Styles

Introversion/Sensing: Let me know the plan	Introversion/Intuition: Let me follow my own lead
1. Set clear expectations and goals 2. Show me examples 3. Provide the steps in the process 4. Answer my questions as I have them 5. Give me time to think 6. Let me work with and memorize facts 7. Avoid too many surprises 8. Build on what I know 9. Let me know along the way if I'm doing things right 10. Connect content with past efforts and experiences	1. Let me delve deep into things that interest me 2. Avoid repetition and routine 3. Let me figure out for myself how to do things 4. Give me choices 5. Listen to my ideas 6. Let me learn independently 7. Let me start with my imagination 8. Help me bring what I envision into reality 9. Give free rein to my creativity and curiosity 10. Provide references for me to build my own knowledge base

Extraversion/Sensing: Let me do something	Extraversion/Intuition: Let me lead as I learn
1. Start with hands-on activities 2. Give me steps I can follow 3. Let me think out loud and work with others 4. Tell me why I'm learning something 5. Give me chances to talk and move 6. Set a realistic deadline 7. Give me examples 8. Provide clear expectations 9. Go light on theory 10. Let me use my experience and skills	1. Start with the big picture, not the details 2. Let me dream big without penalties 3. Let me find a new way to do it 4. Let me interact with others 5. Give me choices 6. Keep changing what we do 7. Let me teach or tell someone what I've learned 8. Let me be in charge of something 9. Let me talk or work in groups 10. Let me come up with my own ideas

LEARNING STYLES AND STAFF DEVELOPMENT

This learning styles framework allows you to carefully construct workshops to meet the energy and informational needs of all of the teachers in the room. You can also make it clear from the start that it's a differentiated workshop and they will probably find some activities more to their liking than others. If they were happy the whole time, some of their colleagues would probably be miserable! Here's a typical agenda for a workshop to introduce type as a common framework. Planning the first 30 minutes of a day in this way accomplishes the following:

IS: Clear goals set and handouts provided that clarify what will be covered.

IN: Goals are tied to a robust theory.

ES: Reality of type preferences is demonstrated and connected to the work of teachers.

EN: Possibilities opened for what type might mean for their classrooms.

1. Agenda (without strict time frames), goals for the day (Introversion/ Sensing).

2. Five-minute theory talk on Jung, Myers, and concept of preferences (Introversion/Intuition).

3. Active exercise: J-P continuum, described on page 82 (Extraversion/ Sensing).

4. Structured explanation of Judging and Perceiving (Introversion/ Sensing). A similar explanation for each preference pair follows the related hands-on exercises.

5. Group project: designing ideal classrooms (Extraversion/Intuition).

6. Creative writing exercise to explain Sensing-Intuition preferences (Introversion/Intuition).

7. Active exercise (teachers on their feet) to explain T-F preferences (Extraversion/Sensing).

8. Group project: type-alike group discussions on teaching and learning (Extraversion/Intuition).

Throughout the day, additional information meets the needs of each quadrant as shown below:

Introversion/Sensing	Introversion/Intuition
Examples that tie type to their current practices, curriculum, and other staff development focuses	Tie-ins to theory and research, as well as making other resources available for them to go deeper
Extraversion/Sensing	**Extraversion/Intuition**
Real-life examples from student work, literature, lesson plans, etc.	Tie-ins to the big picture of how they might use type, theoretical connections

Does it work? After the first Judging-Perceiving exercise validates that all preferences are equally valued, teachers participate willingly. They work in groups through lunch. They stay *past* the close of the workshop, continuing to discuss the implications of personality type. And the vast majority ask to learn more.

LEARNING STYLES AND CHANGE

How important are the learning styles in getting teacher buy-in to change? Consider these reactions:

- One Extraversion/Sensing teacher (ESTP, which, according to the CAPT database, is the least frequent type in teaching) told me that the dislike of theory rang true for her. She said she couldn't really concentrate when staff development covered background material or trends rather than her day-to-day needs.

- Another Extraversion/Sensing teacher mentioned that she'd loved a hands-on training class on classroom management. The trainers had them on their feet, trying different techniques. An Introversion/Intuition principal reported to me that the same training class was excruciatingly painful. He felt that although much of the content was worthwhile, the trainers treated participants like rats in a maze. He recommended that I read their book rather than attend the training, which is typical of his learning style.
- As we conducted a learning styles workshop, an Extraversion/Intuition trainer taught in her natural style as she explained a cooperative learning endeavor, asking the teachers to assume the roles of their students for the moment. Partway through her instructions, an *Introversion*/Intuition teacher raised his hand and said, "I've been wondering all week whether any of this applies to me and I finally get it—your instructions are boring me to tears; I just want it in writing!" The class compared reactions and sure enough, the Extraverts were enjoying her explanation and the Introverts were not.

Why is this level of differentiation necessary with adults? Consider for a moment the Concerns-Based Adoption Model (CBAM). Hall and Hord (2001) identified stages of concern about a change. These acknowledge the typical viewpoints teachers may have toward an innovation and the fact that these viewpoints reflect a process of engaging with the innovation, not static attitudes. The first stages involve self-concerns, such as understanding how the change affects teachers personally. The next stages involve the management of the innovation, including time and administrative constraints. In the final stages, teachers consider the impact of innovations on students, collaboration possibilities, and ways to refocus or improve their efforts.

However, as we saw in Chapter 2, teachers have different informational needs in times of change. This learning styles framework helps meet those needs, thus enabling teachers to move more quickly through the stages of concern. In the first 30 minutes of the workshop, touching on each of the learning styles gives information to influence the educators to believe that the topic is of some concern to them. They become *interested* in whether the workshop might be of use to them.

Another way to look at the need for learning styles is to consider what happens when the needs of the various styles are not met. Although other factors enter in—such as the experience level of the teachers their rapport with the school's administration, their current needs, and the amount of support they will be given in making the change—the following forms of resistance are common:

- If Introversion/Sensing teachers are not convinced that the changes will be better than their current methods, and if they do not receive enough details to implement the changes, then they will often close their classroom doors and continue to teach as they always have. Note that this style correlates with Concrete learning styles.

- Extraversion/Intuition teachers often embrace change, enjoying variety. However, if they have no say in the changes, or do not get a chance to customize the changes, or if the underlying premises are poorly supported, they may actually lead resistance against the change. Note that this style correlates with Abstract learning styles.

- If Introversion/Intuition teachers do not receive the time and resources to reflect on changes, they may delay implementation or search on their own for better alternatives. Note that this style correlates with Abstract learning styles.

- If Extraversion/Sensing teachers do not see the practical implications and how to implement the changes, they may pay little attention to the proposed changes. Again, this correlates with Concrete learning styles.

In other words, each quadrant has its own flavor of resistance. Further, different factors, events, and information will trigger that resistance.

USING LEARNING STYLES TO MOTIVATE CHANGE

The following chart shows common patterns in teacher beliefs. Using charts like this in coaching can help teachers understand that their beliefs aren't wrong per se, but are incomplete because of the boundaries of their strengths and experiences.

Common Patterns in Teacher Beliefs

IS: orientation toward skills	IN: orientation toward depth, creativity
• Tried-and-true methods help students learn • Choice often leads to chaos • Explain concepts, then let students try them • Order leads to learning	• Learning is an individual process • Choice and creativity help students learn • Let students think about concepts, then try them • Interest leads to learning
ES: orientation toward practicality	EN: orientation toward breadth, creativity
• Learning can be structured • Basic skills come first • Let students experiment with concepts • Learning should be hands-on	• Learning is an active process • Engage students and they'll learn • Choice can be structured • Variety is enriching

For most people, one of the quadrants seems most like their style, but they find elements that match them in the adjacent quadrants as well. It is the opposite one in which we struggle most. Before a group of teachers had any in-depth understanding of type, I asked them which students they had the most difficulty reaching. The chart on page 13 shows how teacher strengths affect how they viewed their students. In each case, their frustrations come from students whose learning styles were opposite to their own. Here are some typical responses when teachers examine the learning style of students opposite to them:

- An Introversion/Sensing teacher expressed to me how open-ended assignments or experiential learning overwhelmed her. She felt that she often overscaffolded those tasks to help students get the "right" answer.
- An Extraversion/Sensing teacher looked at the opposite Introversion/Intuition statements and said,

> How can I manage this? Maybe the IN students don't like repetition, but I like to know what to expect. If they're working in depth, how do I monitor to make sure they're doing a good job? What if their imaginations don't fit my plans? And how do I fit their needs with my time schedules? There's a certain way to do so many things—it makes me nervous if I'm not there to tell them *specifically* how to do it.

- An Introversion/Intuition teacher, looking at the opposite Extraversion/Sensing statements, said, "I definitely struggle to take things from the theoretical to the practical because I'm already satisfied that I found out something new or that it was interesting or the information led me to think of other stuff."
- An Extraversion/Intuition teacher, looking at the Introversion/Sensing statements, said, "It's the step-by-step instructions that are tough for me to provide. I concentrate on designing a creative lesson and fall short on working out the details."

In each case, the common framework allows a coach to say, "Your methods work for students like you. Let's explore how to adjust them for others."

Looking back at the model for staff development,

- The teachers now have a common framework for unbiased discussion of education. They can express *why* something works in their classroom. Although teachers are still free to individualize their classrooms, they can better understand what kinds of learners their favorite practices reach. They also see which other staff members—their opposites—are their best resources.

- They understand their own strengths and beliefs. As one teacher put it, "I realized that how I learn something isn't the best way for all my students. I learned how to hook students differently. I learned how to adapt my teaching. It helped with my guilt when I wasn't successful, which made me happy."

- They've seen evidence, partly from the reactions of other teachers who do not share their preferences, that these type differences are real and should influence their beliefs.

- In follow-up sessions, teachers can look at adjusting how they teach, using the common framework to dialogue with colleagues. This hands-on planning lets them choose their focus, or the problem they're most interested in solving, or the area they're most interested in changing, rather than abstract lesson planning or problems that don't concern them.

- In these sessions, they receive experience in what Level III collaboration has to offer, complete with a common framework that helps them delve below the surface of their beliefs, yet respect their colleagues' strengths.

To enact the sixth element of teacher-focused staff development, *coaching,* I work with individual teachers, the subject of the next chapter. Before moving to differentiated coaching, let's briefly review how the other preference pairs, Phases II and III, enter into staff development. Remember, the learning styles model emphasizes just Extraversion and Introversion (Energy) and Sensing and Intuition (Information). Trying to learn the entire model at once takes too much time before teachers can make immediate applications. The following chart describes the phases:

Purpose	*What*	*Why*	*Type preference used*
Phase I For staff development planning	Learning styles model	• Meet teacher informational needs • Model what we're asking them to do with students • Establish common framework • Neutralize biases	Quadrants of the type table: • Introversion/ Sensing • Introversion/ Intuition • Extraversion/ Sensing • Extraversion/ Intuition

Purpose	What	Why	Type preferences used
Phase II For planning, coordination	Time and project management Student work completion	To make it clear that there are two different, effective ways to approach projects and that people do their best efforts in their own style	Judging and Perceiving
Phase III For coaching	Communication model	• Receptivity • Understanding • Differentiating coaching techniques	Columns of the type table (coaching styles): • Sensing/ Thinking: coach as useful resource • Sensing/Feeling: coach as encouraging sage • Intuition/Feeling: coach as collegial mentor • Intuition/ Thinking: coach as expert

NOTES ON PHASE II:
ADDING JUDGING AND PERCEIVING

Our schools operate out of a Judging preference: think of schedules, due dates, quarterly grades, and class agendas. At all levels of education, there are more Judging teachers than Perceiving teachers. The Perceivers may sometimes feel inadequate as they struggle with curriculum mapping, grading, and other scheduled tasks. Complicating this is the fact that over 85 percent of K–12 principals have a preference for Judging (70 percent are just four types: ISTJ, ESTJ, INTJ, ENTJ).

Because Judging types like closure, finishing administrative tasks is easier for them. In contrast, if Perceiving teachers (and Perceiving students) aren't introduced to planning methods that use their own strengths, they may begin to feel inadequate as deadline after deadline catches up with them.

Some teachers I've worked with have begun using this dimension of type before the learning styles framework. Again, the phases are flexible, depending on the problems teachers are most concerned with solving.

PHASE III: ADDING THINKING AND FEELING

Adding Thinking and Feeling to the coaching model allows consideration of communication styles, motivations, decision-making strategies, and the coachee's preferred relationship style with a coach, as discussed in Chapter 8.

Studies, many of which I mentioned above, show that Thinking and Feeling can be just as important in academic success as the quadrants of the type table (IS, IN, ES, EN). However, making them a separate factor for teachers to consider makes differentiation through personality type seem more manageable. The following table provides some basic considerations:

When coaching a Thinking type (or working with Thinking students), remember:	When coaching a Feeling type (or working with Feeling students), remember:
They prefer to be in charge. Allow them to debate, ask "Why?" and occasionally have the last word.	They need to know they are liked. *If they experience criticism without being sure they're liked, they may shut down.*
They need to be competent. They thrive on competition and performance goals. *If they aren't sure they can succeed, they may avoid trying.*	Show that you value their work. Feeling types often need praise along the way as they work on assignments so they know they're headed in the right direction and doing good work.
They respond best when the subject or assignment is logical, objective.	They are interested in people and helping others. Add people-oriented hooks to theories *or* incorporate cooperative learning into subjects requiring logic to help them stay motivated.
Although fairness is an important concept for all of us, Thinkers may discount a coach's or teacher's expertise if he or she doesn't seem to uniformly enforce stated rules or seems to play favorites.	They thrive in harmonious atmospheres. Whether put-downs come from coaches or peers, or are directed at the Feeling person or others, disharmony distracts them.

Within whatever common framework you use, administrators and coaches can begin using type concepts with teachers without knowing their styles because most staffs have people with all preferences. The next chapter provides concrete suggestions for adjusting staff development and coaching based on (1) determining whether the reform or change efforts are biased in favor of certain preferences and (2) examining what teachers with different preferences need during change.

NOTE

1. Recall that the preferences are not evenly distributed. Estimates are that in the United States, for example, 70–75 percent of the population prefers Sensing and 25–30 percent prefers Intuition.

7 Coaching Your Whole Staff for Change

You can enhance the effectiveness of whole-staff development efforts by using your common framework to

- Understand the teachers' strengths and beliefs about education. Do the proposed changes mesh more easily with any particular learning style or belief pattern?
- Tailor the information given through staff development efforts to meet the needs of teachers who will need to change the most.

Coaching isn't a panacea for staff development. Sometimes large-group sessions *are* the most effective way to deliver information. For districtwide or schoolwide initiatives, an initial informational or instructional session gives leaders a chance to introduce their vision and ensure that everyone hears a consistent message. However, as we've seen, people with different learning styles may hear different messages even when they're in the same room.

These sessions can decrease resistance through planning that uses the school's common framework to predict how teachers might react and therefore what information and activities might be most useful. This process has two parts, tying right back to the first key elements for effective staff development:

- Using a common framework for unbiased reflection on education. Again, this forms the foundation for the other elements.
- Understanding the teachers' strengths and beliefs about education. Compare the nature of the proposed changes to your common framework. Do they mesh more easily with any particular learning style or belief pattern?
- Providing information and evidence that can influence those beliefs. What information will ensure that your staff development efforts meet the needs of teachers who will need to change the most?

However, this process needs to begin with self-examination. How do the changes in practices, curriculum, goals, or school structure mesh with the strengths and beliefs of the administrators, coaches, or other leaders? Is the change effort a natural direction for them? Did they thoroughly examine options that might be more attractive for teachers whose learning styles are opposite theirs? Where might they be overselling it? What haven't they considered?

Often, honesty brings more acceptance by the teachers. For this step, review the page for your own personality type in Appendix A. What are your strengths? Your needs during change? Your picture of an ideal classroom? How do you naturally complete statements such as

- In a good classroom, students are . . . the teacher is . . .
- Assessments should . . .
- Classroom management is . . .
- Building relationships with students means . . .

We all have biases, either because of our strengths or past educational experiences, or because of the educational theories we've learned. Admitting our biases often increases acceptance. When one principal, who preferred Extraversion and Intuition, admitted to her staff that she loved change and couldn't help but continue to introduce new options, what had been a source of grumbling about "It's one thing after another" became a point of shared humor, with smiles rather than grimaces at each "Here we go again, changing!"

Once the leaders understand their own strengths and beliefs—and examine whether their plans for change need adjustments in view of their biases—they can turn to the second key element in staff development.

THE SECOND KEY ELEMENT IN STAFF DEVELOPMENT: UNDERSTANDING THE STRENGTHS AND BELIEFS OF THE TEACHERS

For this key element, personality type allows you to (1) evaluate the impact of the change on teachers with different styles and (2) draw some conclusions about who might find the changes most difficult. You can then tailor the overall process as well as the information provided to better accommodate those teachers. Key questions include

- Which students will this change serve? All? Or ones with certain learning styles? Conversely, who might it leave out? (Think back to the whole language–phonics debates.)
- As discussed above, are the proposed changes tied in any way to the strengths and beliefs of the administration? What natural objections might people with the opposite learning style have to those changes? Which of those objections are legitimate?
- Which teachers need to change the most? In other words, do the proposed changes require them to work out of their weaker areas? Hargreaves (1994) points out,

> To ask whether a new method is practical is therefore to ask much more than whether it works. It is also to ask whether it fits the context, whether it suits the person, whether it is in tune with their purposes, and whether it helps or harms their interests. It is in these things that teachers' desires concerning change are located; and it is these desires that change strategies must address . . . The more reformers systematically try to bring the *devices* of change in line with teachers' own *desires* to change, the more they may stifle the basic *desire* to teach itself. (p. 12)

Let's look at four examples of important initiatives many schools are trying to implement to make the practicality of this analysis clear: curriculum mapping, collaboration, standardized curriculum, and standards-based instruction. Looking at common sources of stress for each type (Hirsh & Kise, 2000) helps show how some types might need more coaching than others for these initiatives.

Curriculum Mapping

With the current emphasis on standards and assessments, curriculum mapping is an essential tool for aligning content, skills, and assessments with mandated standards and tests. Several personality types generally find planning processes naturally distasteful, even though they usually learn to do it very well. Perceiving types often struggle with overly structured schedules and plans, partly because plans seldom match reality. Sensing/Perceiving types are especially stressed when pressured to make decisions that have long-term implications. Although a curriculum unit may be right for one group of students, they might say, it might not interest another. The entire process can go against their natural desire for flexibility to meet each child's needs.

Teachers with preferences for Introversion/Intuition thrive on independence and innovation. Although they may comprehend the global need for curriculum mapping, it still violates their internal drive to continually innovate.

However, curriculum mapping is essential because it ensures that important topics are covered without being repeated! Students do not appreciate having to read the same novel or produce country reports two years in a row. Several things can help curriculum mapping serve everyone:

- *Distinguishing between "flexibles" and "nonnegotiables."* At one school, for example, language arts teachers struggled to agree on which novels they should teach each year. Finally, they reversed their discussion and designated five or six "don't touch" novels for use only at specific grade levels. Teachers were left free, then, to choose among dozens of books that met the district standards without feeling locked in to a narrow map.
- *Adjusting the level of detail.* When it comes to the timing of units and the material to be covered, how much detail is needed? For coordination across teams or grade levels, do units need to be taught in the same order, or can two or three be reversed in order? Does the topic need to be set, or can the map say "themed literature circles" or "laws of motion science project" without designating the theme or project? Rather than dictating this from above, consider using the language of type to negotiate what is appropriate, given the needs and stress factors for different preferences.
- *Adjusting schedules for completion.* Use mini-deadlines and progress checks to help teachers pace their efforts, and provide some flexibility if teachers are progressing but at a slower pace.

Collaboration

Teachers with preferences for Introversion/Intuition like to choose their work partners and may struggle (especially without type knowledge) to team with other teachers. Teachers with preferences for both Introversion and Perceiving often truly prefer to work alone—in fact, in workshops, when asked to design their ideal classrooms, they often draw rooms without any students! Teachers with preferences for Extraversion and Judging may be so used to leadership roles that collaboration is difficult. Although all of these types can and do work effectively on teams, some people thrive on collaboration, whereas others need practice or skill development to do so.

Chapter 4 contains suggestions on how coaches can help build collaborative learning communities. The framework of type, though, often helps teachers understand their struggles with teaming.

Standardizing Curriculum

Structured curriculum is a safe haven for some types and a prison for others, especially Intuitives who often don't want to teach the same thing twice. Even if they adopt a curriculum, they may constantly add new ideas until it bears little resemblance to what was standardized.

On the other hand, teachers with a preference for Sensing may balk at a new standard curriculum if (a) they've had success with the current curriculum or (b) no one has shown them that the new curriculum is better. Coaching suggestions include the following:

- Present an analysis of the curriculum in terms of type. Are there reasons some teachers aren't embracing it? One science curriculum did *not* meet the needs of Introverted learners. The teachers discussed ways to adapt it by adding journaling and individual work to the cooperative learning activities.
- Pay careful attention to each teacher's informational needs, as discussed on pages 27–30.
- Prepare a comparison of the old and new curriculums, emphasizing where old lessons or activities might still fit.
- Designate "essentials" teachers need to teach in terms of type. For example, with one elementary mathematics curriculum, teachers routinely skipped playing the "games" that went with many units. Those games were actually basic skills practice that matched Sensing student needs but also caught the attention of Intuitive students. The mathematics coach emphasized their importance.

Standards-Based Instruction

Feeling teachers may understand at a deep level how standards hurt some students. Thinking teachers may balk at anything subjective because ensuring fairness is so difficult. Sensing types may be overwhelmed by the amount of material they are expected to cover. Intuitive teachers may object because the standards take up so much time that they feel compelled to drop favorite units and activities. Two techniques may help:

- Allow teachers to dialogue about working with the standards in type-alike groups. What is healthy about using standards? What is difficult for them? What teaching skills help with implementing standards? Comparing their responses often promotes understanding of their varying struggles.
- Marzano (2003) estimates that "schooling would need to be extended from kindergarten to grade 21 or 22 to accommodate all the standards and benchmarks in the national documents. In other words, the change required is impractical if not impossible to implement" (p. 26). He recommends identifying essential content and ensuring that there is adequate instructional time available, sequencing and organizing the material to give teachers and students a fair chance to cover it all.

    Current standards actually set schools up for failure, and savvy teachers know it. How much better to agree upon a manageable curriculum. When we don't, teachers feel compelled to spend small amounts of time on standards that might be on the state test but are unimportant. Think of how this affects Sensing students who need time to understand a concept completely before moving on. Rushing through a curriculum that is too broad doesn't honor their needs.

    For example, one of the Minnesota math standards is to distinguish between the "odds" and the "chances" of winning. A search through four college statistics books didn't produce a clear difference. In a discussion, one math teacher suggested following Marzano's suggestions, but others protested, "The items we leave out might be on the test!" Finally we agreed that more students would succeed if they thoroughly understood what teachers *did* cover than if they heard briefly about every possible test item.

Providing teachers with knowledge of how their personality type might react to changes often validates their concerns in ways that help them name the uneasiness they're already feeling. At one organization, those with preferences for Extraversion/Intuition said, "Now that we know we naturally enjoy change, we'd better review the initiatives a bit more critically." The Introversion/Sensing employees said, "Now that we know we frequently worry about whether change will go smoothly, maybe we should look at this a bit more open-mindedly." Employees in both quadrants did a better job of analyzing and preparing for the changes.

Again, the goal is a review of the proposed changes or reform efforts, using an *unbiased framework to reflect on education*—the underlying key to any effective staff development effort. With this analysis in hand, the focus turns to planning the sessions to meet the teachers' needs.

THE THIRD KEY ELEMENT OF EFFECTIVE STAFF DEVELOPMENT: PROVIDING INFORMATION AND EVIDENCE THAT CAN INFLUENCE TEACHER BELIEFS

To explore how the framework of psychological type could be used in change efforts, Barger and Kirby (1995) asked 2,000 workshop participants the question, "What does this preference need during a time of change?" The responses showed clear differences in the kinds of information people with different personality preferences need to receive, how they process and react to that information, and what factors make change more stressful. They noted that resistance to change increases when these needs are not met and found that leaders failed to recognize and deal effectively with these needs. They suggested that organizations use a checklist for change that considers the needs of each preference, allowing people to focus on their strengths in adapting to changes (Barger & Kirby, 1997).

Clancy (1997) studied patterns of resistance in Sensing/Judging/ Thinking (STJ) managers, often cited in other studies as the types that are the most resistant to change. Instead, Clancy found that "the behaviors that are being experienced as resistance are actually a result of STJ type preferences not being thoroughly understood, valued, and incorporated into the change process" (p. 416). Her analysis indicated a benefit to reframing certain forms of resistance as indications of different needs in the change process, using the lens of type to understand those different needs. Drawing from learning style characteristics, the needs of STJ teachers would include

- Concrete, not theoretical, evidence that the changes will work
- Immediate classroom applications that address their needs
- Clear expectations and examples
- Step-by-step processes for change
- Realistic deadlines
- Information that builds on their experience and skills.

How does this compare with most change projects? In their review of change literature, Hirsh and Kise (2001) reported,

Most of the current literature on introducing change to organizations gives advice best suited to NT [Intuition and Thinking] types. Rational analysis (Thinking) and big-picture frameworks

(Intuition) are emphasized with little regard for the specifics (Sensing) of how change will be carried out or for its impact on people (Feeling). Often, taking quick action, networking with people, and keeping an eye on outside factors (Extraversion) are recommended, along with being flexible and foregoing structure to change directions quickly (Perceiving). In other words, much of the literature and many of the guidelines for introducing change suggest that everyone become ENTP's! (p. 135)

Making everyone act like ENTPs during change efforts would require most of us to work out of our weaknesses, a surefire way to create stress, not change! Instead, change efforts can be constructed to meet our differing needs.

PATTERNS FOR SUPPORTING PEOPLE DURING CHANGE

The following guidelines for the different informational and processing needs of people with different preferences during change are based on Barger and Kirby's (1995) survey of over 2,000 people regarding what they need in times of change and Hirsh and Kise's (2000) coaching framework:

Extraversion	Introversion
Is there time for productive conversations about the changes?	Is information available for reflection before teachers have to respond or act?
Are there active roles for those who want them?	Are there one-to-one opportunities for communicating, both to share thoughts and to ask questions?
Is action as well as talk taking place?	Is there time to internalize the meaning of the change before having to act?

Remember that Extraversion and Introversion are about gaining energy. If these needs aren't met, the energy around a change effort dissipates. Further, the Extraverted need for conversation will happen covertly, perhaps fostering inaccuracies or outright resistance to a change program. On the Introverted side, if they aren't given time to process the changes, they may well retreat behind the doors of their classroom until they've taken the time to reflect and evaluate—or they may retreat and continue to teach as they always have.

Sensing—what's the best of the past?	Intuition—where do we want to go?
Is real data available to demonstrate why the change is necessary and why it is better than the present?	Have you provided the big picture— the underlying theories and the long-term vision?
Are there specific details about schedules, costs, and responsibilities?	Are there options for implementation?
Have you made specific connections between the proposed changes, past practices, and other change efforts?	Do teachers have opportunities to influence the change effort design?

Note similarities to the CBAM for staff development (page 119); the Sensing concerns parallel Stage 1 Informational Concerns and Stage 2 Personal Concerns. Many Intuitives, if they know that an innovation will affect their classroom, instead start at Stage 6 Refocusing, defined as "the exploration of more universal benefits from the innovation, including the possibility of major changes or replacement with a more powerful alternative. Individual has definite ideas about alternatives to the proposed or existing form of the innovation" (Hall & Hord, 2001, p. 63). Although Sensing teachers predominate, Intuitive teachers, who often thrive on change and variety, may be resistant if they have no say in what is happening—or receive only parts of the puzzle. The CBAM suggests using different modules during professional development to meet the different stages of concern. Using the lens of type to develop those modules would help differentiate for varying teacher needs. Further, the lens of type helps explain why not all teachers pass through all stages. They have different motivations and informational needs, depending on their preferences.

Thinking—what's the worst of the present?	Feeling—what are we afraid of losing?
How clear is the logic of how the change measures were chosen? What about the internal logic of the proposed changes?	Is the change consistent with the values of the organization and people involved?
Has leadership demonstrated competency in implementing change?	Do plans take into account people's needs?
Has leadership shown the fairness and equity of the proposed changes?	Do those most affected have a voice in the implementation plan?

Often, because a decision has already been made about the school reform measures to be implemented, neither Thinkers' nor Feelers' needs are met. Thus, they form their own opinions about the changes, often with insufficient information. This is especially true of many districtwide or even schoolwide reform efforts. When we ignore these needs, we miss the opportunity to troubleshoot implementation issues. The Feeling perspective often provides new insights as to how the changes will affect people and points out implications for individual students, teachers, or subject areas, and whether buy-in is sufficient for success. The Thinking perspective ensures that we examine the right criteria, that choices are fair, that we consider future consequences, and that we weigh the impact on other priorities. Chapter 9 covers the roles of Thinking and Feeling in decision-making more thoroughly.

Judging	Perceiving
Are there clear goals and time frames for the change process?	Is the plan open-ended enough that goals and time frames can be adjusted as the process unfolds?
Are priorities clear? What will be left undone in order to implement this program?	How will the change effort stay open to new information?
Are surprises being minimized?	Is there flexibility for how each person implements these changes?

Note that the Judging and Perceiving concerns, which are rooted in our approach to work and to life in general, are in conflict with each other. Most leaders struggle against setting up implementation efforts that reflect their own preference for Judging or Perceiving. Remember, too, the discussion on page 82–85; we do our best work when allowed to pursue it in our own style.

Think of a change effort you've participated in. Did it meet the informational needs of all of the preferences in ways that matched their learning styles? In some cases, the nature of the changes themselves makes this hard to do.

- For districtwide mandates, it may be difficult to allow for the participation those with preferences for Extraversion and Intuition desire.
- When decisions are already made, administrators may see meeting Thinking and Feeling needs as a waste of time.

- Allowing for Perceivers to be flexible conflicts with the need to evaluate implementation uniformly.

Think back to the "paralyzed pilot team" in Chapter 3. The methods used to help them adopt new strategies for reducing student failure met the needs of the various type preferences during a change effort (Hirsh & Kise, 2001):

- Team time to talk through the ideas (Extraversion)
- One-on-one time after teachers reflected on the suggestions and initial experiences with them (Introversion)
- Details concerning how to make the changes (Sensing)
- Opportunities to adapt the proposed strategies (Intuition)
- Synthesis of the proposed strategies with other frameworks and explanations of the logic of the suggestions (Thinking)
- Dialogue about how the changes might affect both teachers and students (Feeling)
- Clear agenda, expectations, and goals (Judging)
- Choices as to how to use the strategies to meet those goals in their individual classrooms (Perceiving).

Think of using these type preference needs as a checklist to increase buy-in for change efforts. When used with wisdom, type information isn't a methodology for manipulating resisters, but a way to acknowledge teacher wisdom and learn from their concerns.

PROCEEDING AT THE RIGHT PACE

By reviewing the information and processing needs of different personalities during change, type provides a framework for looking at how to meet those needs before moving on to the implementation phase. Using this model, instead of "innovators," one sees that teachers with preferences for Extraversion/Intuition are often wired for change and thrive on jumping right in. Instead of "laggards," one sees that change efforts seldom provide needed information for people who prefer Introversion/Sensing, such as details, structure, clear time frames, and connections with current work.

However, expecting all teachers to progress at the same pace is as unrealistic as expecting all first graders to learn to read at the same pace or all sixth graders to run the mile at the same speed. No matter how excellent and thorough these initial staff development efforts are, the proposed changes will still be harder for some teachers—those who require the greatest change in practices or beliefs.

Differentiated coaching adds needed scaffolding for these teachers, helping them understand why they feel resistant to change and motivating them to look more closely at the merits of what the change efforts require of them. The language of personality type leads to efficiencies in coaching, facilitating

- Examining in advance what information teachers will need to make sense of change.
- Normalizing the fears and difficulties teachers face in change. Instead of doubting their own efficacy, teachers can place the changes within the framework of strengths and needs of teachers like themselves.
- Providing support where it is most needed.
- Focusing discussions on how the changes will serve students with varying learning styles rather than which methods are "right" or "wrong."

Yet because coaching deals with the heart of teachers—who they are, their strengths, their beliefs—there is an ethical way to coach involving the whens, hows, and whys of the process, which is the subject of the next chapter.

8 Differentiated Coaching for Teachers

The Power of a Strengths-Based Model

> The framework of personality type helps coaches understand how to
>
> - Help individual teachers build on their strengths
> - Anticipate how a teacher might struggle with a given change
> - Adjust communication and suggestions to match a teacher's learning style
> - Neutralize critique, making the teacher more open to change
> - Build trust by focusing on the problems the teacher wants to solve.

A principal asked me to conduct a team-building workshop before school started for the year. She told me, "I'm most concerned about Matt, one of the newer English teachers. I swear, he's responsible for 50 percent of the students who get sent to see me. He can't handle his classroom, and what's more, he ignores all of the advice I give him. I've scheduled a performance warning meeting with him right away this year because he's up for tenure."

I used personality type as the framework for the team-building workshop. At the end of our session, the teachers met in "type-alike" groups to discuss their strengths and commonalities around teaching and learning.

As everyone left, the principal caught me and whispered, "No wonder Matt doesn't take my advice—he's my exact opposite! I bet none of my suggestions make sense to him."

The next week, for what should have been a tense performance warning meeting, Matt nearly danced into her office, his type information in hand. "I think I know what's wrong in my classroom. My preferences are for Introversion/Perceiving, and I've been trying to teach like Extraversion/ Judging. It's not working."

The common framework helped Matt embrace his own strengths and use them as pathways for growth. Matt still found it hard to make changes, but the principal could support him in ways that met his needs and helped him rethink his beliefs. When teachers understand *why* change is difficult, they find it much easier to commit to the hard work it requires.

Coaching 30 to 60—or a hundred—teachers in a building may seem overwhelming, let alone providing the needed support for a districtwide effort. However, it is no different from the expectation that a classroom teacher will be able to meet the individual needs of each learner—especially at the secondary level, where as many as 150 children may pass through a classroom during the day. Just as teachers need a strengths-based model for differentiating, so do coaches and administrators. The National Staff Development Council (2004) points out that "Because people have different learning styles and strengths, professional development must include opportunities to see, hear, and do various actions in relation to the content" (p. 1).

For decades, executive coaches have used personality type as a coaching framework in business settings, using it to build on strengths, identify patterns of resistance, and help people reach their potential. However, before working with type as a coaching model, let's consider the role of a coach and how to determine whether coaching is an appropriate intervention.

COACHING DEFINED

Coaching is the art of identifying and developing a person's strengths. Even when a teacher needs to build skills in areas that are natural weaknesses for them, coaches help them do that through techniques that utilize strengths. Frameworks such as type provide a neutral way to identify those developmental needs and customize strategies for personal development. Compare the norms of coaching to mentoring and peer coaching models:

- Coaching is a partnership between the coach and the person being coached. Plans develop through conversation.
- Coaching recognizes that individual differences will and should occur in how most changes are implemented in the classroom. A coach works to understand how a practice fits with an individual teacher's style and then helps that teacher develop his or her own strategies within the parameters of a school reform effort.
- Coaching is *not* a method for squelching resistance to change without understanding the underlying causes of that resistance. Instead, it is a tool for understanding the fears and obstacles, real or imagined, that teachers face and then addressing those obstacles in ways that provide support for the teacher.
- Finally, coaching is far from a "white rat" supervision tool, where once the coach identifies a teachers' type or learning style, he or she applies a given set of practices. Each teacher comes with not just a personality type, but concerns, educational experiences, models of excellence, tried-and-true methods, and prior successes and failures that also influence how they teach—and how they need to be coached.

As a coaching model, the theory of personality type goes beyond learning styles and provides a holistic approach, recognizing many facets of what a teacher brings to a classroom. What motivates them? How do they communicate? How do they like to receive feedback? What are their natural approaches to leadership, time management, and relationships? What tasks are naturally easy for them? How can they best manage the stress of teaching?

WHEN TO COACH? WHO CAN COACH?

Neither coaching nor personality type works in all situations. Further, coaching may sometimes be best accomplished through someone who is external to an organization. At other times a peer teacher or administrator may be able to serve as the coach. There are at least four factors to consider.

First, both the coach and the coachee need to be committed to the process. Coaching is seldom a one-time event. Consider whether the time and resources needed to move toward the desired outcome are present. Also, the teacher needs to have a desire to change and be open to receiving feedback on what isn't working in the classroom. A coach can increase a teacher's enthusiasm for change by meeting the above informational needs for his or her preferences, described on pages 133–135.

Obviously, commitment to coaching doesn't happen without mutual trust, the second factor to consider. The coachee needs to be confident that the coach is on his or her side, not just on the administration's side. Issues of confidentiality need to be resolved so that honest communication is possible. An outside coach may be seen as a more trustworthy recipient of honest sharing of concerns about a change process.

Third, the coaching process requires clear goals. Although the administration may wish to dictate how the teacher will change, it is often more effective for teachers and the coach to reach goals through mutual agreement, beginning with the problems the teacher is most interested in solving, as discussed in Chapter 3. A coach might help "resistant" teachers discover which part of the change effort is most helpful for them. This can increase buy-in.

Fourth, those involved need to agree on what success means. Often, the administration wants a certain practice implemented. The teacher views success as whether students learn more, not whether they implement that practice. Coaches often engage in the art of translation—setting a goal that motivates the teacher but will eventually meet administrative needs as well.

Sometimes the initial meetings uncover an indicator that coaching isn't appropriate. For example, occasionally a teacher has deeper issues to deal with that are best served by meeting with a counselor or a therapist. At other times, a teacher needs a basic skill such as classroom management; taking a class or workshop chosen to fit their learning style may be the best option.

If coaching is appropriate, the following model allows for differentiation.

COACHING AS A STAFF DEVELOPMENT STRATEGY

Looking again at the key elements of staff development, coaching becomes appropriate when the changes requested of the teacher involve changing essential educational beliefs. Changing those beliefs often requires providing personality-appropriate information in the teacher's own learning style. If large staff meetings can't meet those needs, coaching may be the most efficient alternative. Further, coaching provides a way to increase the teacher's level of buy-in by focusing on how the proposed changes will be most helpful for that particular teacher's classroom. Differentiated coaching then becomes a tool for assisting teachers who need more information, support, or training to implement the changes.

Differentiated coaching would be cumbersome without the framework of personality type. By following the processes described in Chapter 7, leadership has already identified which teachers may struggle the most with changes and provided as much relevant information as possible. Coaching then becomes the art of working with individual teachers, tailoring methods and resources to their individual needs, which is the fourth key element of effective staff development.

THE FOURTH KEY ELEMENT OF EFFECTIVE STAFF DEVELOPMENT: MEETING THE NEEDS OF EACH TEACHER

Adjusting Your Own Style

After identifying differences in beliefs, the next step is identifying differences in style. As discussed in Chapter 4, coaches have to be chameleons, leaving their natural communication styles behind to effectively meet the needs of teachers. To coach those whose personality preferences are different from your own, consider how their natural communication style differs from yours.

Examine the following chart. How closely do your own preferences for coaching match your personality?

How Each Type Likes to Be Coached

ISTJ	ISFJ	INFJ	INTJ
• By an experienced coach who has used the teaching methods • Step-by-step, practical methods, clear schedules and goals • Build on past knowledge and successes	• By a practical, organized, supportive coach • Step-by-step sequences leading to mastery • Build on past experiences, what has worked for others	• By an open, creative, prepared coach • In-depth exploration through reading, study • Big-picture focus with room for imagination, creativity	• By a serious, competent, intellectually equal coach • Independent study and analysis, connections with theory • Acknowledge competency, design of own ideas and plans

ISTP	ISFP	INFP	INTP
• By a pragmatic, experience-based yet witty coach • Hands-on experiences • Logic to back whys and hows	• By a warm, supportive coach who can model • Flexible time frames and goals • Tangible, relevant learning in small steps	• By an empathetic, collegial coach • Methods for reflection, research, creativity • Connections to big picture, values, human growth	• By a logical, tough, competent coach who invites skepticism • In-depth, independent experiences • Objective critique, debate
ESTP	**ESFP**	**ENFP**	**ENTP**
• By a talkative, flexible, practical, entertaining coach • Immediate, practical skill development • Relevant ideas and subject matter	• By a coach/friend who offers praise, encouragement • Concrete tasks, hands-on, revised as needed • Variety, with praise, not theory or reading	• By a humorous, inventive, sincere coach/friend • Creative methods, brainstorming, "What if?" • Tie learning to helping others grow and change	• By an inventive, energetic, intelligent coach • High standards, competitive goals • Provide novel, open-ended ideas and theories that they can improve on
ESTJ	**ESFJ**	**ENFJ**	**ENTJ**
• By an experienced, prepared, competent coach • Problem-solving approach with tangible benefit to each activity • Clear plans, time lines, goals	• By a personable, supportive coach • Conversations about learning, experiences, concerns • Variety of structured methods	• By a friendly, inspiring coach • Bring variety of information and ideas, time to discuss them • Concentrate on potential for growth, values	• By a challenging, exciting coach • Be a sounding board, sage for their strategies, goals, and ideas • Emphasize cutting-edge strategies and long-range implications

To consider how important this is, look at an opposite pairing (i.e., ISTJ and ENFP, or INTJ and ESFP). How would each one like to be coached? How would each have to adjust to coach the other? *Hargreaves (1994) listed mismatches in the beliefs and teaching style of peer coaches and the teacher being coached as one of the biggest factors in the lack of successful implementation.* Using learning styles information to tailor coaching practices is a first step in understanding different underlying beliefs concerning classroom practices and opens the way for productive conversations about meeting the needs of all students.

Here are some considerations for adjusting one's style when coaching someone with different preferences:

Tips for Coaching Someone With Different Personality Preferences

If you're an Extravert coaching an Introvert:	*If you're an Introvert coaching an Extravert:*
• Increase the amount of time you allow for people to answer • Set agendas or thought questions in advance • Provide written material or data collected for reflection before the session • Anticipate that the Introvert may be slower to disclose personal information or feelings • To allow the option of reflection, use phrases such as, "You don't have to answer this now, but . . ."	• Encourage talking so his or her ideas can evolve call or meet face to face instead of using e-mail • Show enthusiasm and outward energy • Remember to sometimes say what you're thinking rather than keep him or her in the dark, even if you're still processing • Seek reflection time between observations and giving feedback to teachers • Prepare notes on how you want to give feedback
If you're a Sensing type coaching an Intuitive type:	*If you're an Intuitive type coaching a Sensing type:*
• Save the details until asked • Provide choices whenever possible • Consider using analogies to convey thoughts and ideas • Tie specific practices to theories and trends in education—the big picture • Use a variety of information sources	• Provide clear goals and procedures • Bring ideas that have immediate classroom applications • Translate theories into examples from the teacher's own classroom • Tie changes to what the teacher is currently doing • Ask where clarification or more information is necessary

If you're a Thinking type coaching a Feeling type:	If you're a Feeling type coaching a Thinking type:
• Start with the positive • Concentrate on what the teacher is doing right, as he or she will often take too much of the blame • Show how new practices will help students • Listen carefully to concerns about how specific students will be affected • Remember that examples of student work and stories of student success may be more persuasive than data and theories	• Use only specific praise • Assume your ideas will be debated—don't take it personally • Explain how strategies relate back to theories • Collect objective data to persuade • Consider cause/effect and if/then reasoning to explain ideas • Assume the relationship will stay "business first"
If you're a Judging type coaching a Perceiving type:	If you're a Perceiving type coaching a Judging type:
• Keep some flexibility in your schedule to allow for extended conversations • Expect some deviation from the stated lesson plan and goals • Provide options; allow processing time for selection • Break goals into mini-goals, tasks into steps, and help with planning how to meet them • Consider deadlines as suggestions when teachers are still processing changes	• Set clear goals so the coachee understands what brings closure to each process • Be extra conscientious about timeliness • Limit the number of options you suggest • Plan further ahead than you normally would as to topics to be covered • Ask permission before changing a plan and provide a clear reason for the change

Meeting the Needs of the Teacher

The above chart deals with general communication and work style considerations. Differentiated coaching also helps with tailoring content and coaching techniques to match the teacher's style—the four coaching styles described in Chapter 2. Reflect back on the "paralyzed pilot team"; their types are as follows:

- Sara, ESTP. The "Coach as Useful Resource" (p. 34) met her needs for hands-on, relevant lessons to try that provided tangible results.

- Josh, ESFP. The "Coach as Encouraging Sage" (p. 35) met his needs for encouragement, clear goals, and concrete tasks.
- Kay, INFP. The "Coach as Collegial Mentor" (p. 35) met her needs to understand the theories and use her creativity.
- Pete, ENTP. The "Coach as Expert" (p. 36) met his need to probe suggestions, fit them into his own mental models, and then improve on them.

Note that these teachers are in different *columns* of the type table. The four types in each column have the same middle letters—either Sensing or Intuition and either Thinking or Feeling. The columns are a useful framework for communicating, which is a key component in coaching. Considering the columns lets you select information that fits the teacher's needs for taking in information and making decisions:

- Usually, Sensing teachers prefer to begin with details and concrete experiences. Usually, Intuitive teachers need the big picture with room for creativity.
- Then, whereas Thinking teachers consider you an expert or a resource—business first—Feeling teachers often want to get to know you—relationships first. Thinking teachers may not trust a coach who is overly friendly. Feeling teachers may react timidly or feel inept if a coach is too brusque or businesslike.

We can summarize the styles as follows:

The Four Coaching Styles

	To Meet Their Needs:
Coach as Useful Resource *Teacher preferences:* **S**ensing and **T**hinking *As a coach you need:* A bag of tricks, multiple methods all tailored to specific subjects and situations.	• Provide hands-on, relevant lessons that produce tangible results. They want to test something out to see if it works. If it *does* work, they'll take the time to learn more. • Provide evidence of effectiveness of these lessons as used by others—the ST does not want to waste time on "maybes." • Give examples that are easily customized to their subject areas. They may discount workshop examples that do not deal with the specific subjects they teach.

	To Meet Their Needs:
	• Listen carefully to their concerns about new methods or theories. Often their informational needs have not been met. Further, they naturally prefer to see results rather than read about theories.
Coach as Encouraging Sage *Teacher preferences:* **S**ensing and **F**eeling *As a coach you need:* Time, enthusiasm, on-the-spot suggestions, encouragement, modeling, and follow-up monitoring	• Meet the teachers' needs for encouragement, clear goals, and concrete tasks. They take personally the day-to-day events in their classrooms, assuming that deviations from perfect student behavior or performance are their fault. • Offer to join them in the classroom. Show them what is going right and make concrete suggestions to fix molehills that seem like mountains because of their desire to help each child. • Don't provide too many choices—they may be overwhelmed. • Model one new strategy at a time and document the skills that students learn. Keep the focus on the overall objective; otherwise, teachers may get sidetracked by perfectionism over details.
Coach as Collegial Mentor *Teacher preferences:* **In**tuition and **F**eeling *As a coach you need:* Patience and listening skills, skills in adding structure to ideas, objectivity regarding root causes of difficulties	• Engage in conversations to help these teachers use their creativity. Let them generate ideas that you can critique together rather than work only from a coach's suggestions. • Show them how to give concrete examples of abstract concepts and techniques, providing demonstrations and directions for each technique. • Demonstrate how to provide structure while allowing for student creativity. Techniques include step-by-step assignment procedures and graphic organizers to help them keep students and themselves on task. Also, provide classroom management tools and techniques.

(Continued)

(Continued)

	To Meet Their Needs:
	• Let them talk through several scenarios before deciding on teaching or assessment strategies.
Coach as Expert *Teacher preferences:* **In**tuition and **T**hinking *As a coach you need:* Depth of knowledge, objectivity, persistence, and an ability to not take intellectual challenges personally	• Provide credentials and references to establish trust in your expertise. They expect a coach to answer any question to satisfy their informational needs. • Provide methods for balancing theory and creativity with hands-on experimentation and structure. NTs can assume that everyone is as interested in models as they are. • Allow them to probe suggestions, fit them into their own mental models, and then improve upon them. A response of "That's plausible" to your most brilliant idea is *high praise* from these teachers. Sometimes, teachers with this learning style are viewed as contrary, resistant, or abrasive rather than the deep thinkers they are. • Meet their needs for evidence and data. If they embrace a change as valid and important, they often become enthusiastic.

Then, a teacher's preference for Extraversion or Introversion influences the amount of face-to-face time they want with the coach. The Judging-Perceiving preference influences the amount of structure they prefer. The chart on pages 144–145 shows those differences and how to handle them.

Coaching allows you to fine-tune instruction far beyond the learning style of the teacher. And, since it is the teacher who is being asked to change, the coach needs to flex to meet the teacher's need—or send a coach with a different style.

A Coaching Example

I recently worked with another coach whose Sensing/Thinking preferences balanced out my Intuitive/Feeling approach to classroom observation. For this particular assignment, we observed, then coached, two mathematics teachers who happened to each prefer Sensing/Feeling. *Both* of us had to adjust our styles. With my preference for Feeling, I concentrated on noticing specific, positive feedback I could provide. With her preference for Sensing, the other coach recorded the sequencing of the lesson. We tailored our observation data to ensure that we gave the teachers the information they'd need:

- As Feeling types, they needed positive feedback first, as well as acknowledgment of the obvious good rapport they had with their students. This is part of my natural Intuitive/Feeling style and easier for me to do as a coach than for my Sensing/Thinking colleague.
- They needed clear examples for each comment we made. Sensing/Feeling types deal in specifics, not generalities. This is *not* part of my natural style, but rather more natural for my colleague.
- They needed tangible guidelines and suggestions. The other coach and I had agreed on a specific rubric to use to provide feedback. Before meeting with the teachers, we brainstormed concrete ideas for each area in which they might consider changes to how they were teaching. The rubric also provided a specific list of criteria for focusing our comments about their lessons and student interactions.

How did the teachers respond? The session lasted longer than we'd planned because the teachers insisted on working through additional action steps and ideas for research. They saw the strategies as useful for problems they wanted to solve.

THE FIFTH KEY ELEMENT FOR EFFECTIVE STAFF DEVELOPMENT: RELATING OR APPLYING WHAT TEACHERS ARE LEARNING TO THE PROBLEMS THEY WANT TO SOLVE IN THEIR CLASSROOMS

As discussed in Chapter 7, type provides a framework for assessing in advance what concerns teachers might have with a change. Although many concerns are individually based, and have little to do with type, the framework can also identify general difficulties or concerns with a change effort.

Appendix A provides specific information on each type that can be used to anticipate their biggest concerns as well as explore possible connections between the problems they want to solve and the school's goals. A coach might

- Examine the "at their best in the classroom" information to understand what the teacher hopes to see. What might concern him or her most about the changes, given this view of teaching? What fears might the changes bring to the surface?

- Look at the "common stressors" and "needs during change" to consider how best to approach the teacher.
- Consider how to use the teacher's "general strengths" to help him or her make the changes.
- Study the "coaching suggestions" to develop action steps that fit the teacher's learning style.

Type-based information often serves to depersonalize critique. For example, take the general problem of helping teachers change curriculum when the teaching processes are substantively different. In mathematics, for instance, the National Council of Teachers of Mathematics (NCTM) recommends curricula with a constructivist approach, placing students in the active role of discovering the concepts rather than the passive role of receiving formulas and procedures. They also identified six key pedagogical factors that decrease the cognitive demands of a mathematical task, i.e., traps teachers fall into in using constructivist curriculum (Stein, Smith, Henningsen, & Silver, 2000). As I reviewed those practices, I postulated that teachers' preferences might affect their comfort level with this mode of teaching. The chart below shows some of my hypotheses about the first three factors:

Factors associated with decreasing the cognitive demands of the task	*My analysis of how teachers with differing preferences might struggle to avoid these traps*
1. Problematic aspects of the task become routinized (e.g., students press the teacher to reduce the complexity of the task by specifying explicit procedures or steps to perform; the teacher "takes over" the thinking and reasoning and tells students how to do the problem).	• Sensing teachers may struggle to avoid providing procedures because they've often developed reliable methods.
2. The teacher shifts the emphasis from meaning, concepts, or understanding to the correctness or completeness of the answer.	• Sensing teachers could tend to look first for accuracy in student answers because of its efficiency and their value for accuracy. • Intuitive teachers may not require students to sufficiently justify answers because their own insights often come through hunches.

3. Not enough time is provided to wrestle with the demanding aspects of the task, or too much time is allowed and students drift into off-task behavior.	• Judging teachers may struggle to ignore the clock, even if students are on task, because of their desire for closure. • Perceiving teachers may be content to go with the flow, sometimes missing whether students are progressing enough.

I met with a teacher who used very little of the chosen math curriculum. Her type preferences were Sensing/Thinking/Judging; note how the above chart highlights her possible concerns. When I showed her the chart, she exclaimed, "This is exactly why I hesitate to use this curriculum. I've developed step-by-step processes that seem to work and I don't want to abandon them—I don't want to experiment on my students. I have a responsibility to prepare them for their basic skills tests. Further, the unit sequence doesn't make sense to me. And where's the extra practice for students like me who learn that way?"

These are all valid, change-stopping concerns. Further, none of the initial staff development programs about implementation had provided enough of the information Sensing/Thinking teachers needed. Finding that the programs addressed none of her concerns, despite specific requests for clarification, she retreated to her classroom and continued to teach, for the most part, as she always had. Her students continued to do approximately as well as those taught with the new curriculum, partly because she continued to teach from her strengths.

Upon seeing the above chart, our discussion turned to an honest assessment of the steps she'd need to take to feel competent in teaching the new curriculum and where it would still be appropriate to supplement from her tried-and-true textbooks.

Remember, change is hard. The teachers who have to change the most will probably find that the changes go against their strengths. Further, the changes may make the least sense to them. They'll need the most help, provided in their own style.

Remember, too, that this isn't a "white rat" tool. Many Sensing/Thinking teachers embraced the new curriculum for mathematics discussed above, perhaps because they received thorough training or mentoring in ways that met their needs. Another Sensing/Thinking teacher explained her acceptance of the curriculum:

In high school I did well in math, but when I got to college I found I'd never really understood the underlying mathematics of the problems I'd easily solved. I'd just memorized how to do them. I had to relearn everything! So when I saw the new curriculum, it made perfect sense to me. There'd be nothing for students to unlearn!

Creating an Action Plan

The final step in coaching brings clarity to goals, action steps, and desired outcomes. "Make the change" may be the ultimate goal, but coaches help articulate the intermediate steps that will help teachers accept and implement those changes. Action plans include

- Specific, measurable goals articulated by the teacher and the coach
- Action steps that take into account the teacher's learning style
- A clear picture of the role the coach will play—providing resources, modeling, coplanning, or advising
- Criteria for measuring progress, including examining student data if appropriate
- Action research activities.

Action plans are most effective when the teacher and coach write them in partnership. Working through the key elements of staff development provides the information needed to tailor the plan to the teacher's needs. Besides addressing the teacher's fears and concerns, the plan should take into account

- How quickly a teacher might progress. Compare Sara's style of jumping right in and trying my lessons to Kay's style of reflective processing before designing a lesson herself.
- What matters most to the teacher, incorporating the concept that one way to "sell" change is to first concentrate on the problems he or she wants to fix, relating those to school goals.
- What steps will provide the kind of evidence needed to influence teacher beliefs. Sensing/Thinking teachers might say, "Show me a tangible difference." Sensing/Feeling teachers might say, "Show me how I can do this." Intuitive/Feeling teachers might say, "Show me the potential," and Intuitive/Thinking teachers might say, "Show me the rigor."
- How success will be measured. In change, the measurements need to balance whether the teacher completed the step with how it affected

students. The teacher, remember, may still be weighing the wisdom of the change. In Chapter 1, I knew through observation that Josh had completed the action step of developing and using a station-based unit. Josh, though, measured success by looking at student grades on the unit and their journal entries concerning their enjoyment of the unit to gauge its impact on student engagement. Similarly, I knew that Amy in Chapter 3 implemented the structured transition time to establish a more academic atmosphere, but reaching the more important goal, as far as Amy was concerned, came two weeks later when she reported that the students were respectfully sharing their responses. Finally, she could hold class discussions.

Appendix C contains two case studies on coaching—chances to work through the above process. At first, understanding beliefs, meeting needs, focusing on problems, and adjusting your style may seem overwhelming. Remember, though, that your common framework predicts patterns in behaviors. The more you use it, the more natural adjusting for those patterns becomes.

As an incentive to master differentiated coaching, remember that whether teachers change—whether they try new techniques or continue their habitual practices behind the closed doors of their classrooms—may depend on whether you meet their needs.

And, as helpful a tool as differentiated coaching is, remember that collaboration is the sixth key element of effective staff development. Deep change seldom takes place in isolation; further, the coaching suggestions in Appendix C reveal that coaches often play a role in helping teachers learn to collaborate. The next chapter explains how to focus on problems the teachers want to solve, using a process that encourages and facilitates deep, reflective practice.

9 A Framework for Solving Problems

Individuals and teams can solve problems more effectively by paying attention to each step of a process that brings together the strengths of each personality:

- Defining the problem and identifying the facts (Sensing)
- Considering the possibilities (Intuition)
- Weighing the consequences (Thinking)
- Understanding the impact on people (Feeling).

Let's assume that you've differentiated your staff development efforts to provide the right content and coached teachers to deliver that content in their own styles. Still, you're not seeing a groundswell of support for the mandated changes or common framework. As we saw in Chapter 3, teacher resistance to change decreases when we focus on the problems they wish to solve. However, unless you take a careful, systematic approach to solving those problems, one that produces the kind of evidence needed to change teacher beliefs, you may make no real progress.

Further, educators hear all too often, "This will solve all your problems." Yet, how many times has a school staff thought they'd derived a good solution, only to discover that the solution created new problems they'd never dreamed of? If problems are easy to solve, they aren't really problems.

Dewey (1910) believed that humans aren't by nature good problem solvers. Without deliberate training, our natural habits of thought go astray, leading to inadequate solutions or false beliefs. Myers's (1998) personality type theories add another force that makes change difficult: our innate personality preferences aid in forming our beliefs and habits. Both Myers and Dewey believed in creating experiences that would influence people to question their beliefs.

Think back to the problem of student failure in Chapter 3. This problem was constantly on the pilot team's minds, yet they weren't trying to solve it. On the one hand, the teachers wanted all of their students to succeed and were putting in long hours in hopes of helping as many as possible. On the other hand, they felt that they were using every possible tool to help students succeed and thought that no other solutions existed, a twist on the learned helplessness they saw in their students. The step of framing our task in terms of a problem to be solved united the teachers around a common interest. We could then attack the problem through a method for reflective thought suggested by Dewey (1910), which is parallel to Myers's (1998) problem-solving model.

Reflective Thought and Problem Solving

Besides their own experiences, the teachers carried out their work in an environment that reinforced their belief that factors outside their control accounted for student failure rates. Conversations among teachers, local newspaper articles, and national debates on the achievement gap pointed to the effects of home environment, class size, and the impact of such policies as automatic promotion. Dewey (1910) noted how circumstances like these often filter the information we use, leading to false conclusions. As a tool for forming correct habits of reflection, he laid out a five-step process to help people find specific connections between beliefs, actions, and consequences.

Myers (1998) developed a similar system for thinking through solutions to problems, but her approach encompassed the fact that we are naturally better at certain steps of problem solving than others. Myers designed hers to help us access the strengths of our less preferred processes. For example, type theory holds that the second steps in Dewey's and Myers's models, generating possibilities, is often a natural strength for Intuitives (as is the first step, delineating the facts, for Sensing types). However, research into the processes Intuitives use to generate possibilities has produced steps for Sensing types to use to succeed at this point in the process (and has also produced steps for Intuitives to use in identifying facts). The questions in the table on pages 156–157 are one such tool for helping us use our nonpreferred processes.

Even though problem solving seems straightforward, Hirsh and Kummerow (1998) point out that without a step-by-step process, "people have a tendency to skip over the parts of the process that require them to use their less-preferred functions" (p. 30). They recommend consulting people with different preferences to most effectively carry out all of the steps in Myers's model. Their concerns mirror the importance Dewey placed on training people in good methods of reflective thought; we don't naturally do it well. In other words, collaboration is best for effective problem solving.

THE SIXTH KEY ELEMENT OF EFFECTIVE STAFF DEVELOPMENT: DEEP, REFLECTIVE COLLABORATION

An Effective Problem-Solving Model

Dewey's and Myers's models can be compared as shown below.

Comparison of Dewey's and Myers's Problem-Solving Frameworks

	Dewey (1910, p. 72)	Myers (1998, p. 36)
1.	Location and definition of a problem through observation (Steps 1 and 2 of Dewey's model)	Define the problem (Sensing function): • What are the facts? • What has worked in the past? • What resources are available?
2.	Suggestion of possible solutions, suspending judgment while inference goes on	Consider the possibilities (Intuitive function): • What other ways are there to look at this? • What do the data imply? • What are connections to larger issues or other people? • What theories address this kind of problem? • What are all the possible ways to approach the problem?
3.	Determining the implications of each suggested solution	Weigh the consequences (Thinking function): • What are the pros and cons of each possibility? • What are the logical consequences of each? • Would this option apply equally and fairly to everyone?

	Dewey (1910, p. 72)	*Myers (1998, p. 36)*
		Understand the impact on people (Feeling function): • How does each alternative fit with values? • How will it affect the people involved? • How will each option contribute to harmony and positive interactions?
4.	Further observation and experiment leading to acceptance or rejection, that is the conclusion of belief or disbelief	Make a final decision, act on it, and evaluate the results

Both Dewey and Myers believed that without a structure for approaching problem solving, our natural course would be incomplete; the problems that result from many educational "solutions" point out the wisdom of their beliefs. Myers saw type as a guide to making better decisions.

Using this model helps educators tap the deep value of reflective collaboration as they benefit from colleagues who are stronger in different areas of problem solving. Given how people tend to cluster in different fields according to personality types (remember, 80–85 percent of all administrators have Judging preferences, and 70 percent of all language arts teachers have Intuitive and Feeling preferences), understanding our blind spots helps bring better solutions.

To understand the power of the model, let's look at how teachers have put it to use and how coaches can help them use it well.

Step 1: Defining the Problem: The Realm of Sensing

Although defining the problem may seem like the easiest step, often failure to solve a problem is because the real issues haven't been discovered or properly defined. For this step of the process, coaches often serve as *detective*, adding to the facts.

One teaching team had built up resentments over the issue of timeliness for team meetings. Some of the teachers were chronically 30 minutes late for a 45-minute meeting. The prompt teachers claimed that they'd "tried everything" to help their colleagues be on time, but nothing worked—not

---

Step 1: Defining the Problem

Coach as Detective, adding to the fact base through

- Observation, often teacher-directed
- Individual conversations with teachers
- Checking school policies, data, and trends
- Suggesting other sources of data.

---

even changing the time or the meeting structure. As I talked with each team member, I discovered the deeper problem: The teachers disagreed about how that team time should be used. No wonder some of the teachers were late; they considered the meetings a *waste* of time. The team tackled the real problem first: coming to agreement on their goals for collaboration.

Another team of teaching veterans was at a loss to know how to deal with a particularly difficult cohort of young children. Before making any suggestions, I asked the team to take the time to thoroughly review the facts of the situation. As a first step, I observed each classroom so that I could add to the conversation. Together, we then charted answers to the following questions, based on Myers's (1998) suggestions for tapping into the strengths of Sensing:

- *What are the facts?* Specifically, we examined how their students differed from past classes. Through this discussion, the teachers concluded that these students did not respond to lectures, all-class rewards, or demerits. Responsive classroom techniques failed as well. In observing their classrooms, I also noted that many of the children responded better to visual than to auditory directions.
- *What have teachers tried? Who tried it?* As the teachers made this list, they realized how many things they *had* tried. They felt more effective. They also made note of activities they'd cut from their curriculum because of behavior concerns: activity stations, hands-on projects, and walks through the neighborhood were a few examples. In other words, to control behavior, they'd decreased hands-on activities.
- *What has worked? What hasn't worked?* Through this systematic categorization, the teachers began to identify patterns in what did work, such as silent marching games in the hall that required physical concentration, and allowing students to transition to new activities at their own rates *if* they weren't disturbing others.

Several factors keep teachers from naturally identifying the problem as well as patterns in the facts. First, an outsider is often needed to grasp all of the facts; the teachers are too busy teaching and maintaining classroom control to note subtleties. Second, they seldom have time to categorize the patterns—and many are not naturally adept at this sort of process, thus benefiting from this structured approach. Third, no one person holds all of the pieces in puzzling situations like these. By comparing their classrooms, the teachers gained a much deeper knowledge base of these students. Fourth, in the midst of tense situations (and a preponderance of teachers today are teaching in tense situations), teachers may need the encouragement of seeing all of the strategies they *have* tried or what is actually working. Often, there are more positive factors than they were aware of.

Step 2: Consider the Possibilities: The Realm of Intuition

Another problem in education is that people often champion their own ideas without considering other possibilities. As in any other brainstorming exercise, during Step 2, participants refrain from judging any of the ideas put forth. When participants struggle to refrain from criticism, an effective reminder is the reason that often ideas spark other ideas; even a "bad" idea might help someone think of a great solution.

In the above examples of improperly defined problems, a consistent thread is teachers telling me that they'd "tried everything." Without careful attention to this step of the process, and again very often the needed perspective of an outsider who might have new ideas that they *haven't* tried, workable strategies may remain buried. A coach might function as a *catalyst*, sparking new paths of exploration.

Step 2: Considering the Possibilities

Coach as Catalyst, adding to the possibilities through

- Providing outside resources
- Assessing teachers' learned helplessness, becoming more involved when it exists
- Deflecting "nay-saying."

For the group of difficult students described above, we considered the following steps at this stage:

- *List the possible solutions.* The teachers agreed that the normal step-by-step disciplinary decisions weren't working. They needed a new approach. We also considered new teaching methods, available help from other staff members, how else parents might be involved, what behaviors were and were not tolerable, and many more possibilities.

- *What is this problem analogous to?* This step often shakes up thinking and starts new discussion threads. In this case, we noted the similarities between the behavior of these students and those with Oppositional Defiance Disorder (ODD). We were *not* suggesting that these children all had ODD, but that resources for working with those children might give us new ideas.

   The group also noticed how the students' characteristics were similar to descriptions of normal Intuitive/Thinking children; one of the teachers who shared those preferences talked about how as a child she'd run away seven times before turning fifteen, simply because she was ready to change the world. She had ideas of her own and didn't want to follow adults' agendas for her.

- *What other directions can be explored?* The team realized that because of the stress, they'd mainly concentrated on controlling behavior rather than engineering student learning to engage these students before behavior problems arose. The activities they'd been avoiding were perhaps some of the kinds that these students would best respond to. The analysis resulted in agreement to simultaneously explore two directions: the administrative side of consequences and the classroom side of collaborating on new ways to handle enrichment stations, transitions, and hands-on activities.

To a large extent, the conversation at this stage shifted from "How do we handle these children?" to "What do these children need to succeed?" The teachers were willing to begin examining their own classrooms to see what they might do differently. When the group collaborates on this step, each member goes beyond personal experience and therefore has more information available to make connections to possible solutions.

Step 3: Objectively Evaluating the Possibilities: The Realm of Thinking

Dividing the evaluation stage into two parts—first Thinking, then Feeling—increases the ways of looking at each alternative. Remember, Thinking and Feeling are psychologically opposite processes. Beginning with the Thinking process provides an opportunity to agree on parameters of the decision: objective criteria to be satisfied, the acceptable level of costs, and the actual resources available. With these decisions made, the group has a better common platform from which to consider the pros and cons of each alternative.

> **Step 3: Objective (Thinking)**
> **and Subjective (Feeling) Evaluation of Options**
>
> Coach as Mediator, adding to the process by
>
> - Balancing the two sets of evaluation criteria
> - Defining the strengths of each method
> - Ensuring that both "sides" are heard and understood.

Further, this "logical" step often helps neutralize emotions or polarization on issues, since the personal implications are saved for the next step. Coaches often need to act as *mediators* in this process. Otherwise, most groups favor either Thinking or Feeling criteria. For the teachers working on helping their unruly students, this step gave them a chance to step back from their emotional involvement in helping their students succeed. We considered the following:

- *How practical is each alternative?* The school administrators clarified their availability to help with interventions and ways of involving parents. The group also decided to review the discipline policy. Was it still adequate?
- *Weigh the pros and cons of each alternative.* We considered factors such as the amount of teacher time required for each proposed intervention, the costs associated with each alternative, and the physical limitations of their classroom space (limiting, for example, their ability to separate students).
- *What is the most reasonable course of action?*

Although we may eliminate some ideas at this stage because of very real constraints, final choices are postponed until Step 4.

Step 3 (Part 2): Understand the
Impact on People: The Realm of Feeling[1]

Given the current emphasis in educational circles on scientifically based research, the profound importance of this step is easy to overlook. Further, because Feeling types, who naturally consider the factors that this step formalizes, want to stay harmonious, they may remain silent when Thinkers overlook the Feeling concerns. Some examples of how otherwise "reasonable" educational decisions, often based on fairness or equality, leave this step untouched, are

- Writing test questions. In the drive to be fair, all students must usually answer the same writing prompt. However, students with different personalities and learning styles react differently to the same prompt, resulting in an inherent, unintended bias. One state writing prompt was, "What one thing would you change about yourself and why?" A significant number of adolescent students broke into tears as their thoughts focused on what they hated about themselves. Another prompt was, "If you could be an animal, which one would you be and why?" Several intelligent students, aware that humans are in fact mammals, could only ponder why a human would want to be any-where but the top of the food chain. By the time they came up with an animal to write about, their time was almost gone. Consideration of situations like these could have led the test creators to give a simple choice between two alternatives, lessening the chance that any child would be adversely affected by the subject of any one given prompt.
- Teaching a single novel to an entire class. Often urban schools do this to ensure that students are exposed to certain key pieces of lit-erature. As important as that is, it overlooks the impact on the very students this practice is meant to help. Many of these students don't value reading; if they don't like the chosen novel (a common occur-rence if it's a "classic"), how will they respond if the class spends several weeks on it? Will it foster or discourage reading as an activ-ity of choice for those students? Note that this concern is lessened if students have choices on other novels.

Emphasizing this stage also places the right level of importance on a key element of change: people are not machines. When their wants, emo-tions, and needs are not considered, their productivity decreases, as does their overall level of commitment.

Further, people with a preference for Feeling, whether children or adults, can easily shut down when they perceive that others dislike them, do not value their opinions, or are ignoring the importance of individual and organizational values. This step is essential for gaining buy-in for the chosen course of action.

For the team with difficult students, at this stage we evaluated their own needs in terms of time, energy, and emotional responses. We consid-ered the following:

- *How does each suggestion fit with your personal values? The school's values?* The teachers articulated how close they were to resenting the difficult students because of how ineffective they felt. They even shed a few tears of frustration. This realization actually increased their commitment to find new solutions, as they wanted to stick to their values of helping each child become successful.

- *How will the outcome affect the people, process, or organization?* Conversation turned to the impact of various ideas on other students in the classroom, the implications for teachers who would have the students the following year, and how much time the administrators and specialists could devote to the students given their other responsibilities.

- *What are your personal reactions?* The teachers shared their personal struggles with one of the solutions. For example, a teacher with a preference for Perceiving admitted that the strategy of providing a daily schedule wouldn't work for her. "I change my agenda too often as I see how long things are taking," she said, "and some students get upset if I don't follow what it says, even if I can explain the deviation." Her reluctance took us back to Step 2, brainstorming more possibilities, as we considered ways she could flexibly add structure.

- *Who is committed to carrying out the solution?* We took time to evaluate which aspects of our proposed solutions the teachers felt most wedded to. In this particular case, there was little dissent.

The final question serves as a check on buy-in to proposed solutions. One team thought that all teachers had agreed to ban snacks. However, two teachers hadn't articulated their very real concerns that some of their students were too hungry late morning and mid-afternoon to concentrate. Instead, they closed their classroom doors and continued to hand out snacks. Of course, the rest of the team found out as students disposed of wrappers. At their next discussion of the problem, they considered both the pros and cons of providing snacks, rather than just the cons. The teachers agreed to new rules about what could be served and when, and what would happen if students carried food into classrooms of teachers who would still not be allowing snacks. This time, all members of the team were committed to the new rules.

Step 4: Observation and Evaluation of the Chosen Solution

Before implementing any solution, at this stage there must be agreement on how it will be evaluated and what evidence will show whether it is working or not. In addition to the importance of using scientific methods, consider the choice of evidence that will influence teacher beliefs. At this stage, a coach might act as an *advisor,* guiding discussion of the merits of adding a research component to their effort.

> **Step 4: Evaluation**
>
> Coach as Advisor, assisting in action research by
>
> - Providing technical suggestions for problem definition, acceptable evidence, and data collection
> - Assisting in straightforward research design
> - Setting short-term and long-term benchmarks for progress
> - Analyzing data.

A team may need more than one type of evidence, depending on their personality types. Subjective factors, such as observing student expressions as they work or asking for student feedback, may be just as important as test scores in the short run. Teachers might also consider whether to formalize an action research plan, as outlined in Chapter 4. Might their solution be of significance to others if the evidence shows it to be effective?

A CALL FOR COLLABORATIVE PROBLEM SOLVING

Carefully implementing these steps within a professional learning community helps teachers avoid the traps of contrived collegiality and engage at a level where they

- Question their own beliefs and practices.
- Focus on student needs rather than debating which teaching practice is "right."
- Consider their own reactions to proposed solutions in terms of their own styles. Rather than a quick response of "It won't work," they can work from a deep knowledge of their own strengths and how each proposed solution might be easy or hard for them.

Teachers work hard, very hard, and with the current trends in school funding cuts and accountability, they are constantly being asked to do more with less. With these outside pressures, little time remains for teaming, planning, or considering whether classroom practices fit with what we know about how students learn.

No matter how busy they are, teachers need to take time to articulate the problems they face, generate possible solutions with colleagues whose natural strengths might provide new insights, and then test whether they work. Time for reflection lets teachers understand any ways in which new evidence and experiences support or contradict their beliefs about education. Although it may seem impossible to find this time, the alternative is to continue to be locked into habitual practices and beliefs, using classroom practices that don't provide solutions.

At *every* step of the process, a coach can help teachers improve their skills in problem solving and collaboration by

- *Expanding.* Has the teacher or team probed deeply enough? Should they ask more questions? Do they need more data? Appendix B includes more possible questions for each step of the problem-solving model.
- *Pacing.* Has the individual or team spent enough time at each stage of the process? A coach can help a team ascertain their strengths and weaknesses in using the model: Sensing, Intuition, Thinking, or Feeling. Are any being slighted?
- *Probing.* A coach might probe with open-ended questions such as, "What other possibilities are there?" "Are there other viewpoints to consider?" "What else might happen?" "What might that look like?"
- *Focusing.* A coach might help a team consider whether they're focusing on the right problem. Are there underlying issues? Is the focus related to school goals?
- *Intervening.* Occasionally a coach needs to mediate so that a team can build trust or to point back to the common framework to ensure that everyone is being heard, and that the focus is on which students a practice will reach and not who is "right" or "wrong."

When a collaborative environment uses reflective problem solving, teachers gain opportunities to learn from each other as they compare practices and results. Learning to collaborate takes time, though. As the teachers I work with learn more about each other's personality type preferences, they begin to view each other as resources for lesson planning, coaching, and problem solving.

The usefulness of a common framework can go even further, though, tying together seemingly disparate threads in staff development. The final chapter highlights other ways to use a staff development "backpack."

NOTE

1. Note that Dewey's model does not reference this Feeling step. In analyzing his writings, both content and style, the emphasis on logic, models, and theory indicates a preference for Thinking; Myers's preference was for Feeling (INFP). In other words, their preferences and learning styles influenced the models they created.

10 Organizing Staff Development Efforts in the Same Backpack

Using a common framework for discussing teaching and learning allows schools to integrate such diverse staff development topics as

- Helping students advocate for their own learning needs
- Multiculturalism
- Working with students of poverty
- Brain research
- Strategies for difficult students.

"Last year it was curriculum mapping, then literacy strategies, then learning styles, then we ended up with a new administrator anyway. Don't give us another new and improved way to teach!" Have you heard similar statements from teachers?

It's no secret that many teachers dread staff development efforts. Guskey (1996) points out,

Although professional development in education certainly cannot be considered young and innocent, it still appears to be caught up in infatuations. Ideas, techniques and innovations are latched on to with innocence and naiveté. Devotion to these ideas is passionate and unfettered by criticism. Only positive attributes are perceived, while weakness and flaws pass unnoticed. And as is true in the case of most infatuations, the devotion tends to be short-lived.

As a result, earnest but confused education leaders career from trend to trend. Their infatuations compel them to invest in the perspectives and programs that are currently in vogue, even though their use may not be justified by the current state of theory or sound evidence. Teachers, who are typically the recipients of the in-service du jour, are overwhelmed by the demands of these various programs and become cynical about the "support" provided to help in implementation. (p. 34)

Teachers, as we've seen, often show a healthy skepticism toward staff development, given the many forgotten trends they've suffered through. Whatever common framework you're using, relating each staff development effort back to it helps your staff organize the learning into patterns—not just to reform goals, but to the tools or language you've developed and now share.

So far, for example, we've seen how personality type can organize staff development efforts concerning collaboration, problem solving, coaching, action research, classroom management, and differentiation. Teachers can keep accessing the same concepts rather than using one model for differentiation, another for collaboration, and so on. When new topics need to be included, there is usually a way to tie them back to type. To fully grasp the power of personality type as an overarching framework for staff development, let's review four other major staff development topics in which it has proven successful.

HELPING STUDENTS ADVOCATE FOR THEIR OWN LEARNING NEEDS

A school can implement type as a common framework for team building, collaboration, teacher coaching, problem solving, and lesson planning without mentioning a word about it to students. Including the students, though, adds powerful tools to the school's repertoire for helping students succeed academically and socially, as well as experience personal growth. However, in many of the examples in this book, students did know their preferences. Teachers chose to introduce the language to students so they, too, shared the common framework. Helping students understand why they struggle is far more effective than only giving them strategies to stop struggling.

When teachers instruct students in type concepts, using exercises that demonstrate the preferences, both adults and students "see" the normal differences in how people gain energy, take in information, make decisions, and approach life. Instead of type as a theory, when teachers use it with students, head knowledge converts to the hard "evidence" needed to motivate teachers to change their classrooms.

Using type with students has two goals: (1) helping teachers understand normal differences so that their efforts can turn from managing behavior or misunderstanding attitudes to shaping an academic environment that helps all students learn and (2) helping students understand and advocate for their own learning needs.

This doesn't mean that students should always learn in their own styles. Evidence is quite to the contrary:

- Students do *not* benefit academically by being constantly matched with teachers of their own style (Hammer, 1996), although some students may be more comfortable in classrooms of teachers with styles similar to their own.
- Students also do not benefit by being grouped exclusively with students who share their learning style, although this may be helpful for certain tasks and for short periods (Hammer, 1996).

Teacher concerns. In conversations about teaching type to students, educators generally have two major concerns: that students will be labeled and that students won't understand the concepts.

Three things keep type from serving as a label. First, students select their own preferences. No one tells them which preferences they have. I tell teachers, "If the child claims to be an Extravert and you seldom see them speak—in class or in the halls—refrain from giving your opinion that they're an Introvert." Over time, as students grow to appreciate that all preferences are desirable, many revise their choices and come to better self-understanding.

The second reason type doesn't result in labeling is the fact that all preferences are good ways to be. I do tell teachers that if they don't believe this—if they think that it is better for students to hold one preference or another—then they probably shouldn't use the language with students.

Third, as students learn about type, I remind them that they can stay undecided if they can't decide between two preferences. The worksheets

I use allow them to circle U as a choice. Often, people under the age of 18 are not developmentally mature enough to recognize all four of their preferences.

Using Learning Styles Inventories With Students

The questions about labeling often arise in the context of discussions about whether to use a type or learning styles inventory with students. Some proponents of learning styles models, especially Gregorc (2005), discourage inventories while others have developed instruments.

Although the Internet is full of free learning styles inventories, these are not researched. Several instruments to help students discover their type preferences exist. I use the Murphy-Meisgeier Type Indicator for Children (MMTIC).

The MMTIC is very helpful, but teachers need to be qualified, through taking classes in tests and measurements or through a qualifying program, to use the MBTI or the MMTIC. It is a class B psychological instrument, even though it is not a diagnostic tool. Further, even if students take the MMTIC, they still need to go through a self-selection process: they need to learn about the preferences, decide for themselves which ones they have, then compare their choices to the MMTIC results, and finally choose a "best-fit" type. Students enjoy taking the MMTIC because it's all about themselves, and also enjoy "arguing back with the test," something they seldom get to do. We carefully explain that some students' self-perceptions are more accurate than how they answered questions on the MMTIC.

In summary, a school needs a higher level of commitment to training if they want to use the MMTIC ethically with students. Because of this, it makes sense to work without an instrument for a while until teachers see evidence of the usefulness of the concepts. Then, they might choose to become qualified and learn how to use the MMTIC correctly with students.

Student self-advocacy. As students become more comfortable with their own type, they often start to advocate for their own learning needs. Often, we post signs reminding students, "Type isn't an excuse," and instead emphasize how each of the preferences might approach tasks. For example, when we gave directions for a major project, one that provided lots of choices, a Sensing student told the teacher, "Please, I'm Sensing and I need some concrete examples." Another boy concluded that he was an Introvert and needed quiet to complete assignments. Whenever the class did individual work, he asked to sit away from his friends so that he could stay on task.

After completing a unit that had exercises designed specifically for Sensing students, with clear goals and directions, as well as other open-ended tasks designed for Intuitive students, sixth-grade students journaled about the kinds of instructions they needed, illustrating their understanding of their own learning styles:

- (Sensing) If I get instructions that are not specific, I accidentally mess up and have to do it all over.
- (Sensing) I need instructions that are clear and on paper in case I forget them. I had to go back to the written directions on one task to see how many words I had to write.
- (Intuitive) I like directions with multiple choices where I can choose what I write about.
- (Intuitive) I work best when I get instructions that are not very exact and I'm allowed to do what I want.

The students had completed some of the tasks individually and some in groups, helping them understand their preference for Extraversion and Introversion:

- (Introversion) When I work with a group, I don't work as fast as I would by myself. I don't think as fast as other people. When I was working with another student, she was going faster than I was. I didn't really understand what we were doing. On my own, one day I finished three tasks, and one was one of the hardest ones!
- (Introversion) When I work by myself I work quickly. I usually work faster when I can think alone. For example, I got two stations done with a partner one day and three or four when I worked alone the next day.
- (Extraversion) When I work by myself I do not do well. It's hard to think of an answer.
- (Extraversion) When I work by myself I get bored and become off task. In a group I talk more but still get stuff done.

For many students, learning about personality type brings a sense of relief. In one special education class, all of the students felt that Perceiving described them best. One student told the teacher, "We *aren't* broken." In regular classes, a teacher reported similar results, saying that for students, learning the language of type, "was affirming—they weren't defects. So many kids wonder what's wrong with them that they don't care about deadlines or that rewriting makes a difference. With type they say, 'It's not that I'm a bad student—I just need to work on these skills.'"

Understanding each other. Another goal is to help students better appreciate the variety of activities a teacher might use so that he or she meets the needs of all learning styles. The station-based poetry unit described in Chapter 4, with each of the station's activities designed to meet a different learning style's needs, helps students grasp the styles. The stations are

- IS: writing a haiku about nature, then painting an accompanying watercolor
- IN: choice station—writing a poem, reading poetry, memorizing a poem, etc.
- ES: working as a group to recite a poem with accompanying actions or rhythm
- EN: working as a group to write a poetic parody.

After all of the students have completed all of the stations, we ask them to stand by the station they liked the most. Always, there are some students at every station. Then, we ask them to stand by the station where they learned the most. A large percentage of the students move.

The teacher then points out, "Look around the room. If you don't like an activity I've planned, someone else does. Further, if you changed stations, that shows that sometimes you can be learning a lot even if it isn't your favorite activity." From then on, teachers can remind students of how their classmates reacted to the different poetry stations and that fairness means that everyone will sometimes be doing activities in quadrants that are most and least like them. Teachers report a distinct decrease in complaints—unless they teach to one quadrant for too long. Then, some bright student generally calls them on it, "Hey, we've been doing Introversion/ Sensing all week. When do we get to change up?"

Students being more accepting of themselves, each other, and teachers, and understanding how to advocate for themselves—although teaching type thoroughly and ethically will take time, the benefits are substantial.

MULTICULTURALISM

Page 84 shared examples of the *archetype, stereotype,* and *modal type* within cultures. Which preferences does each culture honor? Within the type community, this style of analysis goes on within the culture, not from without. Type practitioners in Korea, for example, believe that their culture's archetypal preferences include Thinking; further, a 12-year statistical analysis shows that approximately 70 percent of the men and 60 percent of the women have a preference for Thinking (Sim, 2004).

Because of type's universality, it can become a tool for bridging among cultures within a school, distinguishing between the stereotypes we have and real differences in what a culture values. If I am working with multi-cultural groups, I keep my impressions to myself and will often ask them whether they think their own culture matches or differs from the United States archetype of Extraversion, Sensing, Thinking, and Judging (ESTJ). For example, with a group of Native American educators, we talked about the similarities and differences throughout a daylong workshop. They concluded that their own culture's archetype was Introversion, Intuition, Feeling, and Perceiving (INFP)—the total opposite of the larger U.S. culture. One of the leaders quipped, "Right, all these centuries we kept thinking you'd listen."

I mentioned to the group how Jung himself looked at how type appeared in other cultures, partly through anthropological expeditions to the Pueblo Indians of New Mexico and the Elgoni of Kenya. In his *Memories, Dreams, and Reflections*, he recounted a conversation with a Pueblo chief:

> The chief described the alarm that white Americans inspired in him . . . "They are always seeking something. What are they seeking? The whites always want something; they are always uneasy and restless. We do not know what they want. We do not understand them. We think they are mad." Jung asked him why he thought the whites were mad. "They say that they think with their heads," the chief replied. "Why, of course. What do you think with?" Jung asked him in surprise. "We think here," the chief said, indicating his heart. (Stevens, 1991, p. 272)

This seeming description of a Pueblo cultural value around using the Feeling function, rather than the Thinking function, could be interpreted as an archetypal difference in what the two cultures value.

The point was not to stereotype all Native American students as INFP (any more than all white American children match the cultural stereotype/archetype of ESTJ; only about 12–16 percent do). Instead, we were working on using type as a vehicle for helping the students navigate between the two cultures. The discussion grew richer as we looked at learning style characteristics given for Native American students (Shade, Kelly, & Oberg, 1997), which definitely had an INFP flavor.

- Cooperative learning groups
- Getting the big picture before isolated skills
- Settings full of encouragement
- Artwork, metaphors, images, analogies, and symbols rather than dictionary-type definitions

- Visual/spatial orientation rather than verbal
- Brainstorming, open-ended activities
- Student-designed games
- Lessons and exercises that include discussion of values.

During a rich discussion, the educators pointed out that although the descriptors above rang true for Native American traditions, many of their students had lived in the inner city so long that they didn't know much about their own culture. The group hoped that type could help the students "translate" among their cultural values and traditions, their daily life, and the white culture they'd need to negotiate to finish high school.

Using the lens of type does not replace the need for teachers to understand culturally specific values or ways of expression. For example, some of the schools I work with have a significant number of Hmong students. Trueba, Jacobs, and Kirton (1990) highlighted some of the cultural differences in the Hmong community. Of particular importance was the traditional high regard for educators (which is not related to type preferences). However, the resulting reluctance to question teachers and a cultural tendency to never brag or draw attention to oneself often shows as a cultural preference for Introversion in school classrooms. Many Hmong students hesitate to ask questions about assignments, participate only when asked, and would prefer not to give speeches or otherwise speak in front of their classmates. The teachers know this; therefore, when one of these students nods, "Yes," at the question, "Do you understand my directions?" they check back to make sure the student is proceeding well on the assignment.

However, here's the advantage for teachers who may have students from multiple cultures in their classrooms. Instead of looking at each culture separately, teachers can use the language of type to bridge among the cultures; rather than the groups seeming distinct, as important as that is for aspects of self-esteem and important culturally specific knowledge, students see that Extraversion and Introversion, Sensing and Intuition, and so on exist across cultures. And, teachers usually have at least one preference, if not more, in common with each of the cultures. This assists in understanding.

Further, using type hand in hand with cultural responsiveness lessens the chances of labeling students; individual differences stand out more. For example, students of poverty value being entertaining (Payne, 1996), a more Extraverted style. Although teachers need to take that into account in planning lessons, when using type many students self-identify as Introverts and often then use the language to advocate for the introverted time they need to process some assignments. One African American girl used the language of Extraversion and Introversion to explain to her friends how she could be crazy with them in the hallway, yet need time to concentrate in class.

A particularly successful application of using type to bridge among cultures is in encouraging classroom participation. Given the Hmong tendency to not want to draw attention to themselves, these students were not looking forward to a go-round of speech-giving. A teacher explained that although giving a speech appealed more to Extraverts, the Introverts would have several days to gather their materials and practice, so the assignment was fair. All of the students successfully gave their speeches.

Another example of avoiding the masking of individual differences is in how teachers use the culturally responsive information about African American students. Shade, Kelly, and Oberg (1997) report that African American students are more likely to be field-dependent learners, preferring sequential information and tasks; these descriptors also describe Sensing learners. Sometimes this leads to overlooking the needs of students who differ from their culture. In one classroom, a teacher met the needs of Intuitive students by providing choices on an assignment; although many African American students stuck with structured choices, such as taking an open-book test or making a diorama, which they'd done in the past, others chose—and completed—some of the more creative and time-consuming choices. For several, it was the highest-quality work they'd done in that class.

Type, then, helps teachers go beyond the cultural stereotypes that isolated information can produce.

STUDENTS OF POVERTY

When I attended one of Dr. Ruby Payne's seminars on understanding the language of poverty, I was struck by the similarities between her description and suggested practices for students of poverty and type-related suggestions for Extraverted and Perceiving students. Payne (1996) describes the high levels of noise in most households of poverty and the value they place on being entertaining (Extraversion). There's also an orientation to the present moment, lack of planning for the future, and lack of skill in sequencing tasks to work toward completion (Perceiving). When I described the similarities to several teachers, I learned that they'd been to Payne's seminars and that the information had helped them understand the mindset of their students. But they hadn't tried the suggestions; they didn't seem to understand that these were strategies they could teach.

The plan for "No More F's" in Chapter 3 came from tying Payne's work to type suggestions—when I pointed out the connection, the pilot team was willing to try helping students identify steps in an assignment and plan backward. Other teachers have responded in similar ways once they see the tie-ins. Otherwise, they seem to fall into the trap Delpit (1995) describes. She found that under the pressures of teaching, and with all intentions of "being nice," white teachers often essentially stopped attempting to teach African American children. Lipman (1998) echoes this, pointing out the detrimental effects of viewing African American students through a "deficit model." This pattern of thought results in teachers assuming that the problem lies with the child or his or her background rather than with how the teachers provide instruction. The pilot team assumed that they couldn't teach students to be responsible.

Pedagogical practices such as direct instruction are often recommended for students of poverty. Although that will meet the need of some students, using the lens of type highlights how those practices might alienate Intuitive students; they may react by withdrawing, by doing sloppy work, or by openly rebelling. Further, when we add choice and autonomy to assignments, the interest of *all* students increases. Recall in Chapter 1 that when Josh gave students a choice of assignments, several asked if they could do more than one!

Wilson and Corbett (2001), in an in-depth study of urban middle-school students, found the following patterns in how they felt supported by teachers.

> . . . students wanted to be in classrooms where:
>
> - The teacher "stayed on students" to complete assignments.
> - The teacher was able to control student behavior without ignoring the lesson.
> - The teacher went out of his or her way to provide help.
> - The teacher explained things until the "light bulb went on" for the whole class.
> - The teacher provided students with a variety of activities through which to learn.
> - The teacher understood students' situations and factored that into their lessons.
>
> When we say "students wanted" these qualities present in their classrooms, we mean that the overwhelming majority of students reiterated these characteristics at every opportunity in the interviews over the three-year period. (pp. 63–64)

One way to interpret the above research results is that the students want teachers to give them the Judging skills that playing the "game of school" requires. This information, coupled with type information, helped Josh's team feel empowered to "nag" more. The teachers I've worked with use a multistep process to do so:

- They set the expectation that every student will finish assignments. When students have a history of not completing work, teachers make clear that they will find a way for them to complete it—after school, during lunch, or via an alternative, structured assignment if the assignment originally included choices.
- They teach students to identify the steps in a task and to plan backward to complete them. They emphasized that mini-deadlines are as important as the due date for the entire project. Payne (1996) advocates this for students of poverty, and Murphy (1992) advocates these techniques for Perceiving children.
- They provide choice wherever possible. With middle-school students, choice serves as a strong motivator; adolescents enjoy having some power and autonomy over assignments. If we are trying to teach students a certain *form* of work, such as giving a speech or writing a report, we try to allow some choice as to content. If we are trying to assess mastery of *content*, we try to give students some choice over the form in which they present the information.
- Structured correctly, providing choices in assignments helps students take responsibility for the personal choices they are making with regard to their schoolwork. If they stay on schedule, they can stick to their original choice of assignment. The further behind they fall, the fewer choices remain. Often, to avoid doing a teacher-chosen alternate assignment, students ask for lunchtime passes, leave messages on their home phones as reminders of what they need to do, work feverishly during class—anything to avoid the teacher-mandated fallback assignment.

These type strategies give teachers hope that they can help more students succeed. In the secondary grades, one teacher using them alone generally will struggle because of the immense effort needed at the beginning. However, when teams collaborate, uniformly implementing the strategies, the students begin to respond.

BRAIN RESEARCH

Murphy (1992) describes the differing informational needs of Sensing and Intuitive children:

Adults working with sensing children need to respect the sensing child's need to gather as many pieces of information in a sequential way as are necessary to understand the concept. Sensing children may ask many questions while an Intuitive adult is trying to explain something. These questions can be viewed as interruptions or delay tactics. They actually enable sensing children to gather information in a sequential order, which is necessary for them to understand . . . if the bridge from one piece of information to the next is not built, sensing children do not feel comfortable taking the necessary leap and forming what appears to them to be unsubstantiated conclusions.

An intuitive child begins brainstorming various possibilities. If the teacher says, "Where are your facts? How can you support your ideas?" the subtle message is that the idea isn't good until it has supporting evidence.

The problem is that most intuitives gather information to support an intuitive idea. Gathering information without an end as a guide means they have no filter to know which information is relevant and which is not. (pp. 38–40)

Note the similarity between Murphy's description for what happens to the Sensing child and Healy's (1994) discussion of how using the pattern-making areas of the brain is critical to proper development: "Children who don't learn to search for meaning are often good 'technicians' in the 1st and 2nd grade because they can deal with isolated data, but when the demands for comprehension increase, they 'hit the wall.' They simply can't assemble it and make sense out of it. Those who can are often thought of as more intelligent" (p. 50). We've already seen how standardized tests and other trappings of higher education tend to favor the Intuitive learning style. Shade, Kelly, and Oberg (1997) summarize how field-independent learning, which is essentially Intuitive-Thinking learning, is more highly valued than field-dependent learning: "Proponents of this belief system assume that rationality is better than emotionality, print information has more validity than oral information, abstract conceptualizations are better and more superior to concrete conceptualizations, field independence is better than field dependence" (p. 69). Field-dependent learning correlates with the Feeling preference (Hammer, 1996).

There are two dangers here. One is that brain research will be used in a way that overlooks the needs of students with one preference or the other. Murphy's quote above, for example, shows the dangers of assuming that all students need the facts before they can create meaning (Intuitives have a hunch about the meaning and then look for facts to support that hunch), as happens when teachers use Bloom's Taxonomy as a strict model for class discussions. Look at the first level in Bloom's Taxonomy (Bloom, 1956):

Knowledge:

- Observe and recall factual information such as dates, events, places
- Know major ideas
- Master subject matter
- *Question cues:* list, define, tell, describe, identify, show, label, collect, examine, tabulate, quote, name, who, when, where, etc.

All of these describe the steps needed for a Sensing child to successfully pursue interpretation and comprehension of a novel. However, Intuitive minds do *not* start with knowledge. To organize facts, as Murphy points out, they first surmise a theme, the fourth and fifth steps in Bloom's Taxonomy:

Analysis:

- See patterns
- Organize parts
- Recognize hidden meanings
- Identify components
- *Question cues:* analyze, separate, order, explain, connect, classify, arrange, divide, compare, select, explain, infer

Synthesis:

- Use old ideas to create new ones
- Generalize from given facts
- Relate knowledge from several areas
- Predict, draw conclusions
- *Question cues:* combine, integrate, modify, rearrange, substitute, plan, create, design, invent, what if?, compose, formulate, prepare, generalize, rewrite

Because students need to build academic confidence in their own styles, teaching methods in the primary grades need to accommodate *both* styles. In classrooms with older students, when they still struggle with reading comprehension, I often see teachers beginning the entire class with fact-based exploration of the texts. This puts the Intuitive students at a disadvantage; they don't want to look at details unless they understand why those particular details are important. Further, the emphasis on facts doesn't help Sensing students gain practice in looking independently for the patterns in the facts; Healy described the lack of this skill above as "hitting the wall."

Character description assignments, for example, can honor both styles. Intuitive students can list conclusions about the characters, then go back and search for supporting evidence. Sensing students might mark passages that describe a character, then review them and look for the patterns before drawing conclusions. Teaching both strategies, then allowing students to choose, helps them develop their strengths rather than question their natural paths to knowledge.

Similarly, some brain-research studies blur what Introverted and Extraverted students need for learning. Jensen (1998) states that, "Because meaning is generated internally, external input conflicts with the possibility that learners can turn what they have just learned into something meaningful. You can either have your learners' attention or they can be making meaning, but never both at the same time . . . we may want to allow for several minutes of reflection time after new learning. Writing in journals or discussing the new learning in small groups makes good sense for the learning brain" (pp. 46–47). An understanding of Extraversion and Introversion would help teachers plan for both kinds of reflective activities. Further, they might provide Introverted time with the information *before* any classroom activities—Introverts often want to think about things before they do them.

Type also helps add patterns to brain-research information on student motivation. Ford (1992) showed that inner motivation comes through compelling goals, positive beliefs, and productive emotions. Information on type shows that compelling goals differ, depending on a person's preferences:

- Sensing types are often motivated through a sense of order and practicality of what they are learning. How will they use it?
- Intuitive types are often motivated through creativity. How will their outcomes be unique? What new avenues does the information open?
- Thinking types are often motivated through control and competency. How can they take charge in the learning process? Will they be able to master the learning?
- Feeling types are often motivated through how the information will improve relationships or help other people. Will learning help someone else? Is it useful in making the world a better place?

These differing sources of motivation influence how students react to common motivation techniques.

In summary, filtering brain research through type ensures that teachers connect the information with an existing mental model—type—making it easier to use it, *and* ensures that they don't fall into the trap of using brain research as a one-size-fits-all model for learning in areas in which differences exist.

DIFFICULT STUDENTS

Our society is addicted to cause-effect reasoning: If we can figure out the nature of a problem, we can solve it. Although many students have genuine problems such as ADHD or ODD, remember that research indicates that teachers are more likely to view as problem students those whose preferences are least similar to their own (O'Neil, 1986). We leap to "What's wrong with that child?" rather than "How is that child different from me? Am I accommodating those differences?"

Using type to identify how a child's natural style differs from the teachers, and then trying various type strategies designed to help that child learn, can prevent the labeling of students least wired for the Judging world of school. It is an intermediate step before assuming that a child really has a disability. For example, teachers asked the parents of three cousins to have their sons diagnosed for ADHD. All three boys had trouble sitting still, occasionally acted out, and often refused to complete assignments they viewed as stupid. Further, they argued back with teachers. Only one was actually diagnosed with ADHD, but all three had preferences for Extraversion, Intuition, and Perceiving. They were bored by rote work, needed to act and move, and needed chances to be in charge.

Tannock and Martinussen (2001) point out that neither medication nor traditional behavior modification (timeouts and incentives) go far enough in improving academic achievement in students with ADHD. Instructional practices that *do* help match type-based strategies for Perceiving students. These include

- Giving cues for how time is passing and how much of a task should be completed
- Using graphic organizers that show sequences, processes, or assignments
- Teaching self-monitoring strategies such as setting goals for class-time use
- Giving assignment choices that allow for some self-directed, interest-driven work
- Insisting that students meet expectations, providing alternate ways as they learn to take responsibility for their own work.

In other words, by teaching strategies that help Perceiving students, teachers can avoid mislabeling normal differences as ADHD. Further, if the strategies don't work, the evidence may be clearer that the student needs other measures such as medication. Even if this is the case, the student may make even greater progress academically with the strategies. Again, medication may make the student easier to handle in class, but more can be done to improve academics, the ultimate goal.

We can make similar comparisons between ODD and students who prefer Extraversion, Intuition, and Thinking. One of the risk factors for ODD is an inherently difficult personality (Hall & Hall, 2003), which many parents will attest describes their delightful, normal, yet challenging Intuitive/Thinking (NT) children. A few common descriptions from Tieger and Barron-Tieger (1997) include

> Emotionally, ENTP preschoolers tend to get angry more often than they get their feelings hurt. They are very direct and bold children and can make their friends mad when they insist on doing things their way. (p. 140)

> Putting themselves in another person's place is very difficult for most young ENTJs, who have not yet learned the finer skills of diplomacy, empathy, or gentleness. ENTJs tend to rush headlong into life and need to be taught to slow down and notice the impact their directness has on those around them. (p. 115)

In general, NTs

- Need to compete, but can do so by setting goals for themselves.
- View praise with suspicion unless it is specific. If you say, "Johnny, that's such a nice drawing," the student will assume that you're bartering for good behavior. If you say, "Your choice of colors really makes the horse seem like it's moving," he will think you've carefully evaluated his work and deemed it worthy of comment.
- Need leadership roles. If none are provided, they may take leadership in getting others to act out.
- Need autonomy. They naturally resist being told what to do. They respond better to "Do you want to put on your right boot or left boot first?" than to "Put on your boots."
- Are bored with routine—they need adaptations to stay interested in schoolwork.
- May struggle to work in groups because of their strong personalities. They may not understand that other students take critiques personally.

Similar to the relationship between the Perceiving preference and ADHD, many of the suggestions given for working with ODD students run parallel to type suggestions for students who prefer Intuition and Thinking. Consider first whether a child's difficulties in the classroom are because of failure to accommodate that child's natural style, rather than a diagnosable problem; this may lead to faster resolution and prevent unnecessary stress for the student, who often begins to feel like a "bad" child. The strategies include

- *Avoiding "sparkers."* Sparkers of defiant behavior include
  - Direct commands: "Stop it." "No." "Do this."
  - Visible disapproval. These children read the body and facial expressions of adults and respond negatively to disapproval.
  - Idle time. If these students aren't sure what to do next, they may cause trouble.
- *Asking a question* rather than giving a command. "Jenny, what should you be doing right now?" rather than "Jenny, sit down for story time." This leaves the child in control, in his or her mind.
- *Giving choices.* These children need options so they feel in control. Teachers can limit the choices to two options, but choice is important.

Again, students who truly have ODD will need more help than the above suggestions provide (including far more structuring of tasks), but looking first at behaviors through the lens of type may prevent inappropriate labeling of students.

Using type as a unifying framework for staff development keeps new learning from falling through the cracks; the teachers can place it in their "camping backpack" of the organizing theory of type. It establishes a common language for making connections, for finding areas of synergy or concern, for applying learning in new areas, and for looking beyond one's own needs and beliefs to what students require to succeed. The more experience teachers have with the framework of type—and they will *get* enough experience if subsequent staff development efforts tie back to type—the more they will make these connections for themselves.

A FINAL NOTE

> The art for staff development is helping teachers understand where their strengths and beliefs lock them into practices that limit their freedom to help students to succeed. It isn't freedom for teachers to do what they please, but freedom to entertain possibilities and stay open to new avenues for professional growth.

Teaching is an incredibly important vocation. Education plays a vital role in our society. We've seen how teacher-centered staff development—honoring their strengths, beliefs, concerns, and needs during change—sets them free to entertain possibilities and stay open to new avenues for growth. They *will* change their classrooms.

However, the tremendous time commitments are an obvious drawback to implementing these key practices for effective staff development. For school reform, perhaps a starting place for any effort is evaluating the depth of change required. The issue of commitment to change is especially crucial in school settings where funds always seem to be limited and consultants, teachers, and administrators often have to do more with less. Before beginning, let's ask the tough questions.

First, will we commit the time and resources necessary to bring about the changes? In other words, will we try to match reform goals with available resources? Or will we take shortcuts and once again blame teachers when they cling to what has worked for them in the past?

Second, will those involved commit to the change effort long enough for teachers to gain concrete experiences? It may take months or even years if one considers the amount of effort needed to overcome learned helplessness in students—and adults—even when the reform efforts are proven effective in other settings.

And third, if the strengths and beliefs of those in charge are getting in the way of what the teachers need to implement the changes, is there a willingness to reexamine those beliefs? At what cost? Are those costs (and the risk of incurring them) calculated before beginning the effort?

If these are the requirements for effective change efforts—time, long-term commitment, consistency, attention to individuals in the change process, and attention to systems and beliefs prior to requiring changes in practices—it is easy to see why so many school reform efforts fall short. And it is easy to understand why some teachers may have grown skeptical or even hostile toward reforms that take them away from their daily work without adding to their ability to help students succeed. If we don't create conditions that allow the collaborative examination of beliefs and provide scaffolding when we ask teachers to change those beliefs, we may never put the most worthy of reform efforts to the test where it counts—in the classrooms.

However, if we consider structuring the process of change to be as or more significant than the changes themselves, and if we regard the needs of the teachers to be as important as those of the students, then the role of teachers in influencing what and how students learn might return to the high calling of the profession that Dewey (1897/1972) envisioned when he wrote,

> I believe that the art of thus giving shape to human powers and adapting them to social service, is the supreme art; one calling into its service the best of artists; that no insight, sympathy, tact, executive power is too great for such service. (p. 94)

Appendix A

The Sixteen Types: Strengths, Beliefs, and Needs During Change

The following pages contain type descriptions for each of the 16 types. Note that the coaching suggestions cover instructional and interpersonal needs. Often, interpersonal skills form roadblocks to effective collaboration and to change in general.

If you struggle to see patterns in the differences, try examining pages for opposite types, i.e., ENTJ and ISFP. How do their needs differ? How do they want to be coached?

In using these pages,

- Look first at the coaching suggestions for the person being coached. Do the common areas for growth seem accurate? Do they describe some of the changes you are asking the teacher to make?
- Then look at the areas for growth listed for your own type. Are any of these getting in the way of working effectively with specific teachers?

Remember that the coaching suggestions use the teachers' strengths to help them grow and change. Try the following suggestions for differentiated coaching:

- Use the "general strengths" and "at their best in the classroom" information to understand a teacher's beliefs about teaching and learning. Consider how they might use their strengths during change.

- Use the "needs during change" and "coaching suggestions" to tailor coaching methods and resources.
- Consider "common stressors" to anticipate the problems they may wish to focus on. Comparing "at their best in the classroom" to the changes or to your observations can also unearth problems that concern them.

ISTJs

Prefer "Coach as Useful Resource." Provide practical help, step-by-step methods, examples, and clear goals.

General Strengths:	Common Stressors:
• Hardworking, stable, and sensible • Improving what works • Being consistent • Structuring routines • Covering basic skills, essential ideas, and curriculum thoroughly	• Interruptions, schedule changes, uncertainty • Trying to do too much at once • When something goes wrong despite tremendous effort • Changes in textbooks or curriculum standards • Lack of respect from others for their hard work
At Their Best in the Classroom:	**Needs During Change:**
• Assignments that allow for objective grading and clear expectations • Good directions and step-by-step instructions • Structures that help students follow through—outlines, classroom procedures, etc. • Pencil/paper drills, predictable elements to assignments • Teacher-led discussions with emphasis on factual information	• Clear connections between their current practices and new ones • Information that answers all their questions • Careful attention to implementation details—schedules, costs, responsibilities

Coaching Suggestions for ISTJs

Typical Areas for Growth as a Teacher	A Coach Might
Adopting new teaching methods or curriculum (because their lesson plans are complete, already tested)	Encourage ISTJs to list concerns and questions. Answer these carefully. Take one of their favorite elements of the old and show them how to present or adapt it in the new *or* how they can still use their strengths.
Structuring tasks without overscaffolding	Demonstrate strategies that provide general rather than specific structure. Examples include graphic organizers for moving from facts to patterns or ideas, formats for applying problem-solving skills, or tools to help students access prior knowledge.
Building relationships with students	Use descriptions of the needs of Thinking and Feeling students to help build a case for softening task orientation. Teach specific vocabulary and techniques for working with students.
Providing flexibility within the structures they develop	Ask to restructure a worksheet or assignment they use. Add one or two elements that allow for student choice. Discuss results.
Flexing rules to take into account adolescent development	Provide cues for giving students second chances ("Is that what you really meant to say?" "What should you be doing now?") to diffuse situations in which a student may be baiting the teacher. Discuss workable rules that allow exceptions for extenuating circumstances.
Perfectionism—never taking sick days, picking up slack for others, etc.	Help the ISTJ consider how others might benefit from added responsibilities and how to keep from feeling resentful.

ISTPs

Prefer "Coach as Useful Resource." Provide practical information, hands-on experiences, and specific rationale. Be conscious of good use of time.

General Strengths:	Common Stressors:
<ul><li>Being objective, calm</li><li>Pursuing deep knowledge in areas of expertise</li><li>Finding efficient ways to accomplish tasks</li><li>Observing facts and details</li><li>Adapting to unexpected events or circumstances</li></ul>	<ul><li>Changes that don't make logical sense to them</li><li>Lack of time for reflection</li><li>Emotional outbursts—their own or others</li><li>Imposed rules or routines that decrease autonomy</li><li>Being asked to make quick decisions on matters with long-term implications</li></ul>
At Their Best in the Classroom:	**Needs During Change:**
<ul><li>Sequential learning tasks</li><li>Small group demonstrations, providing one-to-one help</li><li>Using data and technology</li><li>Hands-on activities with tangible results, room for trial and error</li><li>Independent projects with flexibility for student</li></ul>	<ul><li>Clear reasons for policies; structures; and any mandated strategies, curriculum, or teaching methods</li><li>Room for flexibility and individuality</li><li>Time to process changes before having to implement them</li></ul>

Coaching Suggestions for ISTPs

Typical Areas for Growth as a Teacher	A Coach Might
Meeting student emotional needs	Help them connect positive feedback with reaching clear goals, because nonspecific praise feels false to ISTPs. Examine student work together to practice giving specific praise. Discuss the Feeling need to see outward enthusiasm from others.
Trying new teaching methods	Use what they do best as a starting point, then adjust for students who learn differently or use other logical rationale for new methods. ISTPs *perfect* things that work for them, so change is hard.
Collaborating with other teachers	Choose an area of interest to them for collaboration or one that immediately increases efficiency. Or, encourage a first collaboration effort with the coach.
Rethinking principles and priorities using values and viewpoints of others	Emphasize using a neutral framework to look at situations in which the ISTPs' stances might not fit the needs of all students or all situations.
Ignoring "dumb" rules	First evaluate the necessity of the rules and then use logic, if-then reasoning, and precedent language to persuade.
Relying on last-minute effort	Teach the ISTP to plan backward, allowing sufficient time for each step of the process, if their work style interferes with that of colleagues.

ESTPs

Prefer "Coach as Useful Resource." Concentrate on applications for their specific classroom. Show enthusiasm and minimize theory in favor of examples of what works.

<table>
<tr>
<td>

General Strengths:

- Making school fun
- Breaking tasks into steps
- Streamlining and improving methods and assignments
- Devising practical solutions to problems, especially in the moment
- Using multiple classroom management practices

</td>
<td>

Common Stressors:

- Planning, especially long-term with details
- Being asked to study theories without clear connections to classroom realities
- Too many restrictions or outside requirements
- Changes that make no practical sense or interfere with what clearly works
- Being rushed to make decisions without sufficient time to explore and analyze options

</td>
</tr>
<tr>
<td>

At Their Best in the Classroom:

- Playful attitude, engaging students through games and contests
- Helping students master basic skills and immediately useful information
- In-the-moment activities and ideas
- Demonstrations and hands-on lessons
- Getting the most out of good curriculum

</td>
<td>

Needs During Change:

- Hands-on, relevant activities to try in their classrooms
- Immediate, tangible payoffs with new curriculum or teaching methods
- Chances to talk through questions and concerns

</td>
</tr>
</table>

Coaching Suggestions for ESTPs

Typical Areas for Growth as a Teacher	A Coach Might
Planning lessons, curriculum mapping	Provide hands-on help, templates, examples, or specific requirements. Point to resources and shortcuts.
Providing projects or assessments that require subjective grading	Help ESTPs prepare checklist rubrics so that requirements and grading parameters are clear.
Taking time for reflection	Use cognitive coaching strategies (Costa & Garmston, 1994) so that reflection can take place in conversation. Draw out their concerns and ideas.
Bluntness—not realizing their impact on students	Use the Thinking-Feeling framework to emphasize the impact of criticism on Feeling students. Role-play starting interactions with positive comments.
Allowing too much fun or noise, leaving Introverted students uncomfortable or drained	Provide specific techniques—journaling, think-talk-write, two-minute wait times for discussions, noise gauges, etc.
Trying new techniques they haven't experienced	Either provide a complete lesson plan or model the technique for them. ESTPs may resist studying or preparing without evidence of usefulness.

ESTJs

Prefer "Coach as Useful Resource." Make benefits, goals, and methods clear. Be logical and specific about why methods or content need to change.

General Strengths:	Common Stressors:
• Hardworking and reliable • Planning and organizing materials and activities • Anticipating problems, troubleshooting • Structuring tasks with clear goals, benchmarks, and standards • Developing responsible behavior in others	• Changes in policies and standards that go against deeply held principles • Having to deal with emotional outbursts • Lack of recognition for their hard work or proven methods • When formal leadership lacks expertise or effectiveness • Finding that a careful plan doesn't work
At Their Best in the Classroom:	**Needs During Change:**
• Keeping students on schedule and on task • Well-planned lessons, often with problem-solving focus, with clear oral directions • Rewards and specific praise for achieving goals • Teacher-led discussions • Hands-on activities with real-life connections	• Clear, logical explanations of any changes to policies, standards, or methods that worked in the past • Specifics about requirements, responsibilities, time frames, and expected outcomes • Data and other evidence, not theory, that the changes will advance goals

Coaching Suggestions for ESTJs

Typical Areas for Growth as a Teacher	A Coach Might
Allowing for differences in individual students	Use a learning styles model to demonstrate variables such as how Perceiving students might require more time for exploration, or how Intuitive students might need a higher level of interest in a task to do it well.
Listening to the ideas of others	Use the type framework for problem solving (Appendix B) to help ESTJs consider other points of view.
Making exceptions when circumstances call for them	Remind ESTJs that Sensing/Perceiving students report how fun it is to "bait" STJ teachers. Discuss three or four surefire exceptions such as excusing a student from homework because of a house fire, then help them adjust their policies to accommodate them.
Lack of empathy/personal relationships with students	Ask them to keep data on interactions with students. Discuss brain research on the emotional side of learning.
Rethinking decisions or entertaining new ideas	Begin by listing clear changes in underlying information—other valid viewpoints, new technology, changes in students, materials that weren't available. Help them adjust for opposite learning styles.
Subjective learning activities, leaving room for imagination	Teach specific use of checklist rubrics, ways to structure subjective tasks. Show examples of strategies that help students move from facts to implications or draw their own connections.

ISFJs

Prefer "Coach as Encouraging Sage." They feel duty-bound to learn and improve, but like clear direction, step-by-step methods, and opportunities to practice until they feel confident.

General Strengths:	Common Stressors:
• Hardworking, reliable, and at ease with details • Being committed to lifelong learning • Organizing materials and developing procedures for efficiency • Emphasizing harmony, cooperation, and mutual support • Listening skills and empathy	• Being asked to change or act without clear direction or probable outcomes • Not having time to prepare for changes, especially when well-established methods or procedures are involved • When others don't appreciate their efforts or want their help • Working too hard to meet everyone's needs • When others ignore common sense or tradition
At Their Best in the Classroom:	**Needs During Change:**
• A respectful, caring atmosphere • Structured tasks with clear directions that involve factual knowledge • Excellent use of curriculum, making real-life connections • Assignments where hard work can bring good grades • Step-by-step tasks with chances for reinforcement until mastery is reached	• Stepping stones from where they are to where they need to be • Clear expectations, procedures, and methods • Examples related to their own personal experiences or those of others in similar situations

Coaching Suggestions for ISFJs

Typical Areas for Growth as a Teacher	A Coach Might
Setting priorities so as not to get lost in sequential progression through tasks	Provide a clear method for setting priorities, tied in with school goals. Help identify "unnecessary" work or how others might help.
Understanding the big picture, letting go of traditions or procedures	Use real-life examples of how the changes have helped others. Practice moving from facts to several possibilities. Refer to their Sensing style to explain why change is hard.
Trying new methods or curriculum	Use modeling, step-by-step procedures, and supportive feedback. Demonstrate ties between the old and the new.
Tailoring curriculum, determining what is relevant for their situation	Use templates for students with different learning styles or backgrounds to help them adjust curriculum by adding materials or skipping nonessentials.
Structuring tasks without overscaffolding	Teach specific methods that stretch student thinking within structures, such as graphic organizers that assist with critical thinking or general problem-solving methods.
Trusting their own creativity	Help them begin by working together to improve something familiar to them rather than starting from scratch.

ISFPs

Prefer "Coach as Encouraging Sage." Provide support as they try new methods, work to boost their self-confidence, and allow for flexibility in how quickly they proceed.

General Strengths:	Common Stressors:
• Being considerate, cooperative, consistent, and caring • Helping others work through their problems • Taking a pragmatic approach to tasks and crises • Working toward harmony, understanding, and inclusiveness • Modeling compassion and kindness	• Disharmony and values conflicts • Being pressured to make important decisions quickly • Being expected to change without receiving concrete information or learning experiences • Overly restrictive rules or procedures that belie individual differences • Changes without demonstration of practical benefits
At Their Best in the Classroom:	**Needs During Change:**
• Nurturing students through quiet help • Demonstrating, then allowing students to learn by doing • Small-group work and cooperative games • Clear, practical tasks with concrete steps • Paying attention to emotional content of learning, allowing for artistic expression	• Practical learning related to their classroom • Concrete steps and procedures that match their ability level • Clear sense of direction, with information on how the needs of all are being met

Coaching Suggestions for ISFPs

Typical Areas for Growth as a Teacher	A Coach Might
Planning beyond curriculum for differentiation, cultural responsiveness, etc.	Give clear steps and examples. Partner in planning, then review student work together. Use examples from other teachers they trust.
Allowing students to work with ambiguous or open-ended tasks	Start with a structured assignment they've used before and help them add choice, what-ifs, or other new elements. Assist in preparing structure for grading.
Developing a "thick skin" for working with students and colleagues	Help them develop self-esteem by clearly identifying strengths and goals for improvement, and then using those goals to objectively hear critiques.
Facing conflict	Use role-playing or a problem-solving model to help them work through conflicts. Help them list consequences of ignoring conflict.
Trying new methods that seem risky to them	Connect the practice to content they've taught before. Let them review steps and ask questions. Offer to model.
Relating goals to theories and models	Put faces on theories and relate them to their classroom and students.

ESFPs

Prefer "Coach as Encouraging Sage." Take time to build a relationship. Partner with them in learning activities that provide in-the-moment skill development.

General Strengths:	Common Stressors:
• Showing enthusiasm, warmth, and energy • Building relationships through personal attention, accepting and including everyone • Adding fun to places and events • Finding useful information and resources to share • Providing practical help to others	• Expectations or standards they don't feel they have the resources to meet • Criticism without accompanying understanding or support • Planning efforts with tight deadlines or too much structure • Working from theory rather than from examples and applications • Speculation and creative problem solving without sufficient facts and other parameters.
At Their Best in the Classroom:	**Needs During Change:**
• Energetic, adding humor and fun • Providing individual help with warmth and encouragement • Hands-on demonstrations and activities with room to explore • Structured activities to help students grasp basic skills • Color, sounds, and activities—a lively classroom	• Practical, concrete tasks to understand new ideas • Support from caring colleagues or coach • Attention to common sense and classroom realities

Coaching Suggestions for ESFPs

Typical Areas for Growth as a Teacher	A Coach Might
Planning without bogging down in details	Be specific about the needed level of detail concerning time frames, lesson content, etc. Provide examples.
Distinguishing important tasks from urgent tasks	Help set priorities based on what the teacher values most for students as well as school goals. Construct an easy-to-remember rule for choosing tasks.
Trying unfamiliar teaching methods	Model, supplying examples and directions. ESFPs often want to observe and then try it themselves. They are open to respectful in-the-moment suggestions and revisions.
Conflict management	Suggest specific training on conflict. Use role-playing for dealing with difficult students or parents.
Engaging students in higher level thinking tasks	Work with the teacher to expand the scope of an existing lesson. Provide graphic organizers, cues, and other examples that use structured ways to go beyond facts and methods.
Seeing patterns in student performance	Collaboratively examine data on student engagement, patterns of response, or grades. Set clear goals and gather new data to see if students met them.

ESFJs

Prefer "Coach as Encouraging Sage." Set clear goals that target specific needs. Allow time for conversation to build a relationship. Use a variety of structured learning methods.

General Strengths:	Common Stressors:
• Organizing time, materials, people, and tasks to meet each person's needs • Improving what works while working within the system • Welcoming each and every person • Setting clear goals, communicating well • Being loyal to tradition, people, and organizations	• Being caught in the middle of disputes • Changes in curriculum or structures that have worked for them • Changes that seem to ask them to compromise their values • When others don't value their personal effort or strengths • Lack of emotional support
At Their Best in the Classroom:	**Needs During Change:**
• Activities that are active but structured—good use of curriculum • Helping each child feel important by meeting specific needs • Teaching procedures, expectations, and courtesy • Creating community, allowing for student interaction • Lessons that help students grasp the importance of values and traditions	• Emotional support and recognition of the efforts they are making • Time to talk through changes, new ideas and expectations, and positive experiences with others engaged in the same process • Clear expectations, methods, and goals with examples from relevant situations

Coaching Suggestions for ESFJs

Typical Areas for Growth as a Teacher	A Coach Might
Letting go of familiar methods or favorite lessons	Try step-by-step instruction, modeling, and role-playing. Start with familiar content and apply new methods to it. Set clear expectations and provide positive feedback.
Structuring tasks in ways that allow for student creativity or critical thinking	Provide examples from relevant situations and subject matter. Demonstrate graphic organizers and other tools of structuring that allow for open-ended student response.
Backing away from their own clear ideas of "right" and "wrong"	Help them use a neutral framework to think through such questions as "What values might the other person hold?" "Which of my own assumptions should I be questioning?"
Distinguishing between when to offer help and when others need to help themselves	Role-play new responses with adults and students, such as "What might you do next?" "What resources are available?"
Assessing the big picture of reasons for change	Use concrete representations such as multigrade curriculum maps or flowchart of student skill development.
Assessing whether activities bring real learning	Help design clear action research to test the effectiveness of paper-and-pencil drills such as "Three weeks later, can a student still diagram a sentence?"

INFJs

Prefer "Coach as Collegial Mentor." Provide materials and tools for reflection, and then meet to dialogue about ideas. Honor their creativity.

General Strengths:	Common Stressors:
• Anticipating what people need, adding ideas to long-range planning • Working independently, in control of time and priorities • Understanding the big picture and overall goals • Encouraging and motivating in individualized ways • Getting people and systems to work together	• Operating in crisis mode with no time for reflection • Situations that require extensive attention to details • Too much noise or activity • Atmospheres thick with cynicism and conflict • When their ideas are ignored or they have no input in change processes
At Their Best in the Classroom:	**Needs During Change:**
• Imaginative projects, often involving creative writing • Interdisciplinary or thematic units focusing on human interactions • Chances for independent study for depth of mastery • Individualized feedback to students • Use of stories, artwork, and other media to help students grasp difficult concepts	• Background information and time to reflect on it • Opportunities to provide ideas and influence implementation • Leadership recognition of people's needs and efforts to meet them

Coaching Suggestions for INFJs

Typical Areas for Growth as a Teacher	A Coach Might
Adding sufficient structure to creative tasks	Emphasize universal tools such as Cornel notes, checklist rubrics, and graphic organizers.
Giving clear directions and procedures	Encourage them to run directions past Sensing teachers. Help them develop checklists for good directions; provide examples and templates.
Sharing ideas while they are still processing them	Point out the advantages of receiving input through collaboration. Suggest they keep an "idea notebook" in which they can record new thoughts, along with questions they might ask others.
Political savvy, assertiveness skills to ensure ideas are heard	For involvement in building or district issues, have them list the people involved, their possible motivations and agendas, and how to present to them.
Following curriculum essentials, paying attention to standards	Map out essentials by focusing on the big picture of shared reform goals and how the standards fit together from year to year for students.
Allowing enough opportunities for students to practice skills	Make sure they understand how step-by-step learning and practice build confidence in many Sensing students. Have them collaborate with you or a Sensing teacher to compare assignments on the same unit. Where might they add structure or practice?

INFPs

Prefer "Coach as Collegial Mentor." Focus on the big picture of human growth. Provide information and ideas, then allow incubation time before expecting discussion or action.

General Strengths:	Common Stressors:
• Showing creativity, self-expression • Idealism, acting as peacekeepers, and upholding values • Helping others clarify and live up to their values • Caring deeply about each person they work with • Focusing on a holistic view of education and human development	• Conflicts over values, especially if changes seem to go against their values • Injustice • Lack of reflective time to explore new ideas or initiatives • Being asked for plans or decisions before they feel ready • When personal expression is discouraged or ideas and concerns are dismissed
At Their Best in the Classroom:	**Needs During Change:**
• Open-ended activities that allow for student creativity and self-expression • Rigorous content emphasizing themes or interdisciplinary approaches • Creative writing or other artistic aspects to assignments • Inclusive discussions, small-group work • Chances for quiet reflection and independent study	• Time for in-depth reflection on the reasons behind the changes and their impact on each student • Review of background material and opportunities for deep discussions • Validation of their concerns and ideas

Coaching Suggestions for INFPs

Typical Areas for Growth as a Teacher	A Coach Might
Adding structure and clear expectations to creative assignments	Bring examples of successful lessons, resources for student organizational techniques, and checklist rubrics. Then ask how you can be of most help to them.
Connecting lesson content with real-life applications	Provide planning tools that make concrete the "so what" connections and graphic organizers or thinking tools for classroom discussions on where and how the information is used, and who is using it.
Dealing with conflict with students, parents, or colleagues	Suggest specific training in conflict management or role-playing after watching others. Add classroom structure such as better transition techniques or material organization.
Collaborating—difficulties come from natural drive for individualism and perfecting ideas before sharing	Provide research on benefits of collaboration, especially tied to the big picture of sustainable school change. Then identify a collaboration effort that would be of most help to them.
Meeting deadlines, often because of pursuit of perfection	Help them plan backward and develop organized shortcuts. Provide a model of what is necessary—level of detail, etc.
Following imposed guidelines or curriculum	Point to the big picture of school goals and help them sort through how they fit in. INFPs are naturally "lone wolves" who have usually thought through their practices in depth.

ENFPs

Prefer "Coach as Collegial Mentor." Relate ideas back to the big picture of personal growth for students and teachers. Bring ideas, but allow time for brainstorming together.

General Strengths:	Common Stressors:
• Initiating and promoting ideas for student growth • Celebrating and appreciating others . • Generating options, finding new resources, and networking • Creating enthusiasm around endeavors • Working to accomplish large-scale endeavors	• Keeping track of details or following structures • Changes in personnel resulting in lost relationships; isolation • Overextending themselves in excitement over new ideas or possibilities • Lack of options • When people don't appreciate each other or honor diversity
At Their Best in the Classroom:	**Needs During Change:**
• Engaging students with their high levels of energy and enthusiasm • Large-scale projects and efforts, often interdisciplinary—plays, fundraising, science fairs, etc. • Providing choices or constant variety of activities with flexible learning modes • Group projects with opportunities to socialize • Imaginative, creative lessons and ideas	• Humor in the midst of stress • Reminders to take care of their physical needs for rest, diet, and exercise • Opportunities to explore options and add creativity in ways that relate to the big picture

Coaching Suggestions for ENFPs

Typical Areas for Growth as a Teacher	A Coach Might
Providing appropriate levels of time, materials, and structure for significant creative assignments	In a collaborative session with other teachers, facilitate a discussion of a lesson so ENFPs can hear their perspectives and viewpoints. Help them plan backward from goals to incorporate needed structure for student success.
Meeting the needs of Introverted students	Provide specific techniques—journaling, think-talk-write, two-minute wait times for discussions, noise gauges, etc.
Meeting obligations of the "details" of teaching—report cards, organizing materials, etc.	Gather suggestions from Sensing teachers. Discuss which ones the ENFPs might be able to adapt to their own needs.
Identifying a manageable level of commitments	Use a grid to set priorities. Where can they have the most influence? What will keep them from saying yes without reflection?
Staying with ideas—not chasing every new fad	Relate this tendency to the big picture of the patterns of educational trends that quickly go out of vogue. Point out the needs of Sensing and Judging students and colleagues.
Meeting standards, curriculum expectations	Map out essentials by focusing on the big picture of shared reform goals and how the standards fit together from year to year for students. Brainstorm ways to continue variety and creativity.

ENFJs

Prefer "Coach as Collegial Mentor." Be ready to be a friend, listen, and discuss ideas. Concentrate on their development as a path to student growth. Provide structure for learning new methods.

General Strengths:	Common Stressors:
• Organizing and leading, with attention to mission and values • Communicating with warmth and enthusiasm • Focusing on meaningful learning for each student, targeting individual developmental needs • Believing in the basic good of human nature • Inspiring others to strive for personal growth	• Failed relationships with students or colleagues • Changes in school personnel that result in lost relationships • Negative atmospheres where they or others are belittled or patronized • When values or needs of people are ignored • Believing that conflicts or failed endeavors are their fault
At Their Best in the Classroom:	**Needs During Change:**
• Creating community and harmony through group work and social interaction • Creative lectures and discussions that engage students • Lessons that focus on people and values • Effective use of cooperative learning and peer coaching • Organizing students to accomplish major efforts	• Recognition of and attention to the human side of change—losses of traditions, relationships, favorite activities, etc. • Acknowledgment of their values and attempts to honor them • Positive conversations around future possibilities for people

Coaching Suggestions for ENFJs

Typical Areas for Growth as a Teacher	A Coach Might
Listening to suggestions, not taking them personally	Start with positive factors. Let them set goals for personal growth and tie suggestions and ideas back to those goals.
Understanding the values and logic of other perspectives, relaxing focus on their own goals	Emphasize watching for reactions of others—when are ENFJs being overzealous? Use their Feeling ability to step into the shoes of others to consider the assumptions and values underlying opposing viewpoints or goals.
Setting limits on helping others to avoid burnout	Help them set limits on tutoring, covering duties for other teachers, or their time in the building. When might others benefit from helping themselves or finding other resources?
Using standardized materials or structured assignments	Point out the needs of children with Introversion and Sensing preferences. How might using some standard materials allow ENFJs to accomplish other tasks?
Anticipating details and requirements for assignments and activities	Help them develop a template for planning, emphasizing materials needed, probable time frames for different steps in the process, and other details.
Dealing with difficult students, especially when relationship-building efforts fail	Provide specific techniques and reasons behind them. Add classroom structure and clear rules. Role-play ways to avoid becoming enmeshed in an argument with a student.

INTJs

Prefer "Coach as Expert." Be ready with theories and suggestions that foster creative thinking. Allow for independent study and debate about long-term implications.

General Strengths:	Common Stressors:
• Going beyond the status quo, looking for better ways • Engaging in deep, independent thinking • Tackling and solving problems • Developing thorough knowledge in areas of expertise • Organizing systems and schedules, strategic planning	• Change without enough warning or planning time • Being told what to do and how to do it • Feeling that they have lost control of an event or a situation • Lack of reflective time to synthesize internal models and principles with change efforts • Planning carefully, yet experiencing poor results or derailments outside of their control
At Their Best in the Classroom:	**Needs During Change:**
• Conveying ideas and theories through clear, informative lectures • Experimenting with new teaching methods, using technology • Allowing for independent study where students pursue their own interests • Speculative thinking and problem solving • Analysis and debate of ideas and values	• Time to reflect and process models, rationale, and implications • Acknowledgment of competencies and contributions • Room for independence, creativity, and strategizing

Coaching Suggestions for INTJs

Typical Areas for Growth as a Teacher	A Coach Might
Patience with students who learn best through practice and concrete tasks	Emphasize a learning styles model to point out patterns in student learning. Analyze student data to find evidence of student needs.
Relational side of teaching, being aware of students' emotional needs	Use the framework of Thinking and Feeling to provide a mental model. Emphasize specific praise, student needs for group work, and brain research on emotions and learning.
Providing clear directions and expectations	Provide examples of universal tools such as checklist rubrics for assignments, graphic organizers to guide student thinking, and general procedures for problem solving and other thinking skills.
Moving from conceptual thinking to everyday examples students can grasp	Talk through ways to capture the attention of students. Use the framework of prior knowledge. Think through real-life applications and visual representations of the concept.
Scaffolding students for big intellectual endeavors	Use information on the needs of Sensing and Perceiving students. Provide examples of breaking assignments into smaller steps, planning backward, and estimating time needs, and how these improve student achievement.
Collaborating with colleagues, building consensus	Point to research on collaboration as a tool for improving student achievement. Start with efforts that will add efficiencies.

INTPs

Prefer "Coach as Expert." Let them explore options, models, and intellectual ideas. Expect to be challenged over their merit. Allow for independence.

General Strengths:	Common Stressors:
<ul><li>Being self-directed, independent thinkers</li><li>Engaging in creative problem solving</li><li>Understanding and/or developing theories and models</li><li>Devising complex strategies with grasp of long-term implications</li><li>Critiquing systems, methods, and ideas</li></ul>	<ul><li>When others doubt their competency</li><li>Emotional outbursts from others or themselves</li><li>Mandated changes with little chance for input or resources for reflection</li><li>Expectations or structures that decrease their autonomy</li><li>Changes without clear logic or rationale</li></ul>
At Their Best in the Classroom:	Needs During Change:
<ul><li>Quest-oriented tasks that challenge the intellect</li><li>Opportunities for self-directed, independent study</li><li>Lectures with Socratic questioning style</li><li>Conveying models and theories</li><li>Assignments with problem-solving focus, options for how students proceed</li></ul>	<ul><li>Involvement in setting standards, examining theories and models</li><li>Room for autonomy or exploration</li><li>Acknowledgment of their ideas, critiques, and competencies</li></ul>

Coaching Suggestions for INTPs

Typical Areas for Growth as a Teacher	A Coach Might
Simplifying major tasks	Use the Sensing-Intuition framework to increase awareness of the Sensing need to move step by step toward big concepts. Provide examples of planning and organization tools, but allow for experimentation.
Building relationships with students	Suggest study of brain research on the emotional aspects of learning.
Balancing critique with praise and skepticism with acceptance	Collaboratively examine student work to look for specific ways to commend progress. Teach techniques for critiquing colleagues, such as counting to 10 or offering a positive comment first.
Adding practical, hands-on tasks to intellectual pursuits	Use a model (brain research, learning styles, or multiple intelligences) to show the need for relevancy and kinesthetic learning. Suggest practice in breaking intellectual concepts into three to five easy-to-remember points.
Collaborating without seeming aloof or overly intellectual	Share research on collaboration. Emphasize the benefits of receiving input on emotional intelligence as well as viewpoints from others.
Mixing intellectual and fun pursuits	Provide resources on relevant, engaging student activities. Allow for experimentation, facilitating comparison and evaluation. Relate activities to higher-level thinking skills and encourage them to do so with students.

ENTPs

Prefer "Coach as Expert." Provide open-ended, creatively challenging methods they can improve on. Allow for critical analysis and debate.

General Strengths:	Common Stressors:
• Seeking the new and novel with boundless curiosity and energy • Understanding theories and models • Solving complex problems, creative thinking • Researching and modeling what works • Fearlessly tackling huge efforts, persuading others to support them with time and resources	• Paperwork, details, and other rote responsibilities • Being fenced in by procedures, mandates, and other external structures • Bureaucratic systems and demands • Situations void of options • Feeling unfairly judged or slighted as incompetent
At Their Best in the Classroom:	**Needs During Change:**
• Fast-paced, engaging activities • Big projects and ideas that call for imagination and problem solving • Students encouraged to take risks and think • Debates and discussions • Chances for students to follow their own interests	• A voice in researching, devising options, and charting the course • Opportunities for discussion, debate, and negotiation of ideas and implementation requirements • Theoretical underpinnings with focus on long-term impact

Coaching Suggestions for ENTPs

Typical Areas for Growth as a Teacher	A Coach Might
Matching tasks to student abilities	Use the concept of flow = interest + ability. Help them conduct a logical analysis of where students have struggled in the past. Are there patterns of not meeting needs of different learning styles?
Providing clear directions and structure	Use models of Sensing and Intuitive learning needs to help them grasp the necessity. Then provide examples and rubrics to aid them in designing assignments.
Listening to and teaming with colleagues	Use research on collaboration, work with the problem-solving model (Appendix B), and point to the logic of collaborating to build support for ideas.
Patience, especially in helping others	Teach specific methods, such as counting to 10 or finding a positive comment before critiquing. Use Thinking and Feeling to increase awareness of the impact of their natural questioning style on others.
Following standard procedures or curriculum	Base nonnegotiables soundly in theory. Use case studies and models to convey concepts. Allow for debate.
Avoiding overcommitment of time and resources	Use criteria to set priorities, referring back to school goals. Suggest collaboration as a tool for a "reality check" on what an assignment or responsibility might really entail.

ENTJs

Prefer "Coach as Expert." Make sure you know your materials and the rationale behind them. Be cutting edge, prepare for debate, and bring challenges that can lead to mastery.

General Strengths:	Common Stressors:
• Leading, organizing, and planning • Tackling problems logically • Being self-motivated, driven toward visionary goals • Thinking strategically • Bringing theories and plans to reality	• Feeling powerless or ignored; not having influence in planning • Bureaucracies, protocols, and paperwork that stifle forward thinking • Emotional outbursts by others or themselves • Being accused of treating people as objects when pursuing a strategic course of action • Inefficient or illogical changes or policies
At Their Best in the Classroom:	**Needs During Change:**
• Innovative, grand-scale endeavors with clear course of action • Planning ahead, helping students do the same • Projects with big-picture emphasis, options for creativity • Encouraging insightful thinking and problem solving • Group work, discussion and debate, competition	• Deep understanding of reasons for change and logic of the chosen course of action • Opportunities for discussion, debate, and providing input • Focus on long-term impact, cutting-edge skills, and paths to advancement

Coaching Suggestions for ENTJs

Typical Areas for Growth as a Teacher	A Coach Might
Patience with those who grasp concepts more slowly	Distinguish between high standards and standards that honor only logical or abstract thinking. Use a learning styles model to demonstrate different methods of processing information.
Understanding "illogical" students, building relationships	Use models from brain research, especially when dealing with adolescent students who tend to react, not plan. Point to the role of emotions in learning.
Providing concrete learning steps and opportunities for practice	Use the model of Sensing (concrete) and Intuitive (abstract) learning to help them understand their opposites. Set the challenge to them of structuring a task so that all students learn.
Meeting the needs of Introverted and Perceiving students	Emphasize teaching skills that help students self-manage, such as planning backward or setting goals for use of class time. ENTJs sometimes equate lack of drive like theirs with laziness and might take over to ensure that students finish tasks.
Being a follower	Remember that they are natural leaders and gravitate toward administrative roles. Teach specific collaborative strategies such as active listening and problem solving (Appendix B).
Rethinking chosen methods, models, and plans in view of new information or ideas	Help them review assumptions and entertain other possibilities. Suggest that they run ideas by the colleague most likely to challenge and debate them.

Appendix B

Problem-Solving Model

As discussed in Chapter 9, the following problem-solving model integrates the work of Dewey (1910) and Myers (1998) to provide a structured, reflective process that uses the strengths of Sensing, Intuition, Thinking, and Feeling. Using the model helps individuals and teams avoid skipping over or rushing through steps that don't use their natural preferences and that therefore may not seem as important.

For a specific problem, choose *three to four* of the most relevant questions from each section. The following method works well for teams with more than five members.

Materials needed: flip-chart paper, markers

a. Use the type chart on page 221 to divide into groups by *dominant* function, the first preference listed for each type. For each step of the process, first answer the questions in the smaller groups, and then compare answers in the larger groups. This allows people to note their strengths and struggles with the process, as well as the strengths of other groups.

b. Have each subgroup write out their responses to the questions for Step 1 on flip-chart paper. When all groups are done, post the responses and allow each group to present them to the large group. Usually the *Sensing* group will have the most information, but not always.

c. Before moving on to the second step, work together as a whole group to come to a clear definition of the problem. Post the definition where everyone can refer to it. *Note: This process is often circular. In the midst of another step, the group realizes that they have not properly defined the problem and moves back to this step again.*

d. Have each subgroup complete Step 2, brainstorming possible solutions. As part of the large-group discussion, transfer all possible solutions to one sheet of paper. Let the group study the list. Ask if anyone has thought of more ideas.

e. Have each group work through Step 3. If the process calls for selecting objective criteria, part of the ensuing large-group discussion will be agreeing on the criteria. Make sure that none of the alternatives are deleted on the basis of these criteria alone; emphasize that sometimes the subjective criteria from Step 4 actually end up carrying more weight.

f. Have each group work through Step 4, and then evaluate the various possibilities on the basis of the identified criteria. As a large group, discuss buy-in and commitment to the top choices.

g. For many problems, Step 5 is simple: implement the chosen solution. For others, a team may wish to set up an action plan or an action research plan to determine whether the chosen solution is effective. Make sure the team agrees to next steps before concluding the meeting.

POSSIBLE QUESTIONS FOR EACH STEP OF THE PROCESS

1. Location and definition of a problem through observation (**Sensing** function)
   - How is the problem best defined?
   - What are the facts? Who? What? When? Where? Why?
   - Which facts are verifiable? (by a clock, a budget, test results, a survey, etc.)
   - How did we get into this situation?
   - What have you or others done to resolve this or similar problems?
   - What already exists and works?
   - What has already been tried or done? By whom?
   - How would an unbiased individual view the situation?
   - What resources are available?

2. Suggestion of possible solutions, suspending judgment while inference goes on (**Intuition** function)
   - What are the connections to larger issues or other people?
   - What other ways are there to look at this?
   - What are the possible solutions or ways to approach the problem?
   - What insights and hunches do you have?
   - What is this problem analogous to?

- What other directions can you explore?
- What would be other possibilities if there were no restrictions?
- What do the data imply?
- What theories address this kind of problem?

3. Reasoning: Weigh the consequences (**Thinking** function)
   - What objective criteria need to be satisfied?
   - How practical are the alternatives?
   - What are the pros and cons of each possibility?
   - What are the logical consequences of the options?
   - What are the costs of each alternative?
   - What is the most reasonable course of action?
   - Would this option apply equally and fairly to everyone?
   - What are the consequences of not deciding and acting?
   - What impact would pursuing each option have on other priorities?

4. Reasoning: Understand the impact on people (**Feeling** function)
   - How does this "fit" with personal and organizational values?
   - How will the outcome affect the people, process, or organization?
   - How will each option contribute to harmony and positive interactions?
   - What are the underlying values involved in each choice?
   - What are your personal reactions (likes and dislikes) to each alternative?
   - How will others respond?
   - Who is committed to carrying out the solution?
   - How will people be supported if this decision is made?
   - How will this affect my own priorities?

5. Make a final decision, act on it, and evaluate the results—action research.

Order of Preferences

ISTJ	ISFJ	INFJ	INTJ
1. Sensing	1. Sensing	1. Intuition	1. Intuition
2. Thinking	2. Feeling	2. Feeling	2. Thinking
3. Feeling	3. Thinking	3. Thinking	3. Feeling
4. Intuition	4. Intuition	4. Sensing	4. Sensing
ISTP	**ISFP**	**INFP**	**INTP**
1. Thinking	1. Feeling	1. Feeling	1. Thinking
2. Sensing	2. Sensing	2. Intuition	2. Intuition
3. Intuition	3. Intuition	3. Sensing	3. Sensing
4. Feeling	4. Thinking	4. Thinking	4. Feeling
ESTP	**ESFP**	**ENFP**	**ENTP**
1. Sensing	1. Sensing	1. Intuition	1. Intuition
2. Thinking	2. Feeling	2. Feeling	2. Thinking
3. Feeling	3. Thinking	3. Thinking	3. Feeling
4. Intuition	4. Intuition	4. Sensing	4. Sensing
ESTJ	**ESFJ**	**ENFJ**	**ENTJ**
1. Thinking	1. Feeling	1. Feeling	1. Thinking
2. Sensing	2. Sensing	2. Intuition	2. Intuition
3. Intuition	3. Intuition	3. Sensing	3. Sensing
4. Feeling	4. Thinking	4. Thinking	4. Feeling

Dominant Sensing Types	Dominant Intuitive Types
ISTJ	INFJ
ISFJ	INTJ
ESTP	ENFP
ESFP	ENTP
Dominant Thinking Types	**Dominant Feeling Types**
ISTP	ISFP
INTP	INFP
ESTJ	ESFJ
ENTJ	ENFJ

Appendix C

Case Studies in Coaching Teachers for Change

The following case studies, each created as a composite of many teachers with the personality type described, are designed to help you put into practice the differentiated coaching techniques described in earlier chapters. They deal with common issues:

- A teacher who isn't implementing a district instructional mandate
- A teacher who isn't collaborating with colleagues.

Each case walks you through the keys for effective staff development and differentiated coaching for the teacher described. There is room for you to respond, using information on that teacher's learning style, educational beliefs, and coaching preferences. Then you can read through a suggested coaching plan.

CASE STUDY 1: COACH AS USEFUL RESOURCE (SENSING AND THINKING)

Mike (ISTJ) has taught sixth-grade language arts for over 10 years at the same high-poverty school. The principal says that Mike is one of the most organized teachers he's ever seen. Mike has few discipline issues in a school where many teachers struggle to keep control of their classrooms.

During an observation, Mike stands quietly with arms folded to signal students to pay attention, and it works. He hands out an assignment on sequencing the main events in the novel the class is reading. He asks students to pay attention for five minutes as he explains it. When he finishes, he allows students to talk quietly as long as he can see that they are working, too. The students stay on task. Later, Mike leads a discussion by asking questions and calling on students who raise their hands.

A few years ago, the school district decided that all middle-school language arts teachers would use literature circles at least three times a year, offering students choices in the novels they'd read.

Mike attended the workshop on literature circles taught by Lisa, the district language arts coordinator. Lisa's preferences are for Extraversion, Intuition, Feeling, and Judging (ENFJ). At the three-hour workshop, teachers received lists of reference books and suggested novels, and graphic organizers that students could use as discussion guides. Lisa displayed various student literature circles' final projects. She then gave an entertaining lecture on cooperative learning and literature circles, including a quick overview of research findings. Mike hadn't read either of the novels she used as examples. Then they broke into groups to plan for using literature circles.

At the start of the school year, Mike experimented with literature circles by forming small groups, but he assigned the same novel, one he'd taught before, to all of the groups. On the first chapter test, students scored below his past classes on vocabulary and comprehension, although they did better on interpretation questions. After seeing the results, Mike went back to whole-class instruction.

When Lisa learned that Mike was still using whole-class instruction to teach novels, she called Mike's principal and reminded him that literature circles were now a district expectation. Here's a summary of what Lisa told the principal about Mike:

> Mike attended the district training workshop. I presented on the research on literature circles—student interest in reading and interpretation skills go way up. Literature circles are about helping students see reading as an enjoyable activity. Students don't seem to have fun in Mike's room—it's all so task-oriented. Mike's using the same worksheets he used five years ago—probably 10 years ago. His notes on the novels he teaches are yellowed and dog-eared. I wonder if he's too lazy to put the effort into using literature circles.

In a private discussion with the principal, Mike defended his practices:

> That training was interesting, but we never had a chance to ask questions. I already have reading "choice" time where students can

read high-interest materials, including comic books if they wish. With literature circles, how can I monitor who's reading and who's copying? How do I keep students on task? How do I spot comprehension problems? Besides, these kids need structure. I have to prepare students for the basic skills tests, which include questions on facts and vocabulary. With literature circles, am I supposed to create worksheets for each book? When?

My students did as well or better on the last set of standardized tests as those who were in literature circles. I've perfected my lessons over several years and students benefit from my experience with them. Besides, I'm here to teach them, not entertain them.

Use the following questions to guide you in constructing an action plan for coaching Mike. Suggestions follow.

Key Element: Use a common framework for unbiased reflection on education

- Compare using literature circles and whole class discussions to your common framework. Which students does each option serve? Which teachers will need to change the most? Why?

Key Element: Understand the teacher's strengths and beliefs about teaching and learning

- In this case, Lisa's preferences are for Extraversion, Intuition, Feeling, and Judging—she shares only Judging with Mike. What does she need to understand about Mike? How do literature circles compare with the ISTJ "at their best in the classroom" information on page 186? How do his concerns reflect his educational beliefs?

Key Element: Provide information and evidence that can influence the teacher's beliefs

- What kinds of information did the district workshop on literature circles provide? Whose needs did the information meet?
- Review Mike's learning style (IS). How could a workshop better meet his needs? Which of Mike's concerns can be addressed by providing different information? Which require other coaching strategies?

Key Element: Meet the needs of the teacher during change

Mike prefers "Coach as Useful Resource," whereas Lisa's natural style is "Coach as Collegial Mentor."

- Review the information on pages 146–148. What advice might you give Lisa that would help her meet Mike's needs? Compare your own coaching style to Mike's style. What would be important for you to remember?
- What coaching techniques might work best in helping Mike take another stab at using literature circles?

Key Element: Relate or apply what is being learned to the problem the teacher wants to solve in his or her classroom

- From the above information, list Mike's concerns about literature circles. Consider the ISTJ information on pages 186–187 and his comments to the principal.

Action Plan

Use the above information to suggest a plan for how Lisa could use Mike's strengths to help him implement literature circles.

Goal	Coaching strategy	Coach's role	Evidence of success
1.			
2.			
3.			

A Possible Coaching Approach for Mike

Key Element: Use a common framework for unbiased reflection on education

- Compare using literature circles to your common framework. Which students does each option serve? Which teachers will need to change the most? Why?

Although literature circles can be tightly structured, Lisa's materials reflected her open-ended Intuitive style. Students who prefer Extraversion often enjoy discussing what they're reading as an energizing break from the quiet. Feeling students enjoy cooperative learning. Literature circles may be hard for Introverted/Sensing teachers, with their preferences for quiet and structure. Sensing/Thinking teachers may feel a loss of direct control over what students are learning. Judging teachers may sense a lack of ways to monitor goals and progress.

Key Element: Understand the teacher's strengths and beliefs about teaching and learning

- In this case, Lisa's preferences are for Extraversion, Intuition, Feeling, and Judging—she shares only Judging with Mike. What does she need to understand about Mike?

  Mike likes to improve what works, not experiment. His lessons cover the essentials; he doesn't want to change without clear direction on how the changes will still cover standards.

- How do literature circles compare with the ISTJ "at their best in the classroom" information on page 186? How do his concerns reflect his educational beliefs?

  Mike likes structure, clear tasks, and teacher-directed work. He'd wondered about assessing student work and structuring the literature circles to keep students on task.

Key Element: Provide information and evidence that can influence the teacher's beliefs

- What kinds of information did the district workshop on literature circles provide? Whose needs did the information meet?

  Referring to the learning styles chart on pages 116–117, the workshop matched Lisa's Extraversion/Intuition style by starting with the big picture, giving choices, allowing teachers to come up with their own ideas, and providing small-group discussion opportunities.

- Review Mike's learning style (IS). How could a workshop better meet his needs? Which of Mike's concerns can be addressed by providing different information? Which require other coaching strategies?

Mike needed more specific step-by-step instructions for literature circles and more detailed graphic organizers or other tools for students to use. Rather than a reference list, he might have preferred to browse through one or two books that Lisa could recommend and choose one as a model. He needed time to ask questions. A video of student discussion within a literature circle might have helped him visualize the process. He might benefit from coaching to revise worksheets he already uses or to add structure to general methods.

Key Element: Meet the needs of the teacher during change

Mike prefers "Coach as Useful Resource," whereas Lisa's natural style is "Coach as Collegial Mentor."

- Review the information on pages 146–148. What advice might you give Lisa that would help her meet Mike's needs? Compare your own coaching style to Mike's style. What would be important for you to remember?

  Build from what he knows. Provide strategies to get him started, then encourage him to improve them. Listen carefully to his concerns and answer them. Remember that he won't want to "experiment."

- What coaching techniques might work best in helping Mike take another stab at using literature circles?
  - Modeling
  - Step-by-step instruction.

Key Element: Relate or apply what is being learned to the problem the teacher wants to solve in his or her classroom

- From the above information, list Mike's concerns about literature circles. Consider the ISTJ information on pages 186–187 and his comments to the principal.

  He's concerned about loss of basic skills practice, holding each student accountable for work, and assessing student participation. He needs tools that explicitly allow emphasis on basic skills within literature circles.

Action Plan

How could Lisa use Mike's strengths to help him implement literature circles?

Goal	Coaching strategy	Evidence of success
1. Develop structuring strategies for literature circles without overscaffolding	• Provide universal tools for basic skills such as creating storyboards, character sketch graphic organizers, clear roles and responsibilities for students, ways for students to generate vocabulary lists, etc. • Bring a ready-to-go module, work together to modify it to meet Mike's needs • Modify worksheets Mike already uses	• Mike uses the tools in a mini-unit using literature circles, with students reading short stories or articles • Examine student work together to look for evidence of basic skills practice, student participation
2. Use literature circles, giving students choices in novels	• Let him observe literature circles in another classroom • Use novels Mike is familiar with • Work together to construct a clear rubric for grading students	• Watch for student time on task • Evaluate an open-ended student survey to understand how they learned or didn't learn in literature circles • Look at data from end-of-unit assessment

Note that the evidence of success consists not only of whether Mike implemented literature circles, but also whether he felt the literature circles helped students learn.

CASE 2: COACH AS EXPERT (INTUITION AND THINKING)

Elise is a 15-year veteran elementary-school teacher, but this year is her first at a suburban elementary school. She and her family moved to town from another state. Her preferences are for Extraversion, Intuition, Thinking, and Judging (ENTJ).

The best word to describe Elise's classroom is BIG. To study the rainforest, she and the students created trees, animals, and rivers out of paint and paper. For a unit on problem solving, she cordoned off the entire room as a "crime scene" one day. The students had to work together to find clues and solve the mystery. Students tackle similar large-scale endeavors to learn about other countries, government, and events in history.

The other teachers complained to the principal, "She makes us look bad. Parents and students can't help but see and wonder why we aren't doing the same. They don't understand that she's skipping the handwriting workbook and units in reading. What will happen to her students in fourth grade? Besides, we should be collaborating."

Elise told the principal, "I offered to share ideas—one teacher even used my rainforest plans. Frankly, though, the others told me it'd be too much work. But they want me to go back to square one, work with them to plan the whole year? I *know* my units help students learn. I'm not jettisoning what works, but they're welcome to join me. You've seen the high work standards my students reach. The parents are thrilled."

Key Element: Use a common framework for unbiased reflection on education

- Consider teaming for reflective collaboration. For which personality types is it most natural? Which preferences might struggle?

Key Element: Understand the teacher's strengths and beliefs about teaching and learning

- How do Elise's classroom methods compare with the ENTJ "at their best in the classroom" information (pp. 216–217)? What might be difficult for teachers with other learning styles?

Key Element: Provide information and evidence that can influence the teacher's beliefs

- What information might persuade Elise to collaborate with her team?
- Review Elise's learning style (EN). Where does collaboration fit in?

Key Element: Meet the needs of the teacher during change

- Elise prefers "Coach as Expert." Compare this to your own style and list key points to remember when communicating with Elise.
- What coaching techniques might work best in helping Elise collaborate?

Key Element: Relate or apply what is being learned to the problem the teacher wants to solve in his or her classroom

- Elise may think her classroom is fine. How might you turn her focus to a bigger focus than her own classroom?

Action Plan

Use the above information to suggest a plan to use Elise's strengths to help her collaborate with her team.

Goal	Coaching strategy	Evidence of success
1.		
2.		
3.		

A Suggested Plan for Coaching Elise

Key Element: Use a common framework for unbiased reflection on education

- Consider teaming for reflective collaboration. For which personality types is it most natural? Which preferences might struggle?

  Look through the coaching tips for the different types. Introvert/ Intuitives value independence and often hesitate to collaborate. ESTJs and ENTJs are used to leading and may struggle to collaborate cooperatively. Further, the elementary-school atmosphere is generally Feeling, and Feeling types often take critique personally, making it difficult for them to understand Thinking types.

Key Element: Understand the teacher's strengths and beliefs about teaching and learning

- How do Elise's classroom methods compare with the ENTJ "at their best in the classroom" information (pp. 216–217)? What might be difficult for teachers with other learning styles?

She uses innovative, grand-scale efforts, plans ahead, and is self-motivated. Further, she's successful at it. Teachers with other styles can find such huge efforts intimidating—they worry about structure, timing, and how to make sure students learn what they are supposed to be learning.

Key Element: Provide information and evidence that can influence the teacher's beliefs

- What information might persuade Elise to collaborate with her team?

  Elise might respond to research on collaboration as an essential part of whole-school improvement—the big picture.

- Review Elise's learning style (EN). Where does collaboration fit in?

  Collaboration provides opportunities to talk through and debate ideas. Elise might need a clear understanding of the other teachers' strengths before she learns to listen to their ideas.

Key Element: Meet the needs of the teacher during change

- Elise prefers "Coach as Expert." Compare this to your own style and list key points to remember when communicating with Elise.
- What coaching techniques might work best in helping Elise collaborate?

  Use the explicit problem-solving model (Appendix B) for discussions so that the process helps her to listen to other viewpoints and not rush to conclusions.

  Teach active listening strategies—rephrasing what has been said to check for her accuracy of understanding. She might also need coaching in showing patience. Sometimes the gestures or expressions of people with preferences for Extraversion and Thinking give away their impatience even when they are trying to listen. They may also need to learn to give positive comments before negative.

Key Element: Relate or apply what is being learned to the problem the teacher wants to solve in his or her classroom

- Elise may think her classroom is fine. How might you turn her focus to a bigger focus than her own classroom?

  If she plans on moving into administration (remember, most principals are TJs), she might be persuaded to look at collaboration as a way to improve leadership skills and practice gaining buy-in for her plans and ideas. Research on collaboration and whole-school improvement might also pique her interest.

Action Plan

Use the above information to suggest a plan to use Elise's strengths to help her collaborate with her team.

Goal	Coaching strategy	Evidence of success
1. Committing to collaboration	• Use the problem-solving model (Appendix B) to help Elise see the other teachers' points of view • With Elise, determine logical reasons to learn to collaborate	• Elise agrees to specific practice to improve her collaboration and listening skills
2. Working on a collaborative team project	• Facilitate the first effort, using a learning styles model as a common framework so that the suggestions of all teachers are heard and appreciated	• The team agrees that the collaboration effort was worthwhile
3. Understand strengths and needs of other learning styles	• Evaluate student work with Elise—are any students consistently underperforming with her large-scale efforts? Did any of them do better work in second grade? How might the other teachers add structure to her efforts?	• Evaluation of student work for one big project; Elise agrees to modifications where necessary. Action research: do similar modifications help with her next big unit?

References

Annenberg Institute for School Reform. (2005a). *Professional development strategies that improve instruction: Instructional coaching.* Retrieved February 7, 2005, from http://www.nsdc.org

Annenberg Institute for School Reform. (2005b). *Professional development strategies that improve instruction: Professional learning communities.* Retrieved February 7, 2005, from http://www.nsdc.org

Barger, N. J., & Kirby, L. K. (1995). *The challenge of change in organizations: Helping employees thrive in the new frontier.* Palo Alto, CA: Consulting Psychologists Press.

Barger, N. J., & Kirby, L. K. (1997). *Type and change: MBTI participant's guide.* Palo Alto, CA: Consulting Psychologists Press.

Bitran, M. (2004, July). *J and P preferences in Chile.* Presentation at the APT International Conference, Toronto, Canada. Retrieved February 5, 2005, from http://www.aptinternational.org/conference_proceeding/files/KN%20J%20and%20P%20Preferences%20in%20Chile.pdf

Bloom, B. S. (Ed.). (1956). *Taxonomy of educational objectives: The classification of educational goals: Handbook I, cognitive domain.* New York: Longmans, Green.

Brookfield, S. D. (1995). *Becoming a critically reflective teacher.* San Francisco: Jossey-Bass.

Clancy, S. G. (1997). STJs and change: Resistance, reaction, or misunderstanding? In C. Fitzgerald & L. K. Kirby (Eds.), *Developing leaders: Research and applications in psychological type and leadership development* (pp. 415–438). Palo Alto, CA: Consulting Psychologists Press.

Costa, A. L., & Garmston, R. J. (1994). *Cognitive coaching: A foundation for Renaissance schools.* Norwood, MA: Christopher-Gordon.

Coward, A. (1990). *Pattern thinking.* New York: Praeger.

Crumpton, S. L. (2000). Helping sensing students understand mathematics. In *CAPT Fourth Biennial Education Conference Proceedings* (pp. 35–42). Gainesville, FL: Center for Applications of Psychological Type.

Delpit, L. (1995). *Other people's children: Cultural conflict in the classroom.* New York: New Press.

Dewey, J. (1902). *The school and society* (rev. ed.) and *The child and the curriculum.* Chicago: University of Chicago Press. (1990 reprinting)

Dewey, J. (1910). *How we think.* Minneola, NY: Dover. (1997 reprinting)

Dewey, J. (1916). *Democracy and education: An introduction to the philosophy of education.* New York: Free Press.

Dewey, J. (1934). *Art as experience.* New York: Perigee.

Dewey, J. (1972). My pedagogic creed. In J. A. Boydston (Ed.), *John Dewey: The early works, 1882–1898, vol. 5, 1895–1898, early essays* (pp. 84–95). Carbondale: Southern Illinois Press. (Original work published 1897)

Dewey, J. (1985). *Ethics.* In J. A. Boydston (Ed.), *John Dewey: The later works, 1925–1953, vol. 7, 1932.* Carbondale: Southern Illinois Press. (Original work published 1932)

Duffy, F. N. (2003). I think, therefore I am resistant to change. *Journal of Staff Development, 24*(1). Retrieved February 9, 2005, from http://www.nsdc.org/library/publications/jsd/duffy241.cfm

Evans, R. (2001). *The human side of school change: Reform, resistance and the real-life problems of innovation.* San Francisco: Jossey-Bass.

Experience-Based Learning Systems. (2000–2005). Retrieved June 8, 2005, from http://www.learningfromexperience.com

Feiman-Nemser, S. X., & Floden, R. (1986). The cultures of teaching. In M. Withrock (Ed.), *Handbook of research on teaching* (3rd ed., p. 512). New York: Macmillan.

Felder, R. M. (1996, December). Matters of style. *ASEE Prism, 6*(4), 18–23. Retrieved July 29, 2004, from http://www.ncsu.edu/felder-public/Papers/LS-Prism.htm

Felder, R. M. (2002). The effects of personality type on engineering student performance and attitudes. *Journal of Engineering Education, 19*(1), 3–17.

Fisher, N. M. (1994). MBTI type and writing-across-the-curriculum. *Journal of Psychological Type, 16,* 42–46.

Ford, M. (1992). *Motivating humans.* Thousand Oaks, CA: Sage.

Fullan, M. (1993). *Change forces: Probing the depths of educational reform.* London: Falmer.

Fullan, M. (2001). *The NEW meaning of educational change* (3rd ed.). New York: Teachers College Press.

Fullan, M., & Hargreaves, A. (1992). *What's worth fighting for?: Working together for your school.* New York: Teachers College Press.

Gardner, H. (1999). *Intelligence reframed: Multiple intelligences.* New York: Basic Books.

Giger, K. (1996). Type goes to school: Reducing school "drop-outs" through the use of type and temperament. In *CAPT Educational Conference Proceedings* (pp. 387–394). Gainesville, FL: Center for Applications of Psychological Type.

Gregorc, A. D. (1999–2005). *Gregorc associates.* Retrieved June 8, 2005, from http://www.gregorc.com

Guskey, T. R. (1996). To transmit or to "construct"? *Education Week, 16*(8), 34.

Guskey, T. R. (2002). Professional development and teacher change. *Teachers and teaching: Theory and practice, 8,* 380–391.

Hall, G. E., & Hord, S. M. (2001). *Implementing change: Patterns, principles, and potholes.* Boston: Allyn & Bacon.

Hall, P. S., & Hall, N. D. (2003). *Educating oppositional and defiant children.* Alexandria, VA: Association for Supervision and Curriculum Development.

Hammer, A. E. (Ed.). (1996). *MBTI applications: A decade of research on the Myers-Briggs Type Indicator.* Mountain View, CA: Consulting Psychologists Press.

Hargreaves, A. (1994). *Changing teachers, changing times: Teachers' work and culture in the postmodern age.* New York: Teachers College Press.

Healy, J. (1994). *Your child's growing mind.* New York: Doubleday.

Held, J. S., & Yokomoto, C. F. (1983). Technical report writing: Effects of personality differences in the laboratory. In *ASEE Annual Conference Proceedings* (pp. 197–201). Washington, DC: American Society of Engineering Education.

Hirsh, S. K., & Kise, J. A. G. (2000). *Introduction to type and coaching.* Mountain View, CA: Consulting Psychologists Press.

Hirsh, S. K., & Kise, J. A. G. (2001). *Using the MBTI tool in organizations.* Mountain View, CA: Consulting Psychologists Press.

Hirsh, S. K., & Kummerow, J. M. (1998). *Introduction to type in organizations* (3rd ed.). Mountain View, CA: Consulting Psychologists Press.

Huelsman, C. B., III. (2002). *Mathematics anxiety: An interdisciplinary approach.* Updated master's thesis, Marylhurst University, Marylhurst, Oregon.

Jensen, E. (1998). *Teaching with the brain in mind.* Alexandria, VA: Association for Supervision and Curriculum Development.

Kaplan, R. E., Drath, W. H., & Kofodimos, J. R. (1985). *High hurdles: The challenge of self-development* (Tech. Rep. No. 25). Greensboro, NC: Center for Creative Leadership.

Kise, J. A. G., Stark, D., & Hirsh, S. K. (2005). *LifeKeys: Discover who you are* (2nd ed.). Minneapolis, MN: Bethany House.

Lawrence, G. (1993). *People types and tiger stripes* (3rd ed.). Gainesville, FL: Center for Applications of Psychological Type.

Lee, V. E., Smith, J. B., & Croninger, R. G. (1995). Another look at high school restructuring. *Issues in restructuring schools.* Madison, WI: Center on Organization and Restructuring of Schools, School of Education, University of Wisconsin—Madison. Retrieved August 30, 2005, from http://www.wcer.wisc.edu/archive/cors/Issues%5Fin%5FRestructuring%5FSchools/ISSUES_NO_9_FALL_1995.pdf

Lehto, B. A. (1990). A comparison of personalities and background of teachers using a whole language approach and a basal approach in teaching elementary reading (Doctoral dissertation, Michigan State University, 1990). *Dissertation Abstracts International, 51/03-A,* 740.

Lipman, P. (1998). *Race, class, and power in school restructuring.* Albany: State University of New York Press.

Little, J. W. (1981). The power of organizational setting. Paper adapted from final report, *School success and staff development.* Washington, DC: National Institute of Education.

Little, J. W. (1990). The persistence of privacy: Autonomy and initiative in teachers' professional relations. *Teachers College Record, 91*(4). Retrieved November 11, 2004, from http://web34.epnet.com

Lortie, D. (1975). *Schoolteacher.* Chicago: University of Chicago Press.

Marzano, R. J. (2003). *What works in schools: Translating research into action.* Alexandria, VA: Association for Supervision and Curriculum Development.

McLaughlin, M. W., & Talbert, J. E. (1993). *Contexts that matter for teaching and learning.* Stanford, CA: Center for Research on the Context of Secondary School Teaching, Stanford University.

Murphy, E. (1992). *The developing child: Using Jungian type to understand children.* Palo Alto, CA: Consulting Psychologists Press.

Myers, I. B., & Myers, P. B. (1993). *Gifts differing: Understanding personality type.* Palo Alto, CA: Consulting Psychologists Press.

Myers, I. B. (1998). *Introduction to type* (6th ed.). Mountain View, CA: Consulting Psychologists Press.

National Staff Development Council. (2001). *NSDC standards for staff development.* Retrieved June 8, 2005, from http://www.nsdc.org/standards/datadriven.cfm

National Staff Development Council. (2004). Learning. *NSDC standards.* Retrieved October 26, 2004, from http://www.nsdc.org/standards/learning.cfm

Neufeld, B., & Roper, D. (2003). *Coaching: A strategy for developing instructional capacity.* Cambridge, MA: Education Matters. Retrieved February 18, 2004, from http://www.edmatters.org

Newmann, F. M., & Associates. (1996). *Authentic achievement: Restructuring schools for intellectual quality.* San Francisco: Jossey-Bass.

Nygren, C., & Nygren, J. (2000). Math success for all types. In *CAPT Fourth Biennial Education Conference Proceedings* (pp. 241–244). Gainesville, FL: Center for Applications of Psychological Type.

O'Neil, B. A. (1986). An investigation of the relationship between teacher/student personality type and discipline referrals in two Massachusetts high schools (Doctoral dissertation, Boston University, 1986). *Dissertation Abstracts International, 47/04-A,* 1141.

Payne, R. K. (1996). *A framework for understanding poverty.* Highlands, TX: aha! Process, Inc.

Peterson, C., Maier, S., & Seligman, M. (1993). *Learned helplessness.* New York: Oxford University Press.

Quenk, N. L. (1993). *Beside ourselves: Our hidden personality in everyday life.* Palo Alto, CA: Consulting Psychologists Press.

Robinson, D. C. (1994). Use of type with the 1990 United States Academic Decathlon program. In *Proceedings: Orchestrating Educational Change in the 90's—The Role of Psychological Type* (pp. 35–41). Gainesville, FL: Center for Applications of Psychological Type.

Rosenholtz, S. J. (1989). *Teachers' workplace: The social organization of schools.* New York: Longman.

Segal, M. (2000). Another look at creativity styles: Reporting on research and a new question. Retrieved September 17, 2003, from http://www.16types.com/Request.jsp?lView=ViewArticle&Article=OID%3A59627&Page=OID%3A59628

Seligman, M. E. P. (1998). *Learned optimism: How to change your mind and your life.* New York: Knopf.

Senge, P., Cambron-McCabe, N., Lucas, T., Smith, B., Dutton, J., & Kleiner, A. (2000). *Schools that learn.* New York: Doubleday.

Senge, P. M., Kleiner, A., Roberts, C., Ross, R. B., & Smith, B. J. (1994). *The fifth discipline fieldbook: Strategies and tools for building a learning organization.* New York: Currency Doubleday.

Shade, B. J., Kelly, C., & Oberg, M. (1997). *Creating culturally responsive classrooms.* Washington, DC: American Psychological Association.

Sim, H.-S. (2004, July). *Reflections on the T/F dimension in a comparative culture context.* Presentation at APT International Conference, Toronto, Canada. Retrieved September 7, 2005, from http://www.aptinternational.org/2004-conference-proceeding/files/KN%20Reflections%20on%20the%20T.pdf

Smith, J. B., Lee, V. E., & Newmann, F. M. (2001). *Improving Chicago's schools: Instruction and achievement in Chicago elementary schools.* Chicago: Consortium on Chicago School Research.

Smyth, J., Dow, A., Hattam, R., Reid, A., & Shacklock, G. (2000). *Teachers' work in a globalizing economy.* London: Falmer.

Sparks, D. (1997). Is resistance to change really the problem? *The Developer.* Retrieved October 26, 2004, from http://www.nsdc.org/library/publications/developer/dev3-97sparks.cfm

Stein, M. K., Smith, M. S., Henningsen, M. A., & Silver, E. A. (2000). *Implementing standards-based mathematics instruction: A casebook for professional development.* New York: Teachers College Press.

Stevens, A. (1991). *On Jung.* New York: Penguin.

Tallevi, L. (1999). How to avoid educational jams over J/P issues. *Bulletin of Psychological Type, 22*(4), 4–6.

Tannock, R., & Martinussen, R. (2001). Reconceptualizing ADHD. *Educational Leadership, 59*(3), 20–25.

Tieger, P. D., & Barron-Tieger, B. (1997). *Nurture by nature: Understand your child's personality type—and become a better parent.* New York: Little, Brown.

Trueba, H. T., Jacobs, L., & Kirton, E. (1990). *Cultural conflict and adaptation: The case of Hmong children in American society.* New York: Falmer.

Tye, B. B. (2000). *Hard truths: Uncovering the deep structure of schooling.* New York: Teachers College Press.

Viadero, D. (2005, January 26). 'Mixed methods' research examined. *Education Week.* Retrieved February 10, 2005, from http://www.edweek.org/ew/articles/2005/01/26/20mixed.h24.html

Voight, C. (1982). *Dicey's song.* New York: Simon Pulse.

Wilkes, J. W. (2004, July). *Why do Intuitives have an advantage on both aptitude and achievement tests?* Unpublished paper presented at the International Conference of the Association for Psychological Type, Toronto, Canada.

Wilkes, J. W. (2005). *A learning styles based course assessment system.* Unpublished paper, Worcester Polytechnic Institute.

Wilson, B. L., & Corbett, H. D. (2001). *Listening to urban kids: School reform and the teachers they want.* Albany: State University of New York Press.

Wilson, M. A., & Languis, M. L. (1989). Differences in brain electrical activity patterns between introverted and extraverted adults. *Journal of Psychological Type, 34,* 36–42.

Witherspoon, R. (2000). Starting smart: Clarifying coaching goals and roles. In M. Goldsmith, L. Lyons, & A. Freas (Eds.), *Coaching for leadership.* San Francisco: Pfeiffer.

Witherspoon, R., & White, R. P. (1997). *Four essential ways that coaching can help executives.* Greensboro, NC: Center for Creative Leadership.

Index

**CORWIN
PRESS**

The Corwin Press logo—a raven striding across an open book—represents the union of courage and learning. Corwin Press is committed to improving education for all learners by publishing books and other professional development resources for those serving the field of PreK–12 education. By providing practical, hands-on materials, Corwin Press continues to carry out the promise of its motto: **"Helping Educators Do Their Work Better."**